Out Here

Out Here

Gay and Lesbian Perspectives VI

Edited by Yorick Smaal and Graham Willett

© Copyright 2011

All rights reserved. Apart from any uses permitted by Australia's Copyright Act 1968, no part of this book may be reproduced by any process without prior written permission from the copyright owners. Inquiries should be directed to the publisher.

Monash University Publishing
Building 4, Monash University
Clayton, Victoria 3800, Australia
www.publishing.monash.edu

This book is available online at www.publishing.monash.edu/oh

ISBN: 978-1-921867-00-2 (pb)
ISBN: 978-1-921867-01-9 (web)

Design

Les Thomas

Cover images

Front cover: Hugh Hood, unknown, Walter Hood (in background), Fitzroy River, Queensland, 1918; Courtesy Wayne Murdoch and the Australian Lesbian and Gay Archives.

Back cover images, left and right: Tommy McDermott Collection, Australian Lesbian and Gay Archives.

Back cover image, centre: Jan Hillier; History Inverted and Australian Lesbian and Gay Archives.

Printer

Griffin Press

Contents

Contributors — vii

Introduction — xi
Yorick Smaal and Graham Willett

'We Blew Our Trumpets and…' — 1
The ACT Homosexual Law Reform Society
Graham Willett

It's Time — 17
The Duncan Case and the Decriminalisation of Homosexual Acts in South Australia, 1972
Clare Parker and Paul Sendziuk

The Okayness of Gayness — 36
Don Dunstan's Record in Homosexual Law Reform
Dino Hodge

Even More Hidden from History? — 56
Male Homosexuality and Medicine in Turn-of-the-Century Australia
Lisa Featherstone

'Homosexual Health Hazards' — 69
Public Discourse on Homosexuality and Medicine in Australia, 1973–1984
Emily Wilson

HIV/AIDS and Gay Community Print News Media in 1980s Australia — 88
Shirleene Robinson

Australian HIV/AIDS Life Writing   104

The Human and the Historic

Geoff Allshorn

When HIV is Endemic amongst Gay Men   120

Michael Hurley

Australian Lesbian Artists of the Early Twentieth Century   135

Peter Di Sciascio

The Bois of King Vic   156

Roberta Foster

Friends and Lovers   168

Social Networks and Homosexual Life in War-time Queensland, 1938–1948

Yorick Smaal

The Influence of Ageism on Relations between Old and Young Gay Men   188

Peter Robinson

'… And the Theatre was Full of Poofs, and I Thought it was Fantastic'   201

Researching the History of Gay Men and the Movies

Scott McKinnon

Contributors

Geoff Allshorn has been involved in teaching for many years and he has produced a variety of resources tackling homophobia in schools. He is also a volunteer in a number of activist groups, and has previously published material on HIV/AIDS and the AIDS Quilt. He is currently undertaking research into the history of HIV/AIDS in Australia.

Peter Di Sciascio is a clinical biochemist and art historian in Melbourne. Peter is employed by a not-for-profit women's health organisation as a Quality Manager. He is also pursuing art history studies at the University of Melbourne. Peter has a particular interest in Australian women's art history.

Dr Lisa Featherstone is a Lecturer in Australian History at the University of Newcastle. She is interested in all aspects of the history of sexuality and the body, and is completing her first monograph, *Let's Talk About Sex: Histories of Sexuality in Australia, 1901–1961*, which will be published in 2011.

Roberta Foster completed her Arts degree at the University of Melbourne, during which she discovered a passion for gender and queer studies. She is currently undertaking the Master of Laws (Juris Doctor) at Monash University and volunteers at Victorian Aboriginal Legal Service, Moreland Community Legal Centre and Fitzroy Legal Service.

Dino Hodge is undertaking PhD research into homophobia during the life and times of former South Australian Premier Don Dunstan. His published work includes *Did you Meet any Malagas?* on Darwin's gay community, and *The Fall Upward*, interviews about spirituality in the lives of Australian lesbian women and gay men.

Associate Professor Michael Hurley is Adjunct Associate Professor at the Australian Research Centre in Sex, Health and Society, La Trobe University, Melbourne. His recent publications include: 'Gay and Lesbian Writing and Publishing in Australia, 1961–2001', *Australian Literary Studies*, 2010; with Garrett Prestage et al., *Pleasure and Sexual Health*, 2010; 'HIV, Sexual Health and Contemporary Gay Cultures', in Jablonski, et al., eds, *Sante Gaie*, 2010; and, with Prestage, 'Intensive Sex Partying amongst Gay Men in Sydney', *Culture, Health and Sexuality*, 2009.

Scott McKinnon is a PhD student at the University of Technology, Sydney. His research investigates the role of the movies in the development of gay male culture, community and identity in Sydney between 1950 and 2010.

Clare Parker is a PhD candidate in the School of History and Politics at the University of Adelaide. Her thesis examines the pioneering legalisation of abortion and male homosexual acts in South Australia in the 1960s and 1970s.

Dr Peter Robinson has taught courses in sexuality and gender studies in universities in Melbourne. His book, *The Changing World of Gay Men*, was awarded the Raewyn Connell Prize in 2010 for the best authored first monograph by an author within the discipline of Sociology. He has a contract with Palgrave Macmillan to write a second book on ageing in the gay world.

Dr Shirleene Robinson is a Senior Lecturer in Australian History at Bond University. She is the author of *Something like Slavery? Queensland's Aboriginal Child Workers, 1842–1945* and editor of *Homophobia: An Australian History*, along with other works. She is currently researching HIV/AIDS and community organisation.

Dr Paul Sendziuk is a Senior Lecturer in the School of History and Politics at the University of Adelaide. His most recent book is *Learning to Trust: Australian Responses to AIDS*, which was short-listed for the Human Rights and Equal Opportunity Commission's 2004 Human Rights Award (non-fiction section).

Dr Yorick Smaal is a Research Fellow at the ARC Centre of Excellence in Policing and Security (CEPS) at Griffith University. He has particular interests in sex and gender, war and society, and the law and criminal justice system.

Dr Graham Willett is a Senior Lecturer in Australian Studies at the University of Melbourne. He is author of *Living Out Loud: A History of Gay and Lesbian Activism in Australia*. He is President of the Australian Lesbian and Gay Archives.

Dr Emily Wilson is a Lecturer in Australian Studies at Bond University. Her current research interest is in the history of medicine and sexuality, with a particular focus on medical attitudes towards homosexuality in Australia during the twentieth century. Her most recent publication is *Prevention is Better than Cure: Eugenics in Queensland, 1900–1950* (Australian Scholarly Publishing, 2010).

Introduction

Yorick Smaal and Graham Willett

The fortieth anniversary of Australian lesbian and gay politics fell somewhere in the period 2009–2010, depending on what gets counted as the founding moment. It has been a period of remarkable achievement which is best understood as a moment in the broader process through which expression of same-sex desire has developed and changed in Australia over the last two centuries, from an initial antipodean version of eighteenth-century British sexual norms and desires, to a developed alternative culture in a modern multicultural Australia.

The contemporary LGBTI culture became well established in Australia during the later decades of the twentieth century, with clearly defined lifestyles, substantial urban ghetto developments in large metropolitan centres, and major public celebrations such as the Sydney Gay and Lesbian Mardi Gras. As we go to print, genuine legal equality is one parliamentary vote away. Lesbians and gay men, along with bisexuals, transgender and intersex people, and queers of all kinds, have moved from the margins of society to places very much closer to the mainstream.

Among those who have responded to these shifts have been historians. Mostly, but not always, queer themselves (though many would reject the term in favour of gay or lesbian), these historians have begun exploring and explaining the antecedents of contemporary behaviours, identities and subcultures, tracing the complex organisation of sexuality and gender back at least to the late nineteenth century. Some studies have shown how nascent subcultures and identities in the late colonial period blossomed throughout the early decades of the twentieth century to become an entrenched, although cloaked, part of Australia's urban landscape by the beginning of World War

II. Others have focused on the political movements which erupted from the late 1960s onwards. A few ambitious chronological histories have brought these developments together, attempting to map changing identities over longer periods of time. Together, this research has given Australia one of the best national accounts of same-sex identity and behaviour; one which embraces the national, regional and local.

The current literature on the histories of (homo)sexuality is expansive. From its modest beginnings, continuing and evolving research over the last four decades has expanded to the point that it is difficult to keep abreast of the new work appearing in monographs, readers and journals, and almost impossible to peruse fully the research scattered across interdisciplinary books and periodicals. Since 1992, the *Gay and Lesbian Perspectives* series has formed an integral part of this literature and the current volume adds to, and consolidates, the claims of Australia's place in this field. This current volume aims to provide an accessible collection of some of the latest scholarship on lesbian, gay and queer histories, privileging a same-sex desire which is often tucked away among discussions of sex and gender more generally. The chapters here began life as papers presented to the annual GLQ history conference, Australia's Homosexual Histories, which has been organised or sponsored by the Australian Lesbian and Gay Archives since 2000. The conference offers the chance for academics, junior scholars and independent researchers to present their work, and that diversity is reflected in the offerings presented here.

This volume covers many of the broad fields of research and is organised around politics, medicine, HIV/AIDS, lesbianism, and finally, the gay male world.

The first section begins with a chapter by Graham Willett. He charts the very early origins of political agitation in Canberra 12 months before CAMP became recognised as the founder of the public gay rights movement in 1970. The next two chapters explore the origins of law reform in South Australia, the first Australian jurisdiction to decriminalise sex between men in 1972. Clare Parker and Paul Sendziuk examine the connections between police harassment, public discourse and law reform, while Dino Hodge explores the role of South Australian Premier, Don Dunstan, in the last stages of this process, which was completed in 1975. It is a sign of the growing maturity of Australian queer history that we are now at the point where competing and complementary studies of the same episodes are being developed. We are still very much involved in what we might think of as the 'primitive accumulation' of knowledge, but as these chapters show, such is the depth of our knowledge on some issues, that we are able, also, to present richer and differently nuanced analyses of the same events and episodes.

Difficulties with source materials (there is no local comparison to the detailed case histories and psychiatric studies one finds in Europe and the US) has meant that local scholars have left medical histories of homosexuality largely untouched. Addressing this lacuna, two chapters explore the place of medicine in the construction of male homosexual identity: Lisa Featherstone locates the male homosexual among nineteenth century medical experts in Australia and Emily Wilson explores the connections between medical knowledge and the media one hundred years later, focusing in particular on the early HIV/AIDS years. Recently released figures showing that 1050 Australians were newly-diagnosed with HIV in 2009 – the highest number in almost two decades – highlight the need for sustained and continuing historical inquiry. A further three chapters on HIV/AIDS are included here: the first, an important study on the role of community print media in 1980s Australia by Shirleene Robinson; the second, an historiographical overview of HIV/AIDS in Australian biographies by Geoff Allshorn; and the third, a chapter on where we are at, and have been for the past 15 years, by leading social reseacher Michael Hurley.

Among the important contributions to this volume are the chapters on lesbian identities which are often marginalised in the writing of LGBTI histories: Peter Di Sciascio explores the interesting and understudied world of lesbian artists in the early decades of the twentieth century while Roberta Foster examines the phenomenon of Melbourne drag kings and the theoretical performativity of gender.

The final section brings together work on the social and cultural practices of male homosexuality. Yorick Smaal starts with a prosecution in Queensland in the 1940s which reveals a dense social network of friends and sexual partners. Peter Robinson and Scott McKinnon move us into the contemporary world and the realm of social research. Both draw on oral histories to explore, respectively, the ageing process in the gay world and the cultural practices of movie-going in Sydney.

All of these chapters employ rigorous empirical research and/or theoretical sophistication and together they draw on a vast array of historical sources. The histories presented here are recovered from government records; policing and legal evidence; archives of political organisations; personal memoirs; media reports; and oral histories. This collection embraces the national approach for which Australian scholarship is lauded, encompassing histories from New South Wales, South Australia, Victoria, Queensland, and the Australian Capital Territory.

We see this as an important collection, but it is one that will entertain and surprise as well, reminding us that history is both a way of knowing the past and enjoying it.

'We Blew Our Trumpets and...'

The ACT Homosexual Law Reform Society

Graham Willett

The formation of the Campaign Against Moral Persecution (CAMP) in Sydney in 1970 has long been regarded as the founding moment of the Australian lesbian and gay movement. And not without reason. Within a year of its foundation, it was a national organisation, with some 1500 members and branches in all states. It put the issues of homosexual law reform and public attitudes on the public agenda to an extent never before seen in Australia and any serious historical analysis must see the following decades of social, political and cultural struggle for gay equality and gay liberation as having their origins in that moment.

The Origins of the HLRS

But CAMP was not the first organisation to raise these issues. It was not even the second. Two other groups which preceded CAMP deserve to be acknowledged. The Daughters of Bilitis (DOB), a lesbian group founded in Melbourne in late 1969 and recently discussed in an important new study by Liz Ross,[1] was undeniably Australia's first political organisation of homosexuals. But there was another group to consider. The Homosexual Law Reform Society of the Australian Capital Territory (HLRS) has not been much noticed in histories of gay politics in Australia, despite the fact that it was, when set up, the most public attempt by liberals to decriminalise male homosexual acts. This indifference is not, perhaps, all that surprising. The group was not a gay group as such – the sexuality of its members was never a matter of public discussion as was the case with CAMP and DOB; nor was it particularly interested in issues other than decriminalisation. Both of these factors mark it off from what was to become the gay and lesbian movement. It makes sense to think of the HLRS as being, in the words of one of its members, the end of a phase of reform politics – a phase located within the rise of modernising liberalism in Australia and of a politics centred on civil liberties and the activism of civil libertarians.[2]

This is especially clear when we look at the group's origins, which lay in a discussion between Dr Thomas Mautner and Mr Dennis Rose in Canberra in 1969 on the subject, not of homosexuality, but of abortion law reform.[3] Mautner was a lecturer in philosophy at the Australian National University, and a long-standing supporter of liberal humanist issues, who had been urged by Beatrice Faust to involve himself in the establishment of an abortion law reform group in Canberra. In the course of a conversation with Rose, discussion turned to a recent newspaper article in the *Canberra Times* concerning two men who had been arrested in a car in the bush and charged with indecent assault. Rose indicated to Mautner that there might be more to the case than met the eye and referred him to one man's solicitor.[4] At a subsequent meeting, Mautner, Michael Landale (the solicitor) and a journalist, Peter Sekuless, discussed the idea of forming a homosexual law reform society. (Sekuless had been approached by Landale after his client had been convicted to get some publicity for the proposed appeal.[5]) The next day a front page newspaper article announced a plan to form a homosexual law reform society.[6] A public meeting was held on 27 July, attended by about 30 people, at which the society was formally established. It adopted four aims and elected a committee of seven which was to be responsible for drafting an ordinance to repeal the anti-homosexual provisions of the Territory's legal code.[7]

The HLRS drew upon the well-established acceptance within liberal circles of an anti-criminalisation stance and it is this which is reflected in the work of the committee elected to prepare the ordinance. The committee (at least three of whom were lawyers) began with a study of the basic documents including the Wolfenden Report, a 1967 public opinion survey, as well as articles and editorials from the *Medical Journal of Australia*, the *Australian Journal of Psychiatry* and the *Sydney Morning Herald*.[8] By the middle of October, under the leadership of Dr Des O'Connor of the ANU Law School, the draft ordinance and an accompanying submission had been prepared. The proposed law, guided by the British *Sexual Offences Act* of 1967, relied upon the notion of the consenting adult in private, but with two main differences from its British model: the age of consent was to be 18 rather than 21 and 'private' was not to be interpreted in the narrow sense of 'in the presence of not more than two people'. Courts would be required to seek a medical opinion before passing any sentence of imprisonment upon a homosexual. The proposal was, then, considerably more liberal than its British model. Once drafted, the proposed ordinance was submitted for approval to a further public meeting, advertised as being open to both HLRS members and others who favoured liberalising the law, held on 15 October 1969.[9]

The HLRS then set out to bring its demands and arguments for reform to the attention of legislators and opinion makers. To help them with this, the committee undertook some public opinion research. This was intended to address the concern that 'the main obstacle [to law reform] is… the belief of politicians that they would become unpopular if they introduced law reform'.[10] The 'Report of a Survey on Homosexuality' by the Faculty of Law at ANU gives the results of a survey of 100 Canberra men undertaken by students. Of the 24 questions, 13 related to homosexuality and found, among other things, that 68% of those interviewed favoured decriminalisation. The research team concluded that 'one thing seems certain – the Canberra public in general is in favour of homosexual law reform'.[11]

The Society also published three issues of a newsletter which had a national mailing list of about 130. The newsletter provided updates on progress, details of the draft ordinance, reports of lobbying activities and it encouraged supporters of law reform to write to the Attorney-General, Members of Parliament (MPs) and parliamentary candidates.[12] Members of the committee also took up the debate in public. Mautner wrote one of three articles for a *Canberra Times* series on law reform, while the journalist Peter Sekuless (who, if not a member of the HLRS, was certainly an active supporter) prepared the other two.[13] In the vigorous debate in the paper's letters column, which began after the formation of the Society was announced, both Mautner and Grieve participated, responding to criticisms of the decriminalisation position.[14] Mautner also addressed the Humanist Society in Sydney on 23 October 1969 and circulated his speech to the press.[15]

Even before they had completed work on the ordinance, members of the committee were able to report on their lobbying efforts. The second issue of the *Newsletter* listed those with whom the committee had consulted: the ACT Law Society, clergymen, members of the medical profession, members of the bench and the general public.[16] Finally, sometime after forwarding the draft ordinance and associated papers, members of the committee met with the federal Attorney-General, Tom Hughes. This was a less than satisfactory experience. Hughes had clearly not read the submission and his adviser produced a string of ludicrous objections to the proposal along the lines of the Territory's responsibility *in loco parentis* to the students at Duntroon military college.[17]

Aside from these activities by the HLRS, its committee and its members, the Society operated as a lightning rod for all those concerned with the issue of homosexual law reform. It was assisted in this by prominent articles by Don Aitkin in the *Canberra Times*, Henry Mayer in the *Australian* and Michael Richardson in the *Age*.[18] All three writers spoke out strongly in favour of homosexual law reform, marshalling the by-then familiar range of liberal arguments. All reported the work of the HLRS and (except for Richardson) provided a contact address. The result was a wave of letters to the HLRS from people praising its efforts, offering support and proposing to set up branches or similar organisations in other cities. Although the committee's view was that the state-based nature of anti-homosexual legislation made a national organisation impracticable,[19] it offered considerable support to those interstate who expressed interest in organising similar groups locally. In Melbourne, Sydney and Adelaide, the committee provided a list of names and addresses to potential organisers.[20] In Melbourne, people who had written to the HLRS met in October 1969. Carl Reinganum, a member of the Humanist Society who was present at this meeting, suggests that nothing came of it – that it petered out or was overtaken by events.[21]

The Humanist societies in various states were important supporters. The formation of the HLRS was reported both at meetings and in print. Humanist Societies in Sydney and Melbourne attempted to set up local law reform groups. At the meeting of 23 October 1969 that Thomas Mautner addressed, some members of the New South Wales branch decided to work as part of a small committee to 'press for reform in NSW'.[22] The committee, which first met in February 1970, was initially encouraged by the favourable publicity received by the ACT HLRS. Hoping to find 'ten really dedicated people', it was disappointed in a number of ways: it found that that the numbers involved in the committee actually declined over the next few months; there were no 'legal, political or sociological experts willing to be active'; and, not least, perhaps, that 'the people to whom this particular social change is of interest – i.e., the homosexual community – [did] not come forward in great numbers'. This, and the result of Wilson and Chappell's 1967 survey which showed a mere 22% support for homosexual law reform among the public, led the committee reluctantly to the conclusion that, 'the climate of opinion is clearly not ripe for change'.[23] The Humanists in Melbourne had somewhat more success. In late 1969 or early 1970, a six person committee set up to 'study and recommend what action should be taken to reform the law on homosexuality' produced a five page pamphlet, *The Homosexual and the Law – A Humanist View*.[24] In Brisbane a committee was set up in 1970 by the Queensland Humanists.[25]

There was little or no adverse reaction to the Society's work. The Society's papers contain no hostile correspondence and, overall, Dr Mautner was able to report to a correspondent in November 1969 that 'it does appear as if there is virtually no opposition to the kind of law reform that we have in mind'.[26] High levels of support were reflected in the debate in the letters column of the *Canberra Times*. Between 5 July (the day after the article announcing the intention to found the Society was published) and 13 August, some 20 letters on the subject of homosexuality and decriminalisation were published. Of these, 14 were in favour of decriminalisation, and six were opposed; and these six were written by only two different people.[27] While this hardly represents a cross-section of the community, it must have struck readers that it was reasonable and common to have a pro-reform position.

Early Responses

In the medium term, significant public figures began to take up the question of law reform. In the churches, although no public statement from any authoritative body seems to have been issued, the Rev. R. W. Lawton, a minister of the Churches of Christ, called for decriminalisation in a radio broadcast, declaring forcefully that '[t]his churchman adds his cry of "shame" at the gaoling of consenting adults, and adds his cry for the repeal of legal prohibitions and penalties'.[28] At the Anglican Synod on 12 August 1969, the Rev. K. Brewer of Canberra moved a motion condemning the law, only to have a motion to close the synod moved and passed. In response to radio reports of this episode, two other delegates dashed off letters to the *Canberra Times* to explain that the decision to close the synod related to a dwindling quorum and the lateness of the hour, rather than any opposition to the content of the motion.[29]

Several months later, on 27 May 1970, the federal Attorney-General, Tom Hughes, in an address to the national conference of the Australian Council of Social Services in Canberra, suggested that homosexual acts ought not necessarily to be within the ambit of the criminal law.[30] (James Grieve scribbled a jokey note to Mautner on a copy of this speech – '*Mon cher Thomas: Salut*! As you see, we blew our trumpets and the walls of Jericho came tumbling down'; reflecting the optimism that the speech evoked.) Better was to follow: the next day editorials in the *Canberra Times* and the *Age* supported Hughes' position and called for law reform.[31] A few months later again Gough Whitlam, leader of the federal parliamentary Labor Party, declared his agreement with Pierre Trudeau's dictum that 'the courts have no place in the bedrooms of the nation' and pledged his support for a free (that is, non-party directed) vote in the Parliament.[32]

Well into 1971, the group was actively seeking opportunities to make its case. Perhaps the most dramatic of these was the attempt to convene a meeting of interested members of the federal Parliament.[33] In October 1971, Dr Mautner wrote to Bill Hayden, a prominent ALP frontbencher who had a long history of support for homosexual law reform. In his letter Mautner noted that the Melbourne Anglican Synod had recently voted for decriminalisation and suggested a briefing for interested MPs.[34]

Hayden responded favourably and called a meeting for the evening of Tuesday 2 November 1971. On that morning, however, the caucus executive discussed the issue of the meeting and Frank Stewart and Charlie Jones, prominent members of the Catholic wing of the party, expressed bitter hostility to the proposal. Hayden's initial reaction was to go ahead anyway – in the absence of any party policy to the contrary, he saw no reason not to at least discuss the matter. Stewart and Jones demanded a special caucus meeting to thrash the issue out, and although this demand was rejected by the executive, the bitterness aroused was by now so intense that Hayden decided to call the meeting off. Stewart was a powerful figure in the New South Wales right and had friends in Queensland (Hayden's home state) and may well have been able to make things difficult for Hayden.[35] Moss Cass, when advised of the cancellation of the meeting and of the reasons for this, organised 11 members of the caucus to reissue Hayden's original circular, convening the meeting for a week later than originally scheduled. Among the signatures were those of senior parliamentary figures such as Lionel Murphy, Jim Cairns and Tom Uren (all members of the caucus executive) as well as, the *Daily Telegraph* noted, four backbench doctors.[36]

Even then the controversy was not finished. On the evening originally scheduled for the meeting, Mautner and his fellow speakers, Moss Cass, Gough Whitlam and several other MPs were standing in King's Hall when Frank Stewart ('a bit under the weather', as both Cass and Mautner recall) passed by. Approached by Cass to discuss the matter, and possibly invited to attend a meeting, he refused, red-faced with fury, any suggestion that he might sit in the same room as any 'bum-fuckers'. In the subsequent exchange of views he threatened to punch Dr Mautner in the nose. Things were defused and a week later the meeting went ahead without incident.[37] Indeed, James Grieve remembers it as a very productive meeting – attended by 18 ALP MPs, with a Liberal (Bob Solomon), who may have been defying a party decision not to attend, sitting away from the table at which the speakers and audience were seated. Mautner, Grieve and Elizabeth Reid presented the case for law reform, rehearsing, yet again, the nature of the draft ordinance and the state of public opinion.[38]

The Limits of Liberalism

In view of the overwhelmingly favourable immediate response to the demands of the HLRS and the apparent escalation of support over the following months, it comes as something of a shock to realise that homosexual law reform was not achieved in the ACT until 1976 – some seven years after the HLRS was established. By this stage, the Society itself had ceased to exist. Its activities had scaled down over the course of 1971 and the federal parliament furore had been something of a last gasp. In July of that year Dr Mautner described the group as 'somewhat inactive' but added that 'individual members keep in touch with Members of Parliament to promote a reform of the law'.[39] A few months later, James Grieve used the term 'a rather dormant body' to summarise its state.[40]

It is not as if the timing was wrong. It was very right indeed. On the very day that the *Canberra Times* reported the case of the two men arrested while having sex in a car, the federal Attorney-General was tabling in Parliament a report prepared that the Law Council had presented to him in February. The report proposed a Draft Criminal Code (DCC) for the ACT.[41] Until this time, the ACT's legal system still rested primarily upon those New South Wales laws which had been in force when the Canberra was established as a separate territory. Amendment of the laws was within the purview of the federal Minister for the Interior who had the power to amend by ordinance the way in which such laws applied in the Territory. This was widely felt to be unsatisfactory and in 1969 the Law Council of Australia had submitted, after five years' work, a draft criminal code for the territories. In its introduction to the draft, the Co-ordinating Committee noted that:

> We are aware that there are some areas of controversy with respect to the criminal law, particularly relating to homosexuality, abortion and

suicide. We have not attempted to answer the problems raised by these controversies, the answer to which must depend upon a government's appreciation of social conditions in the widest sense.[42]

This approach was endorsed by the Attorney-General when he tabled the report and sometime later by F. C. P. Keane, Special Magistrate in the ACT, who acknowledged that the Law Council's Co-ordinating Committee had evaded these hard issues but argued that for it to have taken a stand on such controversial matters would have been a waste of time, because 'there is no consensus of modern-trend thinking acceptable to all sections of the community on these issues'.[43]

The attempt to quarantine the DCC from political debate on these social questions failed entirely. If the immediate trigger for the formation of the HLRS was the prosecution of the man in the car, the DCC provided the focus for much of the public campaign. After all, if the ACT law was to be rewritten, this was the obvious time to decriminalise homosexuality. James Grieve makes the point that it was the co-incidence of the two events that was crucial:

> it had all happened before; there had been many more scandalous, cruel, unjust and stupid prosecutions than this one, yet they had never aroused public indignation nor precipitated the formation of a law-reform society. But this case happened about the time when the Government had published, and invited comment on, the new code of criminal legislation that it intends to introduce.[44]

The opportunity took on a certain urgency once it was realised that, actually, the effect of the code was to *broaden* the scope of the acts that fell under the law's sanction. The proposed offence of 'sexual connection against the order of nature' did not restrict itself to acts committed by men, thus opening the possibility that heterosexual couples could be prosecuted under its terms, and the vagueness of the formulation meant that behaviour that fell outside the established offences of buggery, attempted buggery and indecent assault on a male might be now offences.[45] The DCC, then, was both trigger and target for much of the HLRS' activism, pushing the general issue of the law and society onto the public agenda in a way that made the specific issue of homosexual law reform (and indeed a number of other issues that I have not addressed here) a relevant part of the debate.

Of course, the opportunity presented by the DCC occurred within the broader context of the rise of modernising liberalism. It was a shift that the HLRS was well-placed to take advantage of. The HLRS was at the centre of a complex web of liberal and humanist activists, of which its own founding process is merely one example: from Faust (whom Mautner had met in Melbourne at the time of the Ronald Ryan hanging, and who had herself been involved in support for the homosexual cause through her role as spokesperson for the lesbian group, DOB), to Mautner to Rose to Landale, is an interesting reminder of the way in which small networks of people could mobilise each other around political activity. So, too, is the Landale to Sekuless link.[46] Mautner himself was, as James Grieve says, someone who knew everybody, including prominent figures in the ALP and the media, which provided an invaluable means for lobbying and publicising the issue. Most of the committee members were actively involved in public affairs, with Thomas Mautner and James Grieve having been involved in abortion law reform[47] and two of the other members of the committee being prominent figures in the two main political parties – Landale in the Liberal Party, Gordon Walsh in the ALP.[48]

The Society also had very good contact with and support from the media. The *Canberra Times* had been 'most generous in opening its columns for a detailed and penetrating discussion of the laws on homosexuality'[49] with its six articles in July and August, as well as items on the formation of the Society and many letters. It also published a number of reviews by James Grieve of books regarding homosexuality.[50] As Peter Sekuless notes, the editor of the *Canberra Times*, John Allen, was a Catholic who might have been expected to oppose aims of the HLRS. As a liberal, however, he was keen to have the *Canberra Times* operate as a paper of record and to have it reflect accurately what was happening in society.[51] Michael Richardson, Canberra correspondent for the *Age*, was a keen supporter of editor Graham Perkins, who was pushing that paper into the liberal area of the market.[52] Other newspapers, plus local and national radio and television coverage had also been important.[53]

All of which makes the failure of the HLRS to achieve its goal that much more surprising. But a welcoming political climate and even friends in high places are not, on their own, any guarantee of success. It is often assumed that decriminalisation would be an easy task, compared to the broader goals of shifting public opinion and overthrowing religious and medical paradigms. James Grieve wrote to the founders of CAMP in this vein in September 1970, declaring that CAMP's task of changing public opinion and professional attitudes and policies would be 'a much harder job' and that 'no doubt we shall succeed long before you do'.[54]

In fact, this was not the case at all. And the reason for this is that law reform rests on winning a particular group of people, who may or may not be susceptible to the efforts of the reformers. Public opinion is everywhere; and even the medical profession and the clergy are composed of large diverse groups of people in which pools of supporters and opponents could be identified and targeted. Activists could (and did) operate on many fronts, simultaneously and serially; moving around blockages towards opportunities. Legislators, on the other hand, are a relatively small, tightly-knit and somewhat cautious group. And legislation can only be enacted if a majority of them can be induced to support it. This places quite tight constraints on what a group of activists interested only in law reform can do.

In relation to homosexual law reform in the ACT the main obstacle was not any great hostility to the demand; it was the fact that, despite the pool of support within party political circles, the issue was simply not a pressing one for politicians. The earliest sign of this came with Tom Hughes' unceremonious dumping of the issue. From his cautious but outspoken defence of the idea in May 1970 that homosexual acts ought not necessarily be within the ambit of the criminal law, he retreated rapidly. By September he renounced the idea entirely, declaring that he had been 'kite-flying' to test public opinion and had found more opposition than support.[55] (Michael Richardson, of the *Age*, while not denying that there may have been a flood of hostile letters, saw the chief source of opposition to law reform as being members of the Liberal and Country parties.[56])

The ALP, although having a better record of public support – in July, the Western Australian State Conference had passed a motion calling for law reform[57] – turned out, in power, to be surprisingly dilatory; and, indeed, in the end, it actually failed to decriminalise at all. This despite early positive signs. On 18 October 1973, the House of Representatives voted in favour of a motion that read: '[t]hat in the opinion of this House homosexual acts between consenting adults in private should not be subject to the criminal law'. The motion was a private member's bill moved by former Liberal Prime Minister John Gorton and seconded by ALP Minister for the Environment Moss Cass. A free vote (that is, one in which party discipline was not imposed) resulted in a 64–40 majority in favour of the motion.[58]

Cass was a long-standing supporter of liberal causes, including homosexual law reform.[59] At the suggestion of his staff member, Peter Blazey, he decided to act on the issue and Prime Minister Whitlam was prepared to allow a law reform motion as a private members' bill if a Liberal front-bencher were to co-sponsor it. John Gorton agreed to do so. The motion did not create much interest – Cass remembers little in the way of lobbying, for example – perhaps because it was not expected to pass at all[60] and one of the surprises was the cross-party support that it got. Approached afterwards by Blazey, who noted the number of conservatives who had voted for the motion, Doug Anthony, the leader of the Country Party, laughingly declared that, '[y]ou Labor boys think you're so trendy. But what you don't realise is that a lot of us have been to boarding school!'[61] While this may be part of the explanation, it is more likely that it was the appeal of liberal ideas, as embodied in the key speeches, that carried the vote. Certainly a significant bloc of the opposition came from the right-wing faction of the ALP, reflecting the conservative Catholicism of this group.[62]

This motion had been an expression of opinion only. Because the ACT was expecting self-government, Cass and Gorton agreed that they would not impose law reform, but merely state the Parliament's view that such reform was desirable. The new ACT Legislative Assembly did not have its first sitting until October 1974, and so, in debating the issue on 2 December it was moving promptly on the matter.[63] Unfortunately, it only had advisory powers at that stage and its debate resulted in a motion in favour of law reform, but no actual reform. The final bill for reform was only presented to the Assembly in May 1975 where it passed on 22 July.[64] By the time the federal ALP government fell in November of that year the ordinance had still not been signed into law and in mid-1976 the whole process began all over again under a new Liberal Attorney-General, Bob Ellicott, who had not been happy with the earlier version.[65] The final decriminalisation of male homosexual acts took place in November 1976.

In the end, the reform of the law in the ACT owed much to agendas other than those raised by the HLRS and the liberal humanist imperative. We can see this in the way in which it was argued for during the December 1974 Legislative Assembly debate. Certainly, the well-established liberal arguments were made,[66] but they are supplemented, even over-shadowed, by a more parochial concern with the right of the Assembly to make social legislation. Susan Ryan, the mover of the December 1974 motion, argued at some length along the lines that:

> There is no justification for elected members of Parliament from all over Australia formulating social legislation that affects the lives of the people living here [in Canberra]. We are a community. We are about to have self-government and this is the sort of area where I think we must, very speedily, move into legislation.[67]

Fully three-quarters of the Ryan speech was to do with this aspect of law reform, rather than with the merits of the case itself.

The HLRS had raised the issue of law reform, drafted an impressive proposal and lobbied successfully to elicit statements of support from significant numbers of influential people. It had put the issue of homosexual law reform on the public agenda; it had even undertaken the research to show that there was real public support for decriminalisation. But in the end, it lacked the capacity to overcome the relative insignificance of the issue to those who alone had the power to change the law. Its failure to carry through its task merely affirms that processes of social and political change are more complex – full of vagaries and chances – than a single organisation can necessarily deal with. It was the role of the social movement, which was emerging in the capillaries of society and which was to erupt in Sydney in July 1970, to show just what was required to carry through the reform of Australian laws and attitudes towards homosexuality.

Endnotes

1. Liz Ross, 'We Were Catalysts for Change', *Journal of Lesbian Studies*, vol. 13, no. 4 (2009), pp. 442–458. See also, Lucy Chesser, 'Australasian Lesbian Movement, "Claudia's Group" and Lynx: "Non-Political" Lesbian Organisation in Melbourne, 1969–1980', *Hecate: An Interdisciplinary Journal of Women's Liberation*, vol. 22, no. 1 (1996), pp. 69–91.

2. On modernising liberalism, see, Graham Willett, *Living Out Loud: A History of Gay and Lesbian Activism in Australia*, St Leonards, NSW: Allen and Unwin, 2000, ch. 1. The positioning of the HLRS within the politics of civil liberties was suggested by James Grieve in an interview 21 September 1995.

3. Unless otherwise noted, the information in this section comes from my interview with Dr Thomas Mautner in Canberra, 22 February 1995.

4. Apart from the harshness of the penalty inflicted upon the convicted man (the jury had recommended medical treatment; the judge had sentenced him to six months' prison) the circumstances of the case were also somewhat odd. The *Canberra Times* article ('Sentenced to Gaol', *Canberra Times*, 14 May 1969, p. 8) noted in passing that two men had been found in the car and both had been interviewed; the trial and conviction, however, related to one man only. James Grieve published an article in *Woroni*, the ANU student newspaper, in October 1970 which claimed that one of the men had escaped prosecution because he refused to incriminate himself; the other, surprised by the police, blurted out 'He touched me', which was sufficient evidence to convict. James Grieve, 'Homosexual Law Reform', *Woroni*, 1 October 1970, n. p. [Clipping in HLRS Records]. Peter Sekuless has suggested that, given how isolated the road on which the arrested men had been, there were doubts raised as to how and why the police came to be there in the first place. Peter Sekuless, interview with Graham Willett, 28 March 1996.

5. Peter Sekuless, interview with Graham Willett.

6. 'Moves on Homosexuality', *Canberra Times*, 4 July 1969, p. 1. The article makes no mention of Sekuless' involvement in the meeting, presumably for reasons of professional discretion on the reporter's part.

7   'Homosexual Law Reform', advertisement, *Canberra Times*, 23 July 1969, n. p. [Clipping in HLRS Records]; 'Reform of Law Sought by New Society', *Canberra Times*, 28 July 1969, p. 1; *HLRS Newsletter*, no. 1, 27 August 1969, p. 2; James Grieve, interview with Graham Willett.
8   Thomas Mautner, to Henry Mayer, letter, n. d. [first week August 1969]; Henry Mayer, to Thomas Mautner, letter, 5 August 1969, HLRS Records.
9   Advertisement, *Canberra Times*, 8 October 1969, n. p. [Clipping in HLRS Records].
10 Thomas Mautner, to Mrs L. M. Smith, letter, 17 November 1969, HLRS Records.
11 Faculty of Law, ANU, Report of a Survey on Homosexuality, typescript, n. d., MS2692, National Library of Australia (NLA). The survey was reported in 'Homosexuals: Poll Swings Their Way', *Age*, 24 September 1970, p. 5.
12 *HLRS Newsletter*, no. 1, p. 9.
13 Thomas Mautner, 'Harming Those Who Cause No Offence', *Canberra Times*, 8 August 1969. p. 2; Peter Sekuless, 'The Odd Man Out in the Law's Eyes', *Canberra Times*, 6 August 1969, p. 2; Peter Sekuless, 'The Homosexual in Australia', *Canberra Times*, 7 August 1969, p. 2. Sekuless says that he was probably formally a member of the HLRS and that if he was not, it was only in order to protect himself from accusations of partiality. Peter Sekuless, interview with Graham Willett.
14 James Grieve, letter, *Canberra Times*, 1 August 1969; and, Thomas Mautner, letter, *Canberra Times*, 17 July 1969. Members of the HLRS did not generally identify themselves as such in their letters and the letters' editor did not normally describe the correspondents. It may well be then that there were, among the other correspondents, other members of the Society, though none of the other members of the committee, whose names I know, are represented.
15 A summary of the points made in his address is to be found in the HLRS Records. The speech was reported in 'Draft of Code Criticised', *Canberra Times*, 24 October 1969, p. 3.
16 *HLRS Newsletter*, no. 2, p. 2.
17 James Grieve, to Lena Stevens, letter, 2 January 1970, HLRS Records; Grieve, 'Homosexual Law Reform', n. p.
18 Don Aitkin, 'Between the Lines', column, *Canberra Times*, 9 July 1969, p. 2; Henry Mayer, 'So Why Can't Australia Modernise its Laws on Homosexuality?', *Australian*, 21 August 1969, p. 7; Michael Richardson, 'The Last Great Unmentionable', *Age*, 9 August 1969, p. 7. Peter Sekuless notes that Richardson was a long-standing friend of Landale's and worked to support the issue behind the scenes, as well as in the *Age*, drawing upon long-standing family links to the Canberra community. Peter Sekuless, Comments on draft of thesis chapter, 1997.
19 Thomas Mautner, to Peter Whyte, letter, 15 September 1969, HLRS Records.
20 For Melbourne, see, Thomas Mautner, to James Taylor, letter, 7 November 1969, HLRS Records; for Sydney, see, Dr J. Woolnough, form letter, to nine people, 27 January 1970, copy in HLRS Records.
21 Thomas Mautner, to Mrs F. Thompson, letter, 30 September 1969; Thomas Mautner, to James Taylor, letter, 7 November 1969, Correspondence File, HLRS Records. Carl Reinganum, interview with Graham Carbery and Rob Thurling, 16 April 1989, Australian Lesbian and Gay Archives (ALGA), transcript.
22 'Homosexual Law Reform', *Viewpoints*, November 1969, n. p.
23 Dorothy Simons, 'Homosexual Law Reform', *Viewpoints*, June 1970, p. 47. See also later comment by F. C. Fuller, 'Achievements of the HLR Committee', *Viewpoints*, February 1972, pp. 13–14; and, a letter in reply by Dorothy Simons, *Viewpoints*, April 1972, p. 25.

24 Humanist Society of Victoria, *The Homosexual and the Law – A Humanist View*, Melbourne, 1970. On the committee, see, *Victorian Humanist*, February 1970, p. 2. There are two letters from Reinganum, writing on behalf of the Humanist Society of Victoria, to the HLRS discussing the committee's work. Carl Reinganum, to HLRS, letters, one n. d., and one 5 January 1970. Correspondence file, HLRS Records.

25 'The Brisbane Link (Lynx)', *Camp Ink*, vol. 1, no. 5 (March 1971), p. 7.

26 Thomas Mautner, to Mrs L. M. Smith, letter, 17 November 1969, HLRS Records.

27 *Canberra Times*, letters, 5, 9, 11–12, 15–19, 25–26, 29 July; 1, 4, 6, 12, 13, 15 August.

28 'Church Role on Homosexual Law Defined', *Canberra Times*, 12 August 1969, p. 7. In the same article, an unnamed psychiatrist supported Mr Lawton's stance.

29 (The Rev.) Neville Chynoweth, 'Debate in Synod', letter, *Canberra Times*, 16 August 1969, p. 2; T. R. J. Foster, 'Debate in Synod', letter, *Canberra Times*, 20 August 1969, p.2.

30 T. E. F. Hughes, Deviant Behaviour of a Criminal Nature, unpublished paper presented to the Sixth National Conference of the Australian Council of Social Services, Canberra, 27 May 1970. Newspaper reports include: Peter Sekuless, 'Deviants Viewed More Liberally, Says Hughes', *Canberra Times*, 28 May 1970, p. 1; 'Attorney-General Considers a Change in Sex Law', *Australian*, 28 May 1970, p. 3; 'Homosexual Laws May be Liberalised says A-G Hughes', *Sydney Morning Herald* (*SMH*), 28 May 1970, p.1.

31 'A Case for Change', editorial, *Canberra Times*, 29 May 1970, p. 2; 'In No Man's Land', editorial, *Age*, 29 May 1970, p. 7.

32 'Whitlam Wants Free Vote on Sex Law Reform', *Australian*, 6 October 1970, p. 3; 'No Party Line on Morals, Says Whitlam', *Age*, 1 September 1970, p. 2. The importance of the free, or conscience, vote to the chance of success is emphasised by Dr Moss Cass who explained 'Well, if it hadn't been a free vote, the NSW right would have marshalled and we would never have been able to put the bloody thing in the first place. The only way you could get it up was as a free vote.' Moss Cass, interview with Graham Willett, 7 June 1995.

33 The following is based upon newspaper reports, including, David Solomon, 'Talk on Law Reform Cancelled', *Canberra Times*, 3 November 1971, p. 3; 'Labor Dispute to Recur', *Canberra Times*, 5 November 1971, p. 3; 'Playing the Early Election Card', *Nation Review*, 5–12 November 1971; 'ALP Move Stops Meeting', *SMH*, 3 November 1971, p. 3; 'Camp Meeting Called Off by ALP', 3 November 1971 [Clipping in HLRS Records – I have been unable to locate the original source of this clipping. This article erroneously believes that the speakers were to have been from CAMP]; and on interviews with Thomas Mautner, James Grieve and Moss Cass.

34 Thomas Mautner, to Bill Hayden, letter, 12 October 1971, HLRS Records.

35 Moss Cass, interview with Graham Willett. Hayden himself has no recollection of the incident. Bill Hayden, interview with Graham Willett, 26 September 1995.

36 'New Move to Hear Reform Speakers', *Daily Telegraph*, 5 November 1971, n. p. This article includes the text of the circular as well as a full list of signatories.

37 There was one final exchange of letters between Dr Mautner and Frank Stewart, in which Mautner requested a meeting to exchange views on the issue and Stewart refused. Thomas Mautner, to Frank Stewart, letter, 5 November 1971; Frank Stewart, to Thomas Mautner, letter, 15 November 1971, HLRS Records.

38 James Grieve interview with Graham Willett; Thomas Mautner, Proposal for Introductory Statement at Meeting at Parliament House, unpublished paper, HLRS Records.

39 Thomas Mautner, to Mrs J. Huggins, letter, 1 July 1971, HLRS Records.

40 James Grieve, to Mrs J. Capp, letter, 23 October 1971, HLRS Records.

41 'Territories Law Code Tabled', *Canberra Times*, 15 May 1969, p. 3. There is a useful brief overview of the history of the DCC in Elizabeth Reid, 'Drafting the Code of Repression', *Woroni* [clipping in HLRS Records, n. d., pre-March 1972]. Reid had been a foundation member of the HLRS.

42 'Draft Criminal Code for the Australian Territories', Parliament of the Commonwealth of Australia, Parliamentary Paper no. 44, 1969, p. 3.

43 F. C. P. Keane, 'Repairing a Legal Patchwork Quilt', *Canberra Times*, 29 July 1969, p. 2; F. C. P. Keane, 'Some Ingenious New Approaches', *Canberra Times*, 30 July 1969, p. 2.

44 Grieve, 'Homosexual Law Reform', n. p.

45 Mautner, 'Harming Those Who Cause No Offence'; Grieve, 'Homosexual Law Reform'; Reid, 'Drafting the Code of Repression'. It seems to me that it also opened the possibility of prosecution of lesbianism, though no-one at the time seems to have commented on this aspect.

46 Sekuless and Landale were friends and the court reporter–lawyer nexus provided occasional opportunities to support each other's work. Peter Sekuless, interview with Graham Willett.

47 James Grieve, interview with Graham Willett. For the formation of the Abortion Law Reform Association in Canberra (including the election of James Grieve to the executive body) see, 'Abortion Group Seeks Reforms', *Canberra Times*, 17 September 1969, p. 15.

48 Thomas Mautner, to Henry Mayer, letter, n. d. [late July 1969], HLRS Records

49 *HLRS Newsletter*, no. 1, p. 5.

50 James Grieve, 'A Book to Enlighten', (review of H. Montgomery Hyde, *The Other Love*), *Canberra Times*, 20 June 1970, p. 13; James Grieve, 'A Rough Descent', (review of Ian Harvey, *To Fall Like Lucifer*), *Canberra Times*, 13 November 1971; James Grieve, 'A Jolt For the Liberals', (review of Dennis Altman, *Homosexual: Oppression and Liberation*), 2 September 1972. I am grateful to James Grieve for drawing these to my attention and for providing copies.

51 Peter Sekuless, interview with Graham Willett.

52 ibid.

53 *HLRS Newsletter*, no. 1, p. 5.

54 John Ware and Christabel Poll, to Thomas Mautner, letter, 8 September 1970; James Grieve, to John Ware, letter, 22 September 1970, HLRS Records.

55 'Homosexuality Reform is Off', *Age*, 22 September 1970, p. 3; Michael Richardson, 'Hughes's Great About-Turn', *Age*, 24 September 1970, p. 8. Peter Sekuless reports that he and Michael Richardson of the *Age* went to see Hughes after he made his initial comments and were surprised at his apparent backing away from his position. They came to believe that he had received a 'roasting' in the parliamentary caucus room from conservatives in both the Liberal and Country parties. The fear seems to have been that Canberra would be seen to be setting the pace nationally – a not unreasonable fear, given that this is precisely how the Whitlam government did use its control of the ACT. Sekuless, Comments on thesis draft, 1997.

56 Michael Richardson, 'Hughes's Great About-Turn', *Age*, 24 September 1970, p. 8.

57 'Let Them Do It in Private: Labor', *Age*, 25 July 1970, p. 8.

58 Unless otherwise noted what follows is drawn from my interview with Moss Cass. For the debate, see, *Australian Parliamentary Debates* (*Hansard*), House of Representatives, 18 October 1973, pp. 2327–2335.

59 As we have seen, when Bill Hayden had been forced to withdraw his support for the Parliament House meeting with the HLRS in 1971, Cass had stepped into the breach

by co-sponsoring the meeting in Hayden's stead. He was also an active supporter of the abortion law reform motion which was defeated in Parliament in 1973 and was dismayed and angered that not one Liberal had supported this motion. 'Crabby' in his own words, with the Liberals, he was interested in the suggestion made by a member of his staff that he could press the Liberals on their liberal credentials further by putting up a homosexual law reform motion. The staffer was Peter Blazey – gay, a supporter of gay liberation, but not yet out. It is a nice example of the way in which the movement, being everywhere, could have an impact at odd moments, creating its own opportunities, as well as those generated by others.

60 Gorton expected no more than eight or nine votes from Liberals and none at all from the Country Party; Cass thought that a majority of ALP members would vote against. Moss Cass, interview with Graham Willett.

61 Peter Blazey, 'Big Quakes, Gay Shakes', *OutRage* (March 1994), p. 59.

62 Lex Watson, 'Please Sir, We'd Like Some More', *Campaign*, vol. 3, no. 7, p. 3. One of those who voted against from this position was Paul Keating who, in the 1990s, as Prime Minister, was to actively intervene in Tasmanian state politics to subvert its anti-homosexual laws and to regulate to allow homosexuals to serve in the military.

63 Australian Capital Territory, *Legislative Assembly, Hansard*, 2 December 1974, pp.102–113.

64 Law Reform (Sexual Behaviour) Bill, 1975; Explanatory Memorandum; Memorandum from Gordon Bryant, Minister for the Capital Territory, to the President ACT Legislative Assembly, no. 1975/57, 28 May 1975.

65 Lex Watson, 'Old ACT HLR Saga', *Speaking Volumes*, July – August 1976, n. p.; Lex Watson, 'Federal Poofter Bashing Resumes', *Nation Review*, 20 – 26 February 1976, p.466.

66 See, for example, Australian Capital Territory, *Legislative Assembly, Hansard*, 2 December 1974, Mr Vivian (pp. 106–107), Mr Black (pp. 104–106), Mrs Kelly (pp.110–111).

67 Ms Ryan, Australian Capital Territory, *Legislative Assembly, Hansard*, 2 December 1974, p.103.

It's Time

The Duncan Case and the Decriminalisation of Homosexual Acts in South Australia, 1972

Clare Parker and Paul Sendziuk

On 10 May 1972, the body of Dr George Duncan was pulled from Adelaide's River Torrens. Over the following months, the extensive media interest in the case, which appeared to revolve around the harassment of homosexual men by members of the police Vice Squad, prompted an open discussion of homosexuality never before seen in South Australia. Later that year, the State Government reformed the law regarding male homosexual acts between consenting adults in private, the first reform of its kind in Australia. In this chapter, we examine the circumstances surrounding the South Australian government's reform in 1972. Although the legislation ultimately fell short of full decriminalisation, which would be achieved in 1975, this first reform marks an important turning-point. As well as tracing the key arguments in the debate about homosexuality that ensued following the media's exposé of Duncan's death, we consider the legacy of law reform in 1972 and contemplate why it happened first in South Australia.

There have been a small number of studies of homosexual law reform in South Australia. John Lee has written about male homosexual identity and subculture in pre-World War II Adelaide, and his analysis has been drawn upon and expanded by Chiah Mayne in a recent Honours thesis at the University of Adelaide.[1] Tim Reeves's research into the 1972 decriminalisation debate, including the impact of the Duncan case and the role of the Campaign Against Moral Persecution (CAMP), forms the basis of his Honours thesis at the University of Adelaide, and an essay in the second volume of the *Gay and Lesbian Perspectives* series.[2] Reeves argues that the 1972 decriminalisation Bill was a 'knee-jerk, libertarian reaction' to the controversy surrounding Dr Duncan's death, and as such was unlikely to pass without amendments that would render it impotent.[3] In Reeves' mind, the whirlwind of discussion about the Duncan case and the brief time that elapsed between Duncan's death and the introduction of the Bill did not leave enough time for gay activists to ensure that parliamentarians and the community were sufficiently informed about homosexuality to intelligently debate and pass the Bill in its initial form. He suggests that 'there was no real attempt to examine… the danger of discrimination at work' and that 'the whole social and cultural construction of homosexuality was never considered',[4] but the second of these assertions is contrary to our findings presented here. In a later edition of the *Gay and Lesbian Perspectives* series, Reeves and Malcolm Cowan discuss the law reform debates that occurred between 1972 and 1975, and the events of 1975, which resulted in the complete decriminalisation of homosexual acts between consenting adults. Their analysis draws upon Cowan's Honours thesis on a similar topic.[5] In this and the authors' other publications, it is asserted that Dr Duncan's death and the 1972 law reform 'achieved little',[6] which, we suggest, is an overly pessimistic reading of the evidence. These articles and theses are the only specific discussions of the topic that we have encountered, but the South Australian experience is mentioned in a number of other works with a broader focus, such as Graham Willett's *Living Out Loud*.[7]

Precursors to Reform

Male homosexual acts had always been illegal in South Australia. The law can be traced to the British Buggery Act of 1533,[8] and underwent various changes in Britain and the British colonies over the following centuries. In South Australia, the death penalty for buggery was removed in 1859 (it had never been used), but the range of offences was increased. By 1876, the penalty for buggery in South Australia was anything from 10 years to life imprisonment with hard labour, and allowed for flogging. In 1925, the *Criminal Law Consolidation Act* was amended to state explicitly that homosexual acts 'in public or private' amounted to gross indecency. A further amendment in 1935 reduced the penalty to a maximum of 10 years' imprisonment, with hard labour no longer compulsory.[9] So, while penalties became less severe, the range and exact details of offences became greater. Chiah Mayne argues that this indicates a growing awareness of homosexuality as an identity, and more than just isolated incidences of men having sex with men.[10]

Life for homosexual men in Adelaide before World War II was generally similar to life in other Australian states. Beats were an important part of homosexual interactions, and included the Adelaide parklands, public toilets and, more discreetly, certain eating establishments around town. Police were aware of the major beats, and using them came with an ever-present threat of arrest. It also made homosexual men a target of violence from gangs of youths or vigilantes. The rate of prosecution was not high, and the most commonly reported crimes were sexual violence, indecent assault and rape, often – but not always – against children.[11] Realistically, policing truly private and consensual homosexual acts was virtually impossible.

Apart from certain individual cases before the courts, homosexuality received very little public attention, and remained this way until the mid-1960s. Graham Willett notes that before that time, there was little coverage of homosexual issues in the media, in Parliament, or in medical, legal and religious journals. When it was discussed, 'it was reviled and vilified'[12] as something 'dangerous and repulsive'.[13] Censorship was rife in the era, and any material concerning depictions or discussions of homosexuality was silenced before it could reach an audience.[14] However, later in the 1960s, public discussions of homosexuality began to emerge and became more positive.[15]

In 1954, the British Government commissioned a report into prostitution and male homosexual offences. Published in 1957 and generally known as the Wolfenden Report, it investigated thoroughly the current thinking on the nature, causes and effects of homosexuality, and recommended that the law be changed to decriminalise 'homosexual behaviour between consenting adults in private';[16] a phrase later used in South Australia and elsewhere.[17] This recommendation was adopted by Britain in 1967,[18] and was to have a significant influence on Australian debates.

A notable feature of the British discussions was the firm stance taken by the Archbishop of Canterbury, who spoke in favour of decriminalisation.[19] From the late 1960s, Australian churches began considering their own attitudes towards homosexuality. In 1968, the South Australian Methodist Conference issued a Report on Homosexuality, which was hesitant about recommending law reform: '[t]he Commission does not recommend a change in the law, although some changes appeared to all members to be necessary'.[20]

By 1972, however, the Conference had reached the opinion that the law should be changed, although the emphasis was on encouraging counselling for those with what it called 'homosexual tendencies'.[21] In 1971, the Anglican Diocese of Melbourne issued a report on homosexuality which recommended that the law be changed to make legal male homosexual acts committed in private.[22] The Bishop of Adelaide initially disagreed with the recommendation,[23] but less than six months later the Adelaide daily newspaper, the *Advertiser*, reported that he had changed his mind. The Catholic Archbishop and Executive Minister of the Congregational Union of South Australia agreed. All three made it plain that they regarded homosexuality as immoral and a sin, but that the law was not the best instrument to bring redemption.[24]

Some of the earliest exposure of the experiences of homosexuals was in the student press. One article, 'The Homosexual Villain', by an anonymous homosexual man, appeared in Monash University's student paper *Lot's Wife* in August 1964 and was reprinted in the University of Adelaide's *On Dit* the following month.[25] Four articles about various aspects of homosexuality appeared in *On Dit* in August 1969, written anonymously by members of the University of Adelaide community.[26] They hoped to dispel 'false taboos and fears' and lead to a 'clearheaded debate on such social reforms'.[27] The *Advertiser* also began to run stories in the early 1970s about homosexual men and women.[28] Nationally, the initiation of groups such as CAMP saw the publication of magazines dedicated to information and activism, but their readership was probably confined largely to the homosexual community.[29]

The social shift towards a willingness for the discussion of homosexuality was part of a wider phenomenon of what Willett terms a 'new liberal current in Australian political culture and Australian political life'.[30] This liberalness was particularly evident in South Australia, where a Labor government was elected to power in 1965 after 32 consecutive years of conservative rule. The ascension of Don Dunstan to Premier in 1967 began a period of 'social democracy' in South Australia which saw reforms on issues such as abortion, capital punishment, gambling, consumer protection, and equal opportunity laws. Given the extent of these social reforms, it is in some ways unsurprising that South Australia led the way on the decriminalisation of homosexuality. While Attorney-General in 1965, Dunstan had pushed to decriminalise homosexual acts between consenting adult males, but although it was supported by Cabinet, a Bill never reached Parliament due to the concern of several members of caucus. Dunstan recalls in his 1981 memoir that the Wolfenden Report had not received much coverage in South Australia, and that 'the public "weren't ready for it"'.[31]

Slippery Slopes and Strange Bedfellows: The 1972 Debate

Ready or not, the South Australian public quickly found themselves immersed in a vigorous debate on homosexuality in the winter of 1972. Reporting on the case of an initially unidentified man who had drowned in the River Torrens on the evening of 10 May began slowly, with small articles buried in the centre pages of the *Advertiser*.[32] As more details emerged over the following weeks, the murder of University of Adelaide law lecturer Dr George Ian Ogilvy Duncan became front page headlines.[33] It was alleged that members of the police Vice Squad had pushed Duncan into the river while indulging in 'poofter-bashing' – the area of riverbank where he died was a known beat.[34] Despite this, four weeks passed before the word 'homosexuality' was first mentioned in the media in connection with the case.[35]

Discussion of the matter increased gradually, aided significantly by the *Advertiser*, which dedicated its editorial of 13 June to the Duncan inquest, and asserted that the case had 'touched upon the broader issue of homosexuality and attitudes towards it in our society'.[36] It identified the 'unfortunate' reticence of witnesses in the case to come forward as a symptom of the illegality of homosexual behaviour. It is from this point that the discussion of the decriminalisation of homosexuality began in earnest.

On 26 July 1972, the Liberal and Country League Member of the Legislative Council, Murray Hill, introduced a private member's bill proposing the decriminalisation of homosexual acts between consenting adult males in private (hereafter referred to as the Bill), apparently prompted by a letter urging the relaxation of the law received by all South Australian politicians in late June from a group calling themselves the Moral Freedom Committee (MFC).[37] This group had formed in response to the actions of the evangelical Moral Action Committee (MAC), of which psychologist Dr John Court and Rev. Lance Shilton were outspoken members. MAC railed against society's 'permissiveness' and called for the censorship of 'immoral' material such as the theatrical release of *Oh! Calcutta!*, a production featuring full-frontal nudity and songs about masturbation.[38] MAC ceased to function when members formed new groups such as the Community Standards Organisation and the Festival of Light, by which time the MFC had been provoked into action. The MFC was primarily composed of young, heterosexual, university-trained men and women, many of whom were active in the Humanist Society of South Australia (HSSA).[39] It does not appear to have included homosexual members and was not a front for gay activists. The group was compelled to act by the controversy surrounding Dr Duncan's murder, and the correspondence it issued specially mentioned the case and the unlikelihood of witnesses coming forward while the existing laws against homosexual acts remained in place. Murray Hill, Premier Dunstan, and at least five other Members of Parliament (MPs) directly pointed to the influence of the Duncan case in bringing the issue to light.[40] The ensuing debate about Duncan's murder and, as a consequence, the legitimacy of homosexuality and laws against homosexual acts, divided the community, and took place not only in Parliament, but also in the media and in key interest groups around the state.

Both the pro- and anti-decriminalisation camps put forward a number of arguments, and included among their ranks concerned members of the public, as well as academics, medical professionals, religious leaders, lobby groups, and the parliamentarians who would have the ultimate say. In Parliament, the issue was not argued along party lines. The matter was to be decided by a 'free vote'[41] which allowed debate according to the individual member's conscience, the wishes of their own constituents, or a combination of the two. In the 1970s, as is the case today, conscience votes were allowed on controversial or religious-based issues where party-political stances were not considered appropriate. The debate largely focused on the relevance of religious (moral) traditions on the criminal law,[42] and the possible danger of allowing homosexuality to become regarded as acceptable.

As proponent of the Bill, Hill spoke at length on the need for reform. His speech on 2 August included extensive reference to the Wolfenden Report and the subsequent British parliamentary debates. While he appeared to consider homosexuality as something of a pitiful 'social problem'[43] requiring treatment,[44] he argued that the law was not the appropriate way to deal with the 'psychological nature of homosexuality',[45] and that homosexuals were 'law-abiding citizens in all other respects' and 'surely not criminals'.[46] He was concerned that homosexuals were open to blackmail because of their reluctance to report matters to the police due to threat of their own prosecution.[47]

Hill and other MPs also addressed a number of the concerns raised by opponents to the reforms. Hill observed that 'the only real opposition comes from those who deal solely with the religious viewpoint, and it comes from the extreme literalist group who provide judgmental attitudes, based upon Biblical passages'.[48]

These laws, he said, were made in Biblical times and did not reflect the current scientific understanding.[49] Don Hopgood also refuted the extremist religious argument, pointing out that those who argued that the Bible condemned homosexual acts should also 'require adultery, fornication and Lesbianism to be illegal in order to be consistent'.[50] As these calls were not being made and would be ridiculed if they were, such Biblical arguments were not sound. Attorney-General Len King argued forcefully on a religious basis that he believed homosexual behaviour to be a 'perverted activity' and 'intrinsically evil',[51] but went on to state: 'what we are here concerned with as a Legislature is not precisely the moral question involved in homosexual conduct but what the state of the criminal law should be'.[52] King's attitude mirrored that of the religious leaders who believed that Biblical immorality could not necessarily be directly equated with modern law.

MPs also refuted other non-religious arguments. Referring to the experiences of Belgium and France where homosexuality was legal, Hill assured those concerned about an increase in the incidence of the practice that 'the prevalence of homosexuality seems to be remarkably independent of the state of the law',[53] but did not cite any figures to support his claim. Dr Tonkin asserted that those who feared an increase failed to understand the true nature of homosexuality.[54]

In outright favour of the Bill, a number of members emphasised the unacceptable (and indeed impractical) nature of laws which intruded into individuals' private affairs,[55] and several highlighted the contradiction whereby male homosexual acts were illegal but female acts were not.[56] Finally, two members stated their belief that the law should not punish people who had no control over their sexuality, thereby acknowledging the then current advances in the psychological understanding of homosexuality as being a matter not of choice but of intrinsic nature.[57]

A number of politicians mentioned in their speeches the quantity of correspondence from the public on the issue; several stated that they had received more on this Bill than on any other.[58] Some claimed overwhelming support for the Bill, while one had received a more negative response.[59] F.J.Potter explicitly stated the difficulty of determining true public opinion on the matter,[60] whereas Don Hopgood, despite believing that it was more important to be true to one's own conscience than to bow to public pressure, cited several Australian media polls that pointed to a majority support for homosexual law reform.[61] Hopgood also made an interesting observation about the support of the local media for the reforms: 'generally speaking, the popular press is a little on the conservative side of what people in the community are thinking and, therefore, when we get a progressive statement from the press, we can usually assume there is a fair consensus in the community for it'.[62]

Hopgood's remark on the conservative nature of the local media echoes a commonly held view; both Adelaide daily newspapers, the *Advertiser* and the *News*, were owned by the Murdoch family's News Corporation, a media organisation that is frequently considered to have a conservative outlook.[63]

Support for the Bill was demonstrated in the pages of the print media, most notably in the *Advertiser*. Although there were numerous letters to the editor that spoke vehemently against the Bill (see discussion below), there were a number in support. The correspondents' arguments followed a similar line to those covered in Parliament. Members of the South Australian branch of the Australian Psychological Society wrote of their belief that the legal status of homosexual acts was irrelevant to the successful treatment of such tendencies, and that many people were not coming forward to be treated because of concerns they would be prosecuted. Not only concerned with 'cures', they also wrote that '[p]unishment is likely to intensify the guilt and anxiety which are frequently experienced' and that this caused 'irreparable psychological damage' – and made behaviour modification more difficult.[64]

Dr G. R. Knight and Stan Harris both wrote to the *Advertiser* with their criticisms of the extremist religious views propounded by other correspondents. Like Don Hopgood, Knight argued that '[s]elective quotation from Leviticus is not… any justification for the continued legal persecution of homosexuals',[65] while Harris undermined the legitimacy of the text by noting that Leviticus forbade blind or handicapped clergy, and called for death to those who did not observe the Sabbath, in addition to admonishing homosexuality.[66] Knight also iterated Attorney-General King's argument that 'Old Testament fundamentalists are certainly entitled to express their views' but that there was 'no reason for accepting their views as the basis for law-making in a secular society'.[67] Several days later, Linda Brabham presaged the argument of MPs Potter and Evans by condemning punishment of people who could not help their 'condition'.[68] Correspondent P. S. Delin went further than many and argued that homosexuality was not a problem at all. Expressing a common joke of the time, Delin suggested that what those against reform wanted was for the homosexuals to admit that homosexuality should be made not just legal, but compulsory.[69]

The Vice-President of the South Australian branch of homosexual group CAMP, and the respective Presidents of the HSSA and the South Australian Council for Civil Liberties also wrote in support of reform.[70] This highlights the unusual alliance formed in support of the legislation. On the one hand, psychologists believed that decriminalisation would assist their ultimate aim: to cure homosexuality. On the other hand, activists and human rights groups argued that decriminalisation would be the first step in achieving equality for homosexuals to live their lives in peace. Although their ultimate aims were vastly divergent, decriminalisation was favoured by both groups.

On a numerical basis, one cannot conclude that supporters of the Bill were in the majority; however, the quantity and sophistication of arguments in favour were considerably greater than those against, which tended to focus on limited religious beliefs and a fear of social degeneration. It is notable, however, that although these views were promoted by members of the public, they did not gain significant traction in Parliament. Had they done so in such numbers, the Bill would not have passed. It is also important to note that a meaningful quantitative analysis of newspaper correspondents is notoriously difficult, as editorial decisions are made over what is published, and we can only trust that the printed letters were representative of the quantity and arguments of those that were not.

Similar (if less religious) arguments were raised in Parliament by a number of members who spoke against the Hill Bill. Their key fear was that decriminalisation would lead to an increase in the prevalence of homosexuality, and would be seen as condoning behaviour that was morally wrong. This view was espoused by A. M. Whyte, who said he feared 'an acceptance of something I am not prepared to have publicly flaunted or publicly accepted'.[71] R. C. DeGaris voiced concern about where such relaxation of the law might lead; would incest, for instance, become acceptable? And what of homosexual marriage?[72] M. B. Dawkins and L. R. Hart also feared widespread acceptance, and believed decriminalisation could lead to young people becoming homosexual.[73] Both compared homosexuality to the state's recent debate on abortion, claiming that the legalisation of this practice had led to its increase and normalisation.[74]

Opinion pieces published by the *Advertiser* aimed either to inform the public on the nature of homosexuality (such as a three-part feature by John Miles on various aspects of the 'Homosexual Scene in Adelaide'),[75] or explicitly campaigned in favour of law reform. The paper's editorial on 1 July 1972 was headed 'Legalise Homosexuality' – an unequivocal stance, largely based on the argument that the law had no right to intervene in the bedrooms of private citizens.[76] However, the paper did publish many letters to the editor that argued forcefully against potential reform. John Court, lecturer in psychology at Flinders University, and member of the Christian lobby group Festival of Light, wrote a response to the editorial, arguing that it would be 'Impossible!' to legalise homosexuality. He suspected that such reform was the 'first step to seeking acceptance of totally unrestricted homosexual practices and recognition that they are essentially normal'.[77] Court was one of a small number who wrote in opposition to reform without explicitly referring to religious reasoning. Others to do so included P. P. Kelly, who believed that, like alcoholism, homosexuality was able to be controlled, and therefore did not require relaxation of the law;[78] and Mark J. Posa, who was concerned that legalisation would lead to a general degeneration of society which could result in the acceptance of euthanasia.[79]

The remaining letters all advanced Christian viewpoints. Several quoted Biblical passages from Leviticus in which homosexual acts were described as 'abomination',[80] and passages from the New Testament.[81] Many more argued that God's moral law should prevail. A typical example of this attitude was put forward by Anne E. Joyce, a mother fearing for her children's future who wrote, 'God, in his Holy Word, has set down moral rules for mankind, and if man deliberately and defiantly disobeys, then he will destroy himself'.[82] Andrew McComb similarly advised that the Old Testament was relevant to the framing of modern laws, and warned that 'civilisations which became permissive… frequently degenerated and disappeared from the historical scene'.[83] Dorothy Storr could not bring herself to mention homosexuality, but referred to the 'degrading laws set in our midst', and implored readers to vote for leaders who could set a 'clean Christian standard'.[84] Reverend David L. White of the Seaton Park Baptist Church wrote twice, each time vociferously arguing that 'Homosexuality is NOT normal!',[85] but a 'perversion' that should 'NEVER!' be legalised.[86] He was concerned about a 'moral landslide',[87] and urged the community to show compassion and provide assistance for 'those homosexuals who earnestly want to be normal'.[88] The religious arguments all relied on dramatic vocabulary, fear, and limited sections of Scripture to make their points. These opinions were advanced primarily by laity, and ministers of churches such as the Baptist Church. As mentioned, more liberal clergy voiced support for decriminalisation, even if their reasoning was aimed more towards healing the homosexual man than concern for his rights.

As with the groups who supported the reforms, an unusual alliance also emerged between the groups who opposed the 1972 Bill. On one side, there were those who opposed homosexual law reform altogether, usually on religious grounds, and argued that homosexuality was immoral and unnatural. A number of people took a less overtly religious argument, seeing law reform as the first step on a 'slippery slope' to a 'permissive society'. These groups who opposed any reform at all were joined in opposition to this particular Bill by some gay activists. Knowing that the Bill was highly unlikely to pass in its entirety, Dennis Altman and Lex Watson spoke strongly against certain aspects of the proposed reform at the inaugural South Australian meeting of Gay Liberation in August 1972. They argued that it did not achieve sufficient reform, and advocated full legal equality for homosexuals. Altman described the Bill as 'totally inadequate and probably even dangerous'.[89] Thus, opposition to the Bill came from both those worried it went too far, and those concerned it did not go far enough.

Ultimately, opposition member Renfrey DeGaris moved an amendment to the Bill that undermined its original intent. The Bill passed with this amendment, which meant that being 'consenting adults in private' became nothing more than a defence for the charge of committing a homosexual act, only able to be pleaded before a court.[90] In this case, should conditions of the law be met – namely that the two men be 21 years of age or over, alone, and the sex consensual – no conviction would be recorded. As we have demonstrated, this limited degree of law reform was supported largely because criminal sanctions seemed inappropriate; it did not indicate approval of homosexuality as a legitimate way of life. This was made quite plain by the major Christian denominations and those who echoed their arguments, and all who advocated treatment or cures for homosexuals. Thus, decriminalisation was far from complete in 1972 and did not afford homosexual men any increased privacy. It would take another three years to achieve full decriminalisation, which occurred in 1975 with a Bill introduced by Labor Attorney-General Peter Duncan.[91]

Nonetheless, the 1972 reform was an important first step. In 1965, Don Dunstan, then Attorney-General in the Walsh Labor Government, drafted a homosexual law reform Bill that was blocked by his party's caucus due to concerns that it was against the wishes of the public. Education of the community was required, and the 1972 debate surrounding the mysterious death of Dr Duncan, the reasons for witnesses failing to appear, and the need for law reform, provided homosexual activists and sections of the media with opportunities to enlighten the public and community leaders. These events put the legal status of homosexuality firmly on the public agenda in South Australia, and the rest of the country followed. Those who fought for full decriminalisation later, and for law reform in other states, would have found it much more difficult if they had to work without precedent and without a raised level of public and media understanding of the issues.

The Legacy of Dr Duncan

The murder of Dr Duncan was the catalyst for the decriminalisation debate in 1972. However, as with all catalysts, it alone was not enough to bring about change. There had been a much longer process at work. The gradual post-war liberalisation of societal attitudes formed a foundation for reform. But, in South Australia, it was the political climate of Don Dunstan's progressive Labor Government that made such a reform palatable in many sectors of the community. A combined effort by Dunstan and his predecessor, conservative Premier Steele Hall, had seen the groundbreaking legalisation of abortion only three years earlier, and so the state had already been challenged to consider its views on contentious moral issues. This followed nearly four decades of conservative party governance, dominated by Tom Playford's period as Premier between 1938 and 1965. Others have argued that it was Playford's paternalistic style and inertia on social matters that led to pent up frustration and the rush towards social law reform in the Dunstan era.[92] This situation was unique to South Australia. One might contend that the other states in Australia lagged behind their southern counterpart because conservative parties still held sway there; the Country Party remained in power in Queensland from 1957 until 1989 (the reign of Premier Joh Bjelke-Petersen extended from 1968 to 1987), the Liberal Party governed in New South Wales between 1965 and 1976, and in Victoria from 1955 until 1982.[93] This is not to suggest that it was *inevitable* that Liberal or Coalition Governments would fail to champion or achieve homosexual law reform in the 1960s and 1970s; there were certainly members of those governments whose primary agenda was to relax government and legal controls on individual freedoms and uphold one's right to privacy, rather than defend conservative values on social issues. (The decriminalisation of private homosexual acts occurred in Victoria under a Liberal Government in 1980, although nine Liberal MPs crossed the floor to vote against the proposal while Labor MPs voted as a block in favour.)[94] But small 'l' liberals in Liberal and Coalition Governments were generally not willing to alienate the people who elected them or trade the potential gains they could make in other areas by furthering the rights of gays and lesbians. Instead, as Shane Ostenfeld has argued, the trade union movement (which provided the support base of the state-based Labor parties, as well as many of their candidates), proved most responsive to the needs of gays and lesbians, initially supporting their fight against discrimination in the workplace and then embracing other issues. White-collar and left-wing unions were most active in this respect, while opposition within the labour movement was mounted by Catholic unionists and 'masculinist' right-wing unions.[95] In comparison to the situation in the other states, the South Australian Branch of the Labor Party was more disposed to championing the rights of homosexuals because white-collar and left-leaning public sector unions held sway and Catholic elements within the trade unions and the Labor Party were muted.[96] Indeed, without convicts and lacking a mass migration of poor Irish Catholics in the nineteenth and early twentieth centuries, South Australia has always had a proportionally smaller working-class Catholic population than most of the other states, and this affected the number of Catholics and their influence in trade unions and the South Australian Branch of the Labor Party. Although the law reform vote in South Australia's Parliament in 1972 and then in 1975 was supposed to be one based on 'conscience' rather than dictated by party policy, pressure was brought to bear on Labor MPs to make sure they voted for the decriminalisation bills. Gay activist Roger Knight recalls the final vote for Peter Duncan's homosexual decriminalisation Bill in 1975 and watching Tom Casey, the Labor Minister for Agriculture and a staunch country Catholic who had previously voted against the proposal, be brought into line:

> A message came into the House and indicated to Casey that someone was wanting to talk to him… [Deputy Premier] Des Corcoran, out in the corridor… must have had a few words to say about sticking with Peter's Bill and voting with the Party… Casey came back looking absolutely like thunder… When it came to the division, instead of crossing [the floor to vote against the Bill], he just continued to sit there, looking like thunder, but staying with the Labor Party… It was supposed to be a free vote, it was a conscience vote, a private member's Bill, not a Government Bill, but it was quite obvious that the Labor Party voted for it.[97]

In both 1972 and 1975, South Australian Labor MPs voted in favour of the decriminalisation of homosexual acts. It was members of Murray Hill's party that insisted upon amendments and, having far superior numbers in the Legislative Council in 1972, were able to alter the Bill beyond recognition. Complete decriminalisation was achieved in 1975 once the effects of electoral reform were felt and the Labor Party secured greater numbers in the Upper House.

A further case for South Australian exceptionalism can be made in that the push for homosexual law reform did not emerge from a prior campaign for the introduction of sexuality-based anti-discrimination legislation. Former members of CAMP (SA) and other gay activists at the time are certain about this. Discrimination in the workplace became a primary issue for gay and lesbian activists in other states and this saw their involvement with the labour movement and open engagement with parliamentarians; in states such as New South Wales the campaign against discrimination offered a pathway to homosexual law reform.[98] While this issue was certainly a concern for homosexuals in the southern state, law reform in South Australia predated the push for the introduction of sexuality-based anti-discrimination legislation. It was the controversy surrounding the murder of Dr Duncan that really galvanised the alliance between activists, civil libertarians, select politicians and the labour movement, and which was the principal precursor to law reform. Over the next 25 years, the case would be evoked by gay activists throughout the country and Dr Duncan's name would appear at the head of petitions, on protest banners and badges ('HOW MANY MORE DUNCANS?'), and as graffiti on walls ('DUNCAN IS DEAD – WHY?'),[99] all testament to the importance and ramifications of a terrible event that took place by the banks of the River Torrens in Adelaide in 1972.

Endnotes

1. John Lee, 'Male Homosexual Identity and Subculture in Adelaide Before World War II', in Robert Aldrich and Garry Wotherspoon, eds, *Gay Perspectives: Essays in Australian Gay Culture*, Sydney: Department of Economic History, University of Sydney, 1992, pp. 95–112; Chiah Mayne, The Nature of Male Homosexual Interactions in Adelaide before 1945, BA (Hons) Thesis, University of Adelaide, 2007.
2. Tim Reeves, Poofters, Pansies and Perverts: 1972 Debate on Homosexuality in South Australia, BA (Hons) Thesis, University of Adelaide, 1992; Tim Reeves, 'The 1972 Debate on Male Homosexuality in South Australia', in Robert Aldrich, ed., *Gay Perspectives II: More Essays in Australian Gay Culture*, Sydney: Department of Economic History with the Australian Centre for Gay and Lesbian Research, University of Sydney, 1994, pp. 149–192.
3. Reeves, Poofters, Pansies and Perverts, p. 12.
4. ibid.
5. Malcolm Cowan and Tim Reeves, 'The "Gay Rights" Movement and the Decriminalisation Debate in South Australia, 1973–75', in Robert Aldrich and Garry Wotherspoon, eds, *Gay and Lesbian Perspectives IV: Studies in Australian Culture*, Sydney: Department of Economic History and Australian Centre for Lesbian and Gay Research, University of Sydney, 1998, pp. 164–193; Malcolm Cowan, The Decriminalisation of Homosexuality in South Australia, 1972–1975, BA (Hons) Thesis, University of Adelaide, 1991.

6   Cowan, The Decriminalisation of Homosexuality in South Australia, pp. 79, 127; Reeves, Poofters, Pansies and Perverts, p. 68; and, Reeves, 'The 1972 Debate on Male Homosexuality in South Australia', pp. 178–179.
7   Graham Willett, *Living Out Loud: A History of Gay and Lesbian Activism in Australia*, Sydney: Allen and Unwin, 2000.
8   25 Hen VIII c.6 (*The Punishment of the Vice of Buggery, 1533*).
9   *An Act for consolidating the Statute Law in force in South Australia relating to Indictable Offences against the Person, 1859*, s42; *Criminal Law Consolidation Act, 1876*, (SA), s71–72, 166; *Criminal Law Amendment Act, 1925*, (SA), ss5, 15; *Criminal Law Consolidation Act, 1935*, (SA), s69–71.
10 Mayne, The Nature of Male Homosexual Interactions in Adelaide before 1945, p. 56.
11 ibid., pp. 31–49; Lee, 'Male Homosexual Identity and Subculture', pp. 100–101.
12 Graham Willett, 'The Origins of Homosexual Politics in Australia', in David L. Phillips and Graham Willett, eds, *Australia's Homosexual Histories: Gay and Lesbian Perspectives V*, Sydney: Australian Centre for Lesbian and Gay Research and the Australian Lesbian and Gay Archives, 2000, p. 68.
13 ibid., p. 70.
14 See, for instance, John Tasker, 'Censorship in the Theatre', in Geoffrey Dutton and Max Harris, eds, *Australia's Censorship Crisis*, Melbourne: Sun Books, 1970, pp. 44, 50–51. See also, Willett, *Living Out Loud*, p. 13.
15 Willett, 'The Origins of Homosexual Politics in Australia', pp. 68–70.
16 Wolfenden et al., *Report of the Committee on Homosexual Offences and Prostitution*, London: Her Majesty's Stationery Office, 1957, p. 25.
17 Willett, 'The Origins of Homosexual Politics in Australia', p. 73.
18 ibid., p. 28.
19 See, speech given by Murray Hill, *South Australian Parliamentary Debates (SAPD)*, Legislative Council, 2 August 1972, pp. 469–470.
20 The Methodist Church of Australasia, Minutes of the 67th South Australian Conference, Adelaide, October 1968, p. 134, cited in Malcolm Cowan, '"Knowing" Sodom? Australian Churches and Homosexuality', in Garry Wotherspoon, ed., *Gay and Lesbian Perspectives III: Essays in Australian Culture*, Sydney: University of Sydney, 1996, p. 213.
21 Arnold D. Hunt, *This Side of Heaven: A History of Methodism in South Australia*, Adelaide: Lutheran Publishing House, 1986, p. 399.
22 Diocese of Melbourne Social Questions Committee, *Report on Homosexuality 1971*, Melbourne: Exacto Press, 1971, pp. 14–15.
23 'Bishop Disagrees with Vic. Synod', *Advertiser*, 13 October 1971, p. 10.
24 'Prison No Solution, say Clerics', *Advertiser*, 17 February 1972, p. 20.
25 Anonymous, 'The Homosexual Villain', *Lot's Wife*, 27 August 1964, reproduced in *On Dit*, 25 September 1964, p. 8. See also, Willett, 'The Origins of Homosexual Politics in Australia', p. 72.
26 'Four Essays Upon Aspects of Homosexuality', *On Dit*, 5 August 1969, pp. 5–6, 11–12.
27 ibid., p. 5. Graham Willett suggests that the student press was at least somewhat representative of its readership, citing a sizeable 1968 Melbourne University survey which revealed 66% support for the legalisation of homosexuality. See Willett, 'The Origins of Homosexual Politics in Australia', pp. 72–73.
28 For instance, Shirley Despoja, 'What's it Like… Being a Homosexual?', *Advertiser*, 12 May 1971, p. 30.

29 See, editions of *Camp Ink*, CAMP's official magazine. An early feature article, *Australian Attiudes [sic] Towards Abortion, Prostitution and Homosexuality* by P. R. Wilson and D. Chappell was contained in vol. 1, no. 4 (February 1971), pp. 4–8.
30 Willett, 'The Origins of Homosexual Politics in Australia', p. 71.
31 Don Dunstan, *Felicia: The Political Memoirs of Don Dunstan*, Melbourne: Macmillan, 1981, pp. 126–127. See also, speech by Dunstan, *SAPD*, House of Assembly, 18 October 1972, p. 2205.
32 'Car Keys Clue to Body in River', *Advertiser*, 12 May 1972, p. 9; 'Lecturer's Body in River', *Advertiser*, 13 May 1972, p. 4.
33 Bob Whitington, 'Police Questioned on River Death', *Advertiser*, 20 May 1972, p. 1.
34 'Government Calls for Facts on Duncan Case', *Advertiser*, 2 June 1972, p. 1.
35 Bob Whitington, 'Shock Evidence in Report to Inquest', *Advertiser*, 5 June 1972, p. 1.
36 'The Duncan Inquest', *Advertiser*, 13 June 1972, p. 5.
37 *SAPD*, Legislative Council, 2 August 1972, p. 464. See also, 'Legal Homosexuality Wanted', *Advertiser*, 23 June 1972, p. 6. There has been speculation that Hill was motivated by more personal reasons – a gay family member or friend – for introducing the Bill, however, this cannot been confirmed. Hill certainly was not a typical Liberal and Country League politician. He had belonged to the reformist wing of Steel Hall's LCL government (1968–1970) and throughout his tenure in Parliament sought to protect individual privacy and freedoms in the tradition of classic liberalism.
38 Lance Shilton edited a book titled *No, No Calcuttta* [Adelaide: Brolga Books, c.1971] which encapsulates the group's fears and what it sought to overcome. See also, John H. Court's books, *Changing Community Standards*, Adelaide: Lutheran Publishing House, 1972; *The Permissive Society*, Adelaide: Trinity Publishing Society, c.1972; and, *Law, Light and Liberty*, Adelaide: Lutheran Publishing House, 1975. For further information about the Moral Action Committee and its later incantation, see, David Hilliard and John Warhurst, 'Festival of Light', *Current Affairs Bulletin*, vol. 50, no. 9 (February 1974), pp. 13–19.
39 David Hilliard, personal correspondence, 26 July 2010.
40 *SAPD*, Legislative Council and House of Assembly, August and October 1972. Hill (p. 464), Dunstan (p. 2205), Springett (p. 788), Hart (p. 1800), Tonkin (p. 2193), Hopgood (p. 2200) and Millhouse (p. 2204).
41 Alan Wheat, 'Homosexuals: "Free vote"', *Advertiser*, 8 July 1972, p. 3.
42 See, Reeves, 'The 1972 Debate on Male Homosexuality in South Australia', pp. 150–151.
43 M. Hill, *SAPD*, Legislative Council, 2 August 1972, p. 472.
44 ibid., pp. 464, 473.
45 ibid., p. 464.
46 ibid., p. 472.
47 ibid., p. 466.
48 ibid., p. 471.
49 ibid.
50 D. J. Hopgood, *SAPD*, House of Assembly, 18 October 1972, pp. 2201–2202.
51 L. King, *SAPD*, House of Assembly, 18 October 1972, p. 2213.
52 ibid.
53 M. Hill, *SAPD*, Legislative Council, 11 October 1972, p. 1951.
54 Dr Tonkin, *SAPD*, House of Assembly, 18 October 1972, p. 2193.

55 F. J. Potter, *SAPD*, Legislative Council, 16 August 1972, p. 790; S. G. Evans, *SAPD*, House of Assembly, 18 October 1972, p. 2212; L. King, *SAPD*, House of Assembly, 18 October 1972, pp. 2214–2215.

56 V. G. Springett, *SAPD*, Legislative Council, 16 August 1972, p. 787; D. J. Hopgood, *SAPD*, House of Assembly, 18 October 1972, p. 2201; S. G. Evans, *SAPD*, House of Assembly, 18 October 1972, p. 2211. Dunstan went further and noted that even if it were passed, the law would still be inconsistent, as anal intercourse would be legal between consenting men, but not for a heterosexual couple. He introduced an amendment to rectify this inconsistency. D. A. Dunstan, *SAPD*, House of Assembly, 18 October 1972, p. 2207.

57 F. J. Potter, *SAPD*, Legislative Council, 16 August 1972, p. 90; S. G. Evans, *SAPD*, House of Assembly, 18 October 1972, p. 2212.

58 D. H. L. Banfield, *SAPD*, Legislative Council, 13 September 1972, p. 1256; L. R. Hart, *SAPD*, Legislative Council, 4 October 1972, p. 1799; M. Hill, *SAPD*, Legislative Council, 11 October 1972, p. 1954.

59 *SAPD*, Legislative Council. F. J. Potter (p. 791), R. C. DeGaris (p. 1078), and D. H. L. Banfield (p. 1256) received more in favour; A. M. Whyte (p. 939) reported an overwhelmingly negative response from his constituents.

60 F. J. Potter, *SAPD*, Legislative Council, 16 August 1972, p. 791.

61 D. J. Hopgood, *SAPD*, House of Assembly, 18 October 1972, p. 2200. Both a Melbourne and Sydney poll by Wilson and Chappel, and an ACT poll, indicated that about 62% of people supported homosexual law reform. A 1971 poll in the *Age* indicated that a majority of people felt that homosexuals were not a threat.

62 D. J. Hopgood, *SAPD*, House of Assembly, 18 October 1972, p. 2200. Editorials such as that in the *Advertiser* on 1 July, p. 5, point to this media support (see below).

63 Richard Belfield et al., *Murdoch: The Decline of an Empire*, London: Macdonald, 1991; Denis Cryle, *Murdoch's Flagship: The First Twenty-Five Years of the Australian Newspaper*, Melbourne: Melbourne University Publishing, 2008.

64 A. E. Whitford (Chairman) et al. of SA branch of the Australian Psychological Society, on behalf of all the committee. 'Homosexuality "Not Concern of Law"', letter to the editor, *Advertiser*, 18 July 1972, p. 5. Like Murray Hill, the psychologists believed in the importance of successful treatment as one of the key reasons for decriminalisation. Most of those cited who made these arguments also acknowledged that such treatments should be voluntary and were not always appropriate.

65 Dr G. R. Knight, 'Bible and the Law', letter to the editor, *Advertiser*, 18 July 1972, p. 5.

66 Stan Harris, 'Law from Scripture', letter to the editor, *Advertiser*, 19 July 1972, p. 5.

67 Knight, 'Bible and the Law', letter to the editor.

68 Linda Brabham, 'Own Road to Hell', letter to the editor, *Advertiser*, 25 July 1972, p. 5.

69 P. S. Delin, 'Attitude Queried', letter to the editor, *Advertiser*, 5 July 1972, p. 5.

70 Duncan Hartshorne, Vice-President, CAMP, SA Branch, 'Support Pledged', letter to the editor, *Advertiser*, 5 July 1972, p. 5; John Chandler, President, Humanist Society of SA, 'Law and Morals', letter to the editor, *Advertiser*, 5 July 1972, p. 5; W. B. Fisse, President, SA Council for Civil Liberties, 'Reformed Law', letter to the editor, *Advertiser*, 6 July 1972, p. 5. The SA branch of CAMP took an active role in petitioning Members of Parliament and clergy. See their magazine, *Canary*, vol. 1, no. 2 (October 1972), pp. 8–11.

71 A. M. Whyte, *SAPD*, Legislative Council, 23 August 1972, p. 940.

72 R. C. DeGaris, *SAPD*, Legislative Council, 30 August 1972, pp. 1077–1078.

73 M. B. Dawkins, *SAPD*, Legislative Council, 3 September 1972, pp. 1253–1254; L. R. Hart, *SAPD*, Legislative Council, 4 October 1972, p. 1799.
74 ibid., pp. 1254–1255; A. M. Whyte, *SAPD*, Legislative Council, 23 August 1972, p.940.
75 John Miles, 'Homosexual Scene in Adelaide: Lively Talkers, Stylish Dressers', *Advertiser*, 22 June 1972, p. 5; 'Homosexual Scene in Adelaide: When Police Will Act', *Advertiser*, 23 June 1972, p. 4; 'Homosexual Scene in Adelaide: Two Main Types', *Advertiser*, 24 June 1972, p. 4.
76 'Legalise Homosexuality', *Advertiser*, 1 July 1972, p. 5.
77 J. H. Court, 'A First Step?', letter to the editor, *Advertiser*, 3 July 1972, p. 5.
78 P. P. Kelly, 'Reform of Law', letter to the editor, *Advertiser*, 10 July 1972, p. 5.
79 Mark J. Posa, 'No Change in Values', letter to the editor, *Advertiser*, 6 July 1972, p. 5.
80 J. N. Collins, 'Bible Verse', letter to the editor, *Advertiser*, 6 July 1972, p. 5; Rev. David L. White, Seaton Park Baptist Church, 'Moral Landslide', letter to the editor, *Advertiser*, 15 July 1972, p. 5. The passages quoted from Leviticus are 18:22 ('Thou shalt not lie with mankind, as with womankind: it is abomination') and 20:13 ('If a man also lie with mankind, as he lieth with a woman, both of them have committed an abomination: they shall surely be put to death; their blood shall be upon them'). *The Holy Bible*, King James Version, Oxford: Oxford University Press.
81 Grace Magarey, letter to the editor, *Advertiser*, 21 July 1972, p. 5; Rev. David L. White, Seaton Park Baptist Church, 'The Bible and the Homosexual', letter to the editor, *Advertiser*, 22 July 1972, p. 5; W. J. Meath, 'Religious Views', letter to the editor, *Advertiser*, 4 August 1972, p. 5.
82 Anne E. Joyce, 'Mother's Fears', letter to the editor, *Advertiser*, 11 July 1972, p. 5.
83 Andrew McComb, 'Law from the Bible', letter to the editor, *Advertiser*, 21 July 1972, p.5.
84 Dorothy Storr, 'Christian Values', letter to the editor, *Advertiser*, 20 July 1972, p. 5.
85 White, 'Moral Landslide'.
86 White, 'The Bible and the Homosexual'.
87 White, 'Moral Landslide'.
88 White, 'The Bible and the Homosexual'.
89 '"Gay Lib." Slates Bill', *Advertiser*, 24 August 1972, p. 9.
90 *SAPD*, Legislative Council, 11 October 1972, pp. 1956, 1960.
91 See, introduction of the Criminal Law (Sexual Offences) Amendment Bill, *SAPD*, House of Assembly, 27 August 1975.
92 See, for example, various essays in, Andrew Parkin and Allan Patience, eds, *The Dunstan Decade: Social Democracy at the State Level*, Melbourne: Longman Cheshire, 1981.
93 The Liberal Party was in government in Western Australia between 1953 and 1983 bar three years in the 1970s. Tasmania was the exception to the rule, as Labor held power for the majority of the post-World War II period. Yet the Tasmanian Branch of the Labor Party followed a relatively conservative agenda, especially in terms of social policy. It became the last of the Australian states to decriminalise private homosexual acts in 1997.
94 See, Shane Ostenfeld, 'Sexual Identity and the Australian Labor Movement in Historical Perspective', in Gerald Hunt, ed., *Laboring for Rights: Unions and Sexual Diversity Across Nations*, Philadelphia: Temple University Press, 1999, pp. 179–180.
95 ibid., pp. 157–160.
96 ibid., p. 175.

97 Roger Knight and David Hilliard, '20 Years On, 1975–1995: The Campaign that Led to the Passing of Homosexual Law Reform Legislation in South Australia in 1975', cited in Dino Hodge, 'The Okayness of Gayness: Don Dunstan's Record in Homosexual Law Reform', in this volume.

98 See, Ostenfeld, 'Sexual Identity and the Australian Labor Movement', pp. 157–190.

99 For further discussion of the way in which Dr Duncan has been memorialised and the case used to propel activism, see Reeves, Poofters, Pansies and Perverts, pp. 9–11.

The Okayness of Gayness

Don Dunstan's Record in Homosexual Law Reform

Dino Hodge

The first attempt at homosexual law reform to be introduced into an Australian Parliament was tabled as a private member's bill in South Australia. It was prompted by the murder of Dr George Duncan. In the historical record, however, a sense of confusion and a silencing of details has emerged around the work and efforts of South Australia's decriminalisation of homosexuality.

Late in the evening of 10 May 1972, university law lecturer Dr Duncan and two others were attacked and thrown into Adelaide's River Torrens. Duncan drowned.[1] Don Dunstan, then South Australian Premier, reveals in his memoirs, '[t]he area, apparently, was known to be frequented by homosexuals, and also those who regarded "poofter bashing" as a sport'.[2]

Although the Police Commissioner denied police involvement, reports implicating the force soon emerged. Two constables refused to answer questions at the inquest on 29 June on the grounds that they could be incriminated. The following day the two constables and a senior constable were suspended from the force. One officer resigned immediately, and the other two resigned soon after.[3]

This brutal murder, reports journalist Stewart Cockburn, shocked the South Australian community 'into an ashamed realisation of the extent to which homosexuals were being threatened and persecuted'.[4] Unexpectedly an Upper House member of the conservative Liberal and Country League party, Murray Hill, announced his intention to introduce a private member's bill. The intention was limited in scope 'to protect the privacy only of those people who lived together' and would not legalise homosexuality outside of the home or provide protection against discrimination or vilification.[5]

Following intense debate both in Parliament and the media, the Hill Bill was enacted on 25 October 1972 with drastic amendments.[6] The new law retained the illegality of homosexual acts, but allowed a defence if a person could show that the act was committed in private with only one other person and that both people were over 21 years of age.[7] Don Dunstan opposed these limitations, and recalls that a 'majority in both houses voted for that Bill though attempts by me and others to put in amendments to improve it were lost'.[8] Dunstan considered the eventuating legislation as only a beginning of necessary reform.[9]

The state election in March 1973 saw the inclusion to the Australian Labor Party (ALP) backbench of Peter Duncan. He had studied law in Adelaide during the late 1960s when academic legal circles discussed homosexual law reform as a civil rights issue.[10] Duncan announced his intention to draft a private member's bill and introduced his bill for the full decriminalisation of homosexuality into the House of Assembly in September that year.[11]

Lobby groups quickly established contact with Duncan, including representatives of the Gay Activists' Alliance (GAA) and the Campaign Against Moral Persecution (CAMP).[12] The Council for Civil Liberties (CCL) was lobbying Duncan and providing him with legal opinion.[13] Duncan's bill established a more equitable code of sexual behaviour regardless of sexual orientation and a standard age of consent of 17 years, but it was rejected following the public debate over untimely suggestions by the more radical GAA who proposed talks on homosexuality to senior school students.[14]

Further to another state election in 1975, Duncan re-introduced the bill, which was passed on 17 September 1975, making South Australia the first jurisdiction to decriminalise male homosexual acts.[15] Both bills in 1973 and 1975 received only lukewarm support in the Caucus, explains political scientist Allan Patience. He concludes that the 'Dunstan Cabinet's support for these measures prevailed and their incorporation into the criminal law statutes was a triumph for progressive social reform'.[16]

Difficulties Recalling Dunstan's Achievements

Justice of the High Court, the Hon. Michael Kirby, delivering the lecture *Consensus and Dissent in Australia* in 2007, declared that, 'Don Dunstan began our national process to remove the criminal laws against homosexual men', but gives no further details.[17]

Dunstan died in 1999. His record in homosexual law reform was not cited either in the official memorial service commemorating and celebrating his life and work, or in a tribute special edition of the *Labor Herald* published for the occasion.[18] There is an antecedent to this circumstance, as homosexual law reform was not discussed in the 1981 survey of the Dunstan governments' record in law reform.[19]

Dunstan is regarded as one of Australia's great innovative and reformist premiers, and the memorial service was designed to acknowledge his achievements. Copies of the *Labor Herald* tribute were issued to mourners at the Festival Theatre, and contained testimonies by two former prime ministers and two former premiers, as well as by leading political, community and cultural figures.

During the service Dunstan's achievements were recounted. He reformed not only his own party – he played a central role in removing the federal ALP's White Australia policy and was a long-standing member of the federal executive – but the state's electoral system, too, ending decades of a severe gerrymander.

Dunstan was an early advocate of multiculturalism, introduced the country's first Aboriginal lands rights reforms, abolished capital punishment, established anti-discrimination and equal opportunity measures designed to eliminate racism and sexism, nurtured industrial democracy, initiated consumer rights protection in Australia, and reinvigorated the arts and hospitality industries. Much of his work was ground-breaking, providing models for other Australian jurisdictions, politicians and political parties, and garnering international recognition. The *Labor Herald* testimonies widely reflect upon Dunstan's deep concerns about civil liberties. However, the one achievement not recognised is that of homosexual law reform.

Following the service, journalist Samela Harris lamented this oversight, as well as the failure to welcome to the memorial service Dunstan's male partner of more than a decade.[20] Academic Barbara Baird has also observed that a welcome was extended to the many groups present but not to the gay, lesbian and HIV/AIDS communities. She notes that:

> Dunstan's commitment to the gay and lesbian and HIV/AIDS community politics among the 'causes' to which he was dedicated was another erasure. But most cruelly, and finally in the order of proceedings, was the omission of the name of Dunstan's partner Steven Cheng, in the list of names of those who had cared for him in his last days read out by [Dunstan's elder son] Andrew Dunstan.[21]

And while a journalist at the *Australian* included 'homosexual reforms' amongst Dunstan's achievements while in office,[22] historian Tim Reeves refuted this assertion in a letter to the editor:

> This is misleading.
>
> Three Private Members Bills were introduced in 1972, 1973 and 1975 to decriminalise homosexual male acts... the second and third from an enterprising new Labor member, Peter Duncan.
>
> While Attorney-General in the mid-1960s, Dunstan had advocated decriminalisation but was blocked by Caucus. In the Lower House Labor demonstrated its solidarity as a party in defiance of a conscience vote for each Bill. But Dunstan never took the lead on decriminalisation in parliamentary or community debate. And although in the House he accused police of engaging in entrapment to ensnare homosexuals, he also referred to homosexuals' 'vulgarity and unpleasantness of... behaviour'.
>
> It was Duncan who introduced pioneering legislation that created a code of sexual behaviour regardless of gender or sexual orientation, and a common age of consent, demonstrating the political courage and acumen on this issue.[23]

Here, Reeves was continuing a theme that he wrote about in 1994,[24] which he subsequently pursued with historian Malcolm Cowan in 1998 when they wrote on the gay rights movement and law reform between 1973 and 1975. In this later piece, Reeves and Cowan conclude that,

> [w]hile the Dunstan Governments have been hailed for their commitment to broad social reform, the introduction of Private Member's bills in 1973 and 1975 seeking decriminalisation was the work of a young and enterprising Labor member... Peter Duncan's pioneering legislation sought to create a code of sexual behaviour which established statutory equality regardless of gender or sexuality.[25]

Writing about the murder of Dr George Duncan four years later, Reeves restated his opinion on the eventual enactment of law reform: '[t]he ignorance and prejudices of even those politicians in support was evident during debate; Premier Don Dunstan referred to homosexuals' "vulgarity and unpleasantness" of behaviour'.[26]

Thus by 2002, three years after Dunstan's death and thirty years since the first legislative reform of 1972, Dunstan's role and contributions had been overlooked and even denied.

Homosexual Law Reform Efforts of the 1960s

Innovative law reform was a strong feature of Dunstan's career.[27] A journalist interviewing Premier Dustan in 1968 learnt that '[t]he duties of State Labor Governments must be clear... to pioneer in the area of social reform'.[28] Dunstan, writing in 1970 for *The Australian Humanist*, delineates two principles underpinning his civil rights position:

> The first is that the laws a community enforces should be designed solely to allow the members of that community to live together amicably, and the second is that no-one in the community has the right to lay down that a certain code of behaviour should be observed by everyone in the community, regardless of the effect such a code has on individuals in the community.
>
> Following from this, I believe that the criminal and civil Laws [sic] of the community are to protect citizens from having themselves or their property damaged by other citizens, and for no other reason.[29]

So it is not surprising that one of Dunstan's first initiatives upon his appointment in 1965 as Attorney-General was to secure Cabinet agreement to decriminalise homosexuality. Dunstan recalls obtaining the permission of Caucus to introduce the draft legislation into the Parliament. Before the Bill had been presented, however, several Caucus members expressed concern that the public was not ready. Dunstan understood their position and acknowledged that little had been heard in South Australia about the 1957 Wolfenden Committee report in England which had recommended a similar change in law there.[30]

This early initiative is discussed subsequently during the 1972 parliamentary debate on Hill's proposed law reform. Dunstan reflects on his motivations:

> I had a Bill drawn on this matter when I was Attorney-General but I did not proceed with it then because the climate of public opinion was not such that I believed we could obtain a sufficient consensus of opinion to support an amendment to the law – not that I did not believe it was right to make the change then as I believe it is right to make a

change now, for my experience in the criminal law had been such that I had seen the misery, the harm, the hurt and the injustice that have occurred in this area of the law.[31]

Support indeed was scarce. A 1967 nation-wide survey of 1045 adults by legal academics Chappell and Wilson revealed that less than one quarter of respondents favoured liberalisation of the laws relating to homosexuality. The researchers concluded:

> Those brave (or foolish) enough to advocate reform must combat the fierce traditional antipathy of Australians towards homosexuals, antipathy based almost certainly on a widespread misunderstanding and lack of sympathy…
>
> However, there seems little doubt that few Australians are aware of the nature of the [Wolfenden report] reform effected in England, due largely to the lack of debate on the subject of homosexuality in or outside of the various parliaments of this country.[32]

Dunstan was not deterred and pursued his agenda. Premier Frank Walsh, under the then ALP age rules, was not eligible to contest the coming elections and instead chose to retire while in office.[33] Dunstan was sworn in as Premier on 1 June 1967. In July, Dunstan announced a three-member committee headed by Justice Hogarth to review the criminal law; homosexuality was noted within the committee's terms of reference.[34] But with scarcely nine months in office, this initiative faltered.

Despite losing the 1968 elections,[35] Dunstan persisted. As Leader of the Opposition, he secured the agreement of Caucus to pursue decriminalisation. However, this time Caucus did not want Dunstan to lead the initiative. Instead, it was arranged for Lindsay Riches, another ALP MP and a Methodist lay preacher, to present the matter to Parliament.[36] Dunstan explains that,

> [i]n 1969, while in opposition, I arranged for a motion to be introduced by a senior Labor member to raise the matter publicly for debate, but the then Premier called an election before it was due to be moved.[37]

Working for Reform in the 1970s

Following a campaign during which he declared his support for criminal law reform, Dunstan's second term as Premier commenced in May 1970.

'People should be able to live the way they wish' he announced. He went on to explain that,

> [t]he Labor Party will establish a commission for the revision of the criminal law and its administration, whose specific duty will be to consider the removal of attempts to invade areas of private morality and social welfare.[38]

By now Dunstan had accrued an extensive body of experience as Attorney-General, Premier, and Leader of the Opposition to guide him on how best to inform, educate and persuade others that the intended reform deserved support. In power again, his approach for achieving law reform was more strategically addressed to the political niceties of process: he decided to set up a broad inquiry into South Australian criminal law. A couple of days after the election, Dunstan declared that homosexuality would be dealt with by the anticipated review.[39]

In December 1971 Justice Roma Mitchell was commissioned to chair the enquiry.[40] Specifically, the decriminalisation of homosexuality would be dealt with as one of a number of issues.[41] The process allowed for community submissions, a range of professional input, informed debate and – perhaps most importantly – a set of independent recommendations to the government for its attention and legitimate action. The use of committees of enquiry and Royal Commissions to minimise public reaction to reforms, and to allow the government to argue that its policies were based on sound information, came to be recognised as a hallmark of the Dunstan government.[42]

At this same time the gay liberation movement was becoming established in Australia. The first meeting in South Australia of CAMP had been held in August 1971, and a decision was taken to work on a submission to the Mitchell enquiry.[43] CAMP SA reported in the national newsletter, *Camp Ink*, that 'many observers believe, this committee will recommend the abolition of existing laws against male homosexual behaviour as part of its wider proposals for law reform'.[44] However, following Dr Duncan's murder in May 1972 and Hill's consequent private member's bill, Peter Ward, a senior member of Dunstan's staff, requested a meeting with CAMP. Ward explained that the government would work for the passage of the private member's bill even though the Mitchell enquiry had not completed or reported on its findings; Ward urged CAMP to lobby.[45]

The government by its previous efforts, and with the Mitchell review underway, had nailed its colours to the mast and could not be seen to be influencing community debate. Ward's behind-the-scenes meeting, though, suggests that the government was clearly determined to ensure that at least this time there would be a community debate. The meeting itself is an extraordinary step for a senior member of the Premier's staff to take: it is most unlikely that any staffer from the Premier's office, no matter how senior, would give an undertaking about the government's intentions and provide encouragement to a lobby group without the prior knowledge and permission of the Premier himself. Here, the circumstance of Dr Duncan's death had created a different climate which presented an opportunity, and the government intended to secure a successful outcome. But the conservative elements forced changes to Hill's intended legislation and the result was less than desirable. Consequently, this meant a return to the process of the Mitchell enquiry, and the media reported Dunstan's view that, 'any further alteration to the law on homosexuality would depend on the report of the Criminal Law Revision Committee'.[46]

Dunstan's Support

In the meantime, Dunstan worked to open up discussion within the Labor Party. At the annual state ALP convention in June 1972, the Young Labor Association listed a resolution for the decriminalisation of homosexuality. Social issues had not been discussed at previous conventions on the ground that members should be free to cast a conscience vote on such matters. Dunstan's input facilitated a break with tradition, allowing open discussion at future conventions with the proviso that any decisions were not binding on party members. This step was regarded as one of the most significant moves for many years, and according to one delegate, 'Don's support has given the ALP a new dimension. It will give people searching for guidance something to look to'.[47]

Dunstan's support extended to Peter Duncan, when the latter took his seat on the backbenches following the ALP's win in the state election of March 1973. Peter Duncan recalls his initiative to reform the law:

> Len King [the Attorney-General] wouldn't have touched this with a barge pole. He was a good Catholic boy, and wasn't at all interested in anything that ran across the morality of the Church. Well, that is why I raised it in Caucus before anything happened. And Len King was happy to have it happen as long as he didn't have to be part of it… Len could have early on probably squashed my right to put a Bill up. And I suspect that Don made sure he didn't.[48]

Len King's personal opinion expressed during the parliamentary debates over Hill's 1972 private member's bill was blunt:

> I do not accept a view that has been propounded outside the Parliament that we should repeal the existing law because homosexual practices are themselves no more morally reprehensible than are heterosexual practices... I take the view that the traditional attitude of Christendom, the traditional Judaeo-Christian ethic on this matter, is right and that homosexual practices are intrinsically evil.[49]

Duncan's first Bill unexpectedly was not passed.[50] The difficulties were such that Duncan, 'found it necessary, however, to confirm that the bill was in no way to be seen as condoning homosexual practices or behaviours in public, and made no mention of any homosexual reform groups'. Peter Ward, Dunstan's senior adviser, had telephoned the GAA and advised that 'the Government supported the legislation and GAA should tread carefully to ensure its safe passage'. But, following the furore over suggestions by GAA about educating senior school students on homosexuality, supportive politicians reversed their position and thus Duncan's initiative failed.[51]

The Mitchell Committee's first of three reports was tabled in July 1973, just prior to the introduction of Duncan's first Bill. In this report the difficult issues surrounding sexual offences, especially with minors, and recidivism received attention.[52] The second report, tabled in November 1974, dealt with, 'those street offences which may have political implications and which in our view warrant amendment'. The Committee considered the crime of loitering – the charge most frequently brought against homosexual men – and recommended the abolition of this offence, sounding, suggest Mitchell's biographers Magarey and Round, 'just like... Don Dunstan in the 1960s'.[53]

A looming election, eventually held in July 1975, slowed government response to this second report. Once the election was over, however, Duncan moved quickly to re-introduce his Bill.[54] There was a change this time in the role and method of homosexual activists. As Roger Knight, president of CAMP, recalls:

> it was decided really to avoid any direct gay lobbying of politicians by people who were gay activists, but to move the thing onto a kind of faintly ghostly level known as the Social Concern Committee. Now the Social Concern Committee was born... I think, in Peter Ward's living room... one day in 1975 when a number of people sat around and said, 'Well, okay, let's... get together a group of people

> who would look to be or are concerned citizens in let us say the caring professions in which we'll include religion'; and… finally I think it was probably Peter Ward who came up with the idea of a 'Social Concern Committee'. He thought it sounded nice and that the Methodists would probably like it, and he was dead right. So this was then floated and we got together a committee, which never met of course, which then produced a document which was circulated around parliamentarians… Peter Ward did a wonderful editing job on [the document]… What it skirted around really carefully was this issue… the okayness of gayness. It really never got around to saying that at all. Whenever that issue emerged, the Social Concern Committee galloped away in the opposite direction.[55]

This time Duncan succeeded in homosexual law reform. It must be noted, however, that Duncan's efforts follow on from the initiatives commenced by Dunstan in 1965, and were supported directly through the behind-the-scenes liaison and collaboration with gay liberation groups by one of Dunstan's trusted senior staff.

Leadership and Guidance

As well as this work with lobby groups, there is a suggestion that there was a collaborative effort at play within the ALP's parliamentary wing led by Dunstan. Roger Knight recounts sitting next to Peter Duncan in the Parliament to observe the final vote, at which Tom Casey, the Minister of Agriculture and a staunch country Catholic who had previously voted against the Bill, was again voting.

> And Duncan said 'Just watch this'. What he'd arranged for was [for Deputy Premier] Des Corcoran, who was also a decent old Catholic guy from the country, to go and have a little word with Casey… A messenger came into the House and indicated to Casey that someone was wanting to talk to him and the person who wanted to talk to him was in fact Des Corcoran out in the corridor, who must have had a few words to say about sticking with Peter's bill and voting with the Party and so on, and Casey came back looking absolutely like thunder. And he just sat there, on the benches, and when it came to the division, instead of crossing [the floor to vote against the bill], he just continued to sit there. Looking like thunder, but staying with the Labor Party. It was instructive as to how parties work…

Knight concludes with an observation on these political machinations:

> the lesson I got in the discipline of the Labor Party… It was supposed to be a free vote, it was a conscience vote, a private member's bill, not a Government bill, but it was quite obvious that the Labor *Party* voted for it.[56]

Knight mistakenly attributes the party discipline to Duncan; it is more likely due to Dunstan's role as parliamentary leader. As noted above, Duncan suspected that Dunstan made certain that Attorney-General Len King did not stymie the incursion into his portfolio by a young backbencher. Duncan further declared:

> Don put a lot of political heavyweight lobbying into this. I mean, I don't know the details of individual conversations, but Tom Casey – to put his hand up in the Upper House – he probably had to have his ministerial arm twisted…

> There were two people I knew of in the Parliament, or subsequently knew in the Parliament apart from Dunstan, who were gay or bi. And neither of them went anywhere near this issue, except for putting their hand up in a public sense, because they were obviously terrified of being blackmailed or outed or whatever… And you know, in the context of putting their right hand up at the right time was all I asked of them.[57]

Interestingly, Dunstan confirms his role, but also explains that the Bill, 'passed with strong support from the then Attorney-General, Len King, (now Chief Justice), and myself, and we used our influence to see that although it was a free vote, all members but one of the ALP in both Houses voted for it'.[58]

The success of the 1975 vote on homosexual law reform was assured by the support of Dunstan, not just with his vote in the House, but also with his strategic lobbying and guidance within the ALP parliamentary wing.

Vulgar and Unpleasant?

The historical record surrounding the inference – raised at the time of Dunstan's death and published again in 2002 – that Dunstan's reference to homosexuals' 'vulgarity and unpleasantness' of behaviour demonstrates his 'ignorance and prejudice',[59] also deserves attention. The full context of these 1972 comments in the parliamentary record reveal that Dunstan was describing the attitudes of his own upbringing; he concludes, 'I think most of us have been brought up with a kind of traditional prejudice about this matter'. Dunstan then explains how he came to confront his prejudices advising that, 'I think everyone of us, in life and in politics, needs constantly to question his own assumptions'.[60]

In an interview, also in 1972, Dunstan explained both his and the ALP's position on homosexual law reform. '[T]hat's a matter of individual conscience', he said. 'I should think that the majority of the members of the party would be in favour of it. I've always been in favour of it and I've always made that clear – it's a personal opinion and I'm not expressing my Party's opinion'.[61]

Dunstan was not ignorant of homosexuals or homosexuality, given that he circulated in a sophisticated world of fine arts. His own artistic streak was evident in his teens, writing poetry and short stories as well as drama criticism. In 1945, aged 18, Dustan acted in Colin Ballantyne's production of Shakespeare's *Twelfth Night*. By 1946 Dunstan was on the board of the Adelaide University Theatre Guild, and when Ballantyne established the Company of Players in 1955, Dunstan was co-opted as legal adviser, and he 'sat on the new Company's board formally representing the authors and taking an active part in the enterprise'.[62]

The Company's first production was a set of three verse plays by Brian Medlin, John Bray and Charles Jury.[63] Jury's work, *The Administrator*, first presented by the Company of Players in its inaugural season, is a play about the love between two young men; it has a happy ending. In the same year, Jury published the outcome of more than a decade's work, the play *Icarius*, another love story between two young men. Jury had asked fellow playwright and lawyer, John Bray, for advice on the Latin in the dedication for *Icarius*.[64] Jury and Bray were steadfast friends from their university days.[65]

John Bray was integral to an erudite network of friends, including Colin and Gwenneth Ballantyne and their neighbours, Dimitri Theodoratos and Peter Ward.[66] Ward recalls that living with his male partner in the inner city suburb of North Adelaide was, 'in those days, a defiant statement'.[67] Ward's talents led him to a diverse career in advertising, public relations, and radio and print journalism. When Ward was elected to the position of South Australian Branch President of the Fellowship of Australian Writers in 1960, it was Bray who was his Vice-President.[68] The circles of friendships were cemented with literary 'school' gatherings each week at a hotel, and monthly poetry meetings.[69]

These friendships complemented other working relationships: in the late 1960s both Ward and Dunstan were involved in the CCL.[70] As an executive member of the Council, Ward had raised concerns about police records on homosexuals.[71] Ward also had worked on Dunstan's campaigns prior to joining Dunstan's staff in 1969.[72] It was at Ward's kitchen table that John Bray sat as they worked together drafting the Bill to establish the South Australian Theatre Company.[73] And for the 1973 opening of the new drama theatre at the Adelaide Festival Centre, records Dunstan, 'John Bray the Chief Justice, composed a poem for me to recite from the stage, and Peter Ward added (having announced he was also the premieral bard) some excellent blank verse of his own as an introduction'.[74] Dunstan recalls in his memoirs that, 'Ward steadily became a friend and confidant'.[75] By the time Dunstan had resumed the premiership in 1970, he and Ward frequently would dine at one another's home.[76]

While Dunstan could count homosexual people amongst his friends and colleagues, he also had direct exposure to difficulties that could arise from prejudice. During the 1972 parliamentary debate on Hill's Bill, Dunstan – previously a member of the Actors Equity Guild – explicates:

> As Secretary of my union, since there is a larger proportion of people who are homosexually inclined in the acting profession than almost anywhere else, naturally enough I came in contact with cases… [T]here were people in the community who were apparently, from all observations and any other conceivable criterion, completely normal in their activities, attitudes, modes of living, and the like, but who nevertheless were homosexuals… [T]he problem for them was that, although they were socially useful (they related satisfactorily to other people in the community; they were able to carry out their jobs, and they were often charming, pleasant, intelligent and sensitive people), they lived subject to the constant threat that, since their motives were different from the norm and from the outlooks and tastes of the majority of the community, they were liable to prosecution, persecution and blackmail.[77]

Prejudice was apparent, too, within Dunstan's personal experience. As Attorney-General, Dunstan was inspired in 1967 to appoint Bray to the position of Chief Justice of South Australia, partly because of Bray's worldly knowledge outside of the law and his historical perspective of humanity.[78] Dunstan regarded positively Bray's, 'somewhat Bohemian existence' and associations with 'authors, artists and actors rather than the blue-rinse set'.[79]

Bray's nomination had been cleared by Dunstan with Premier Frank Walsh prior to being tabled in Cabinet. Police Commissioner McKinna, however, was determined to prevent the nomination proceeding and informed Walsh of allegations that Bray was homosexual. Walsh announced in Cabinet that the nomination could not proceed. Dunstan recalls consequently meeting Walsh with McKinna, 'I flew into a temper and demanded to know how he dared to traduce a citizen and endeavour to interfere with Cabinet appointments on such a basis'.[80]

When Bray learnt of the attempt to block his nomination, he misunderstood the detail of McKinna's report. The charge of homosexuality was against Bray, but he mistakenly believed the concern was that he had been linked with a homosexual. Bray supposed this was Peter Ward, and discussed the issue with Ward – who thought that the homosexual could have been any of a number of others. Eventually, Dunstan threatened to resign if the appointment was blocked. Bray became Chief Justice, and his successful term in office came to be highly regarded internationally.[81]

Dunstan's commitment is further evident at the time of the dismissal by the board of the fledgling South Australian Theatre Company of its inaugural director, John Tasker, not quite three years into his appointment. Tasker had been living openly in a homosexual relationship and was convinced that this had been used against him. Ward records that Dunstan considered 'Tasker to have been grievously treated, [and] he found employment for him in the Labor Party's advertising agency writing radio and television scripts in the run-up to the State election, set for March 1968'.[82]

The inference that Dunstan's comments on homosexuals' 'vulgarity and unpleasantness' reflected his ignorance and prejudice is contradicted not only by their context and by his other statements, but also by the personal familiarity and professional respect characteristic of Dunstan's engagement with homosexuals.

Achieving Radical Policies

There is further inconsistency to be found in the statements not by Dunstan but by Duncan. When introducing his private member's bill for the second time in 1975, Duncan declared,

> The first thing to which I want to refer is the question of homosexuals who are living together adopting children. I find that quite abhorrent, and I oppose it strongly... Further, suggestions have been made that homosexuals should go into schools to discuss their attitudes, and I

do not support that in any way... This Bill in no way seeks to assist or approve of homosexual practices.[83]

Duncan's comments, too, seem ignorant and prejudiced. But this contradiction can be teased out. According to political scientist, Dennis Altman, Dunstan's electoral success lay in his, 'appreciation of the symbolic in politics, and the way in which even very radical policies can be achieved as long as the veneer of respectability is preserved'.[84] This is remarked upon by one of the homosexual community members most closely involved in the lobbying process, David Hilliard, who recalls of Duncan's negative introduction to the final debates in Parliament that, '[i]n his second reading speech, [Duncan] tried to mollify conservative critics'.[85]

Duncan remembers that he had to negotiate his way around a number of pressure groups. For example, the General Conference of the Methodist Church in Australasia had previously had passed a resolution stating that, '[i]n the light of the fact that Parliament, society and the church do not consider fornication, adultery and Lesbianism as criminal offences, we consider that homosexual acts between consenting male adults should not be proscribed by the criminal law'.[86] Yet, Duncan recalls, he still had to clarify that decriminalisation would not entail recognition of same-sex relationships as marriages. 'The Methodists... were particularly concerned that gay law reform applied to the Criminal Law and not to the laws of marriage. That may have been why I was so strident in saying that I didn't accept – that I didn't want to see change in that regard'.[87]

Duncan confirms the explanation of these seemingly prejudiced comments in terms of the need to be circumspect, to acknowledge the views of others in the broader community even if they are not one's own, and to minimise the risk of alienating voters in parliamentary debate.[88] And, as discussed above, the conservatives to be mollified were found not only in the wider community and on the opposition benches in Parliament, but also within the government's own members. So it seems that such adverse comments are more appropriately interpreted as statements reflecting in Altman's words, 'the way in which even very radical policies can be achieved as long as the veneer of respectability is preserved'.

But Dunstan's direct position on his role as a legislator in 1970, as stated in the *Australian Humanist*, is consistent with his view given in the Parliament during the 1972 debate:

> one must face the fact that the majority of people who are homosexual do not regard homosexuality as a disease at all, nor do they regard it as

a condition to be cured. They regard it as normal and natural... I do not believe that society has any right whatever to trespass in this area. The purpose of the criminal law is to protect persons from physical harm and from active affront, and their property from harm, also. Outside of that area, I believe the criminal law has no place at all... The law is not a means of enforcing morality.[89]

The full context of Dunstan's reference to homosexuals' 'vulgarity and unpleasantness' of behaviour refutes rather than reflects ignorance and prejudice. In the Parliament, Dunstan speaks clearly about his knowledge of homosexuality and about his personal opinions. By his actions, Dunstan demonstrates his regard for those homosexuals known to him as colleagues and friends. And in leading his government, there is a political appreciation of conservative opinion and voters – both in the electorate and within the ALP – while securing the progressive and ground-breaking outcome desired.

Acknowledging Dunstan

Michael Kirby's belief that, 'Don Dunstan began our national process to remove the criminal laws against homosexual men' has validity.[90] Dunstan was the first Australian politician in government who actively championed the civil liberties of homosexual citizens.

While the assertion that 'Dunstan never took the lead on decriminalisation in parliamentary or community debate' may appear superficially to have substance, the detail of Dunstan's record establishes that he took the lead in other ways before informed parliamentary and community debate became readily possible. Similarly, the assertion that Dunstan merely 'advocated decriminalisation' is inaccurate by its incompleteness. Even though Dunstan's draft bill in 1965 did not make it to as far as the Parliament, his preparation of draft legislation enabled a more complete amendment seven years later: although Duncan introduced pioneering legislation into the Parliament for debate and vote, Dunstan had initiated it a decade earlier, and its eventual passage was achieved with his guidance and leadership.

Looking back, it is apparent that the professional life and work of Don Dunstan was infused with, and enriched by, the skills, contributions and commitment of homosexual men who understood his vision for South Australia, and who shared his political ideals. Later in life, Dunstan would embrace these ideals personally living as a homosexual man. At the time of Don Dunstan's death in 1999, neither Dunstan's solid record in homosexual law reform nor Duncan's ground-breaking Bill were included in the formal recognition given to the many law reform achievements of Dunstan and his government.

Amongst the ALP's tribute to Dunstan's reformist pioneering spirit was the testimony by senior political figure Clyde Cameron: '[w]hen Labor won government in 1965 and again in 1970, Premier Dunstan did more to civilise South Australians than any other Premier in the history of this state'.[91] But erasing *homosexual* from *law reform* not only denies recognition due for Dunstan, it also diminishes our standing as a civil society.

Endnotes

1. *Homosexual Law Reform in Australia*, Parkville, Vic.: Australian Lesbian and Gay Archives (ALGA), 1993.
2. Don Dunstan, *Felicia: The Political Memoirs of Don Dunstan*, South Melbourne: Macmillan, 1981, p. 201.
3. Tim Reeves, 'The 1972 Debate on Male Homosexuality in South Australia', in Robert Aldrich, ed., *Gay Perspectives II: More Essays in Australian Gay Culture*, Sydney: Department of Economic History with the Australian Centre for Gay and Lesbian Research, University of Sydney, 1994, pp. 158–162.
4. Stewart Cockburn, *The Salisbury Affair*, Melbourne: Sun Books, 1979, pp. 75–77.
5. Reeves, 'The 1972 Debate', p. 160.
6. 'Homosexuals and the Law', editorial, *Advertiser*, 13 October 1972, p. 5; Malcolm Cowan, The Decriminalisation of Homosexuality in South Australia, 1972–1975, BA (Hons) Thesis, University of Adelaide, 1990, pp. 67–80.
7. Dean Jaensch, 'Chronicle: South Australia', *Australian Journal of Politics and History*, vol. 19, no. 1 (1973), p. 94.
8. Don Dunstan, 'Dunstan Sets it Straight', letter to the editor, *Sydney Star Observer*, 5 April 1991, p. 11.
9. Dunstan, *Felicia*, p. 202.
10. Susan Magarey and Kerrie Round, *Roma the First: A Biography of Dame Roma Mitchell*, Kent Town, SA: Wakefield Press, 2007, pp. 234–235; Peter Duncan, interview with Dino Hodge, 21 September 2009.
11. Malcolm Cowan and Tim Reeves, 'The "Gay Rights" Movement and the Decriminalisation Debate in South Australia, 1973–1975', in Robert Aldrich and Garry Wotherspoon, eds, *Gay and Lesbian Perspectives IV: Studies in Australian Culture*, Sydney: Department of Economic History and Australian Centre for Lesbian and Gay Research, University of Sydney, 1998, p. 177.
12. Letters to Peter Duncan, Flinders University, Dunstan Collection, Allan Patience Files, 17.
13. J. G. Cummins and Council for Civil Liberties, to Peter Duncan, letter, 21 August 1973, Dunstan Collection, Allan Patience Files, Flinders University, 17.
14. Cowan and Reeves, 'The "Gay Rights" Movement', pp. 177–185.
15. ibid., pp. 164–193; Andrew Parkin, 'The Dunstan Governments: A Political Synopsis', in Andrew Parkin and Allan Patience, eds, *The Dunstan Decade: Social Democracy at the State Level*, Melbourne: Longman Cheshire, 1981, pp. 11, 13.

16 Allan Patience, 'Social Democracy in South Australia in the 1970s', in Parkin and Patience, eds, *The Dunstan Decade*, pp. 294–295.
17 Michael Kirby, *Consensus and Dissent in Australia: Tenth Annual Hawke Lecture*, Adelaide: The Bob Hawke Prime Ministerial Centre, University of South Australia, 2007, p. 8.
18 Gary Orr, ed., *Don Dunstan, 1926–1999: A Labor Herald Tribute*. Barton, ACT: Labor Herald, 1999.
19 Charles Bright, 'Law Reform', in Parkin and Patience, eds, *The Dunstan Decade*, pp. 147–162.
20 Samela Harris, 'Don Dunstan – A Celebration. One Big, Sad Omission', *Advertiser*, 13 February 1999, p. 13.
21 Barbara Baird, 'The Death of a Great Australian', *Journal of Australian Studies*, vol. 71 (2001), p. 75.
22 Roy Eccleston, 'A Decade of Dash and Doing', *Australian*, 8 February 1999, p. 11.
23 Tim Reeves, 'Duncan Led Gay Law Reform', letter to the editor, *Australian*, 16 February 1999, p. 12.
24 Reeves, 'The 1972 Debate', pp. 172–173.
25 Cowan and Reeves, 'The "Gay Rights" Movement', p. 192.
26 Tim Reeves, 'Duncan, George', in Robert Aldrich and Garry Wotherspoon, eds, *Who's Who in Contemporary Gay and Lesbian History: From World War II to the Present Day*, London: Routledge, 2002, pp. 116–117.
27 Peter Ward, 'Donald Allan (Don) Dunstan', in Wilfrid Prest et al., *The Wakefield Companion to South Australian History*, Kent Town, SA: Wakefield Press, 2001, p. 154.
28 Brian Buckley, 'Dunstan', *Bulletin*, 3 February 1968, p. 25.
29 Don Dunstan, 'Civil Liberties in the Seventies', *The Australian Humanist*, no. 14 (June 1970), p. 23.
30 Dunstan, *Felicia*, pp. 126–127; Dunstan, letter to the editor, *Sydney Star Observer*, 5 April 1991, p. 11.
31 *South Australian Parliamentary Debates (SAPD)*, 18 October 1972, pp. 2204–2205.
32 Duncan Chappell and Paul Wilson, 'Public Attitudes to the Reform of the Law Relating to Abortion and Homosexuality, Part II', *Australian Law Journal*, vol. 42 (September 1968), pp. 175–180.
33 Campbell Sharman, 'Political Chronicle: South Australia', *Australian Journal of Politics and History*, vol. 13, no. 2 (1967), p. 270.
34 Jeffrey Scott, 'Political Chronicle: South Australia', *Australian Journal of Politics and History*, vol. 13, no. 3 (1967), p. 428.
35 Neal Blewett and Dean Jaensch, *Playford to Dunstan: The Politics of Transition*, Melbourne: Cheshire, 1971, pp. 156, 168–169.
36 Malcolm Cowan, '"Knowing Sodom?" Australian Churches and Homosexuality', in Garry Wotherspoon, ed., *Gay and Lesbian Perspectives III: Essays in Australian Culture*, Sydney: University of Sydney, 1996, pp. 213–214, 234.
37 Dunstan, letter to the editor, *Sydney Star Observer*, 5 April 1991, p. 11.
38 Don Dunstan, 'Televised Policy Speech', Adelaide Town Hall, 30 May 1970, GRG 75/7/2 Unit 1, Department of Premier and Cabinet, miscellaneous documents 1970–1985, State Records of South Australia.
39 Tony Baker, 'Govt to Study Reforms: Male Sex Law', *News*, 3 June 1970, p. 5.
40 ibid.; Magarey and Round, *Roma the First*, p. 227.

41 'Criminal Law Reform', editorial, *Advertiser*, 15 December 1971, p. 2.
42 Richard Cox, Social Democracy: A Study of the Dunstan Labor Government, PhD Thesis, Flinders University, South Australia, 1979, p. 343.
43 'Homosexuals Seek Law Reform', *Advertiser*, 16 February 1972, p. 22. Greg Walker, 'Homosexuality', *Sunday Mail*, 24 June 1972, p. 93.
44 'Adelaide Scene', *CAMP INK*, vol. 2, no. 2/3 (December 1971/January 1972), p. 19.
45 Reeves, 'The 1972 Debate', pp. 151–164.
46 'MP Abused Over Homosexual Bill: "Reputation Damaged"', *Herald*, 28 October 1972, p. 9.
47 Dean Jaensch, 'Chronicle: South Australia', *Australian Journal of Politics and History*, vol. 18, no. 3 (1972), p. 432.
48 Peter Duncan, interview with Dino Hodge, September 2009.
49 *SAPD*, 18 October 1972, p. 2213.
50 'Schools and Homosexuals', editorial, *News*, 1 November 1973; 'Homosexual Defeat', editorial, *Advertiser*, 22 November 1973, p. 5.
51 Cowan and Reeves, 'The "Gay Rights" Movement', pp. 164–185; David Hilliard and Roger Knight, '20 Years On, 1975–1995: The Campaign that Led to the Passing of Homosexual Law Reform Legislation in South Australia in 1975', Darling House Community Library, 1995, GR 147, 2–3.
52 Roma Mitchell et al., 'Criminal Law and Penal Methods Reform Committee of South Australia, First Report: Sentencing and Corrections', *Parliamentary Paper 91*, Adelaide: Government Printer, 1973, pp. 68–69, 89–94.
53 Roma Mitchell et al., 'Criminal Law and Penal Methods Reform Committee of South Australia, Second Report: Criminal Investigation', *Parliamentary Paper 128*, Adelaide: Government Printer, 1974, pp. 11–16; Magarey and Round, *Roma the First*, p. 233.
54 'A Necessary Reform', Editorial, *Advertiser*, 11 August 1975, p. 5.
55 Hilliard and Knight, '20 Years On', pp. 6–9.
56 ibid., p. 14.
57 Peter Duncan, interview with Dino Hodge, September 2009.
58 Dunstan, letter to the editor, *Sydney Star Observer*, 5 April 1991, p. 11.
59 Reeves, 'Duncan, George', p. 117; and, Reeves, 'Duncan Led Gay Law Reform', letter to the editor, *Australian*, 16 February 1999, p. 12.
60 *SAPD*, 18 October 1972, p. 2205.
61 Julius Roe, 'A State View: Don Dunstan', *Woroni*, vol. 24, no. 12 (1972): Election Special Blueprint, pp. 6–7.
62 Peter Ward, *A Singular Act: Twenty Five Years of the State Theatre Company of South Australia*, Adelaide: State Theatre Company, Wakefield Press, 1992, pp. 11–15.
63 ibid.; Barbara Wall, 'Jury, Charles Rischbieth (1893–1958)', in *Australian Dictionary of Biography*, vol. 14, Melbourne: Melbourne University Press, 1996, pp. 594–595; Michael Hurley, *A Guide to Gay and Lesbian Writing in Australia*, St Leonards, NSW: Allen and Unwin, 1996, p. 152; John Emerson, *First Among Equals: Chief Justices of South Australia Since Federation*, Adelaide: University of Adelaide Barr Smith Press, 2006, pp. 162, 183.
64 Professor Graham Nerlich, (who also acted in one the lead roles in the 1955 production of Jury's *The Administrator*), telephone conversation with Dino Hodge, 11 November 2009.
65 Emerson, *First Among Equals*, pp. 175, 180–181.

66 ibid., p. 184; Magarey and Round, *Roma the First*, pp. 179, 185; Ward, *A Singular Act*, p. 6.
67 Magarey and Round, *Roma the First*, pp. 178–179.
68 Emerson, *First Among Equals*, pp. 170, 182–183, 187.
69 ibid., pp. 184–187; Ward, *A Singular Act*, p. 15.
70 Magarey and Round, *Roma the First*, p. 208.
71 Anne Summers, 'New Questions in the Dossier Affair', *National Times*, 30 January – 4 February 1978, pp. 5, 7.
72 Cockburn, *The Salisbury Affair*, p. 4.
73 Ward, *A Singular Act*, p. 16.
74 Dunstan, *Felicia*, p. 245.
75 ibid., p. 168.
76 GRG 108/1 Unit 1, Transcript of Proceedings – Royal Commission into the Dismissal of Harold Hubert Salisbury, 805–806, State Records of South Australia.
77 *SAPD*, 18 October 1972, pp. 2204–2205.
78 Emerson, *First Among Equals*, p. 162.
79 Dunstan, *Felicia*, p. 116.
80 ibid., p. 133.
81 ibid.; Emerson, *First Among Equals*, pp. 160–163; Magarey and Round, *Roma the First*, pp. 211–213; Ian Purcell, 'Justice Served', *Adelaide Review*, November 2008, pp. 24–25; Bright, 'Law Reform', p. 148; Wilfrid Prest, *A Portrait of John Bray: Law, Letters, Life*, Kent Town, SA: Wakefield Press, 1997, p. 95.
82 Ward, *A Singular Act*, pp. 25–32.
83 *SAPD*, 27 August 1975, pp. 503–504.
84 Dennis Altman, *Coming Out in the Seventies*, Sydney: Wild and Woolley, 1979, p. 225.
85 Hilliard and Knight, '20 Years On', p. 3.
86 *SAPD*, 18 October 1972, p. 2198.
87 Peter Duncan, interview with Dino Hodge, September 2009.
88 ibid.
89 *SAPD*, 18 October 1972, pp. 2206–2207.
90 Kirby, *Consensus and Dissent*, p. 8.
91 Clyde Cameron, 'Young Don', in Orr, ed., *Dunstan: A Labor Herald Tribute*, p. 24.

Even More Hidden from History?

Male Homosexuality and Medicine in Turn-of-the-Century Australia

Lisa Featherstone

In the final years of the nineteenth century, the surgeon Paul Ward Farmer was briefly institutionalised in the Kew Lunatic Asylum, Melbourne. Determined to expose the chronically miserable conditions of the asylum, Farmer wrote a gripping tale of institutional life, a warts-and-all exposé of life amongst the poor and the mad. He chronicled the treatments meted out to inmates, as well as the peculiar and often repulsive behaviour of the mentally ill men, with understanding, humanity and grace.[1]

Where his general benevolence fell, however, was when Farmer witnessed male same-sex desire. Despite his medical training, Farmer was amazed to find homosexuality within the asylum. He recorded:

> One day I noticed a case here which struck me most forcibly, and that was the desire of one man to embrace another. I fear this is a crime not unknown outside from something I saw on visiting a patient in Bourke-street [sic] a little while ago. The idea of such a thing to a sane man is, of course, revolting, and I devoutly hope it is not common in our midst.[2]

Farmer was a trained medical man, yet had no language to describe homosexuality, and no concrete idea of its existence, until a chance encounter with a patient. Homosexuality was almost entirely outside of his educational and moral framework, so much so that he was not quite sure of its very existence.

It is clear that there were emerging, nascent beats and subcultures in urban Australia during this period.³ Yet it is less clear whether or not understandings of sodomy or homosexuality were widespread or integrated into broader colonial culture.⁴ Even amongst medical professionals, knowledge about homosexuality could be very limited. Certainly, in the late nineteenth century, the British sexologist Havelock Ellis claimed that even experienced medical men had no experience of inversion.⁵ When considering medical training at Sydney University, there appears to be no mention of homosexuality or sodomy, or indeed even any space where they might have been discussed. The lack of training might have led to unworldly doctors never conceiving of homosexuality. Dr Farmer felt not only a lack of knowledge, but a clear loathing towards what he discovered: for a man who took most of the aspects of living in Kew Asylum in his stride, and who had a resounding sympathy for his fellow inmates, he was notably repulsed by the very idea of same-sex desire.

The memoir of Dr Farmer raises a broader question: was there a general blindness to sodomy and/or homosexuality amongst medical men? This chapter will explore male homosexuality in late nineteenth century medical discourse in Australia. It will suggest that the Australian experience is in stark contrast to the European frameworks we are familiar with, where medicine was key in defining, marginalising and pathologising the homosexual in the late nineteenth century. It was at this point the homosexual (as opposed to the sodomite) was to become a medicalised type, a 'person with unique psychical and somatic characteristics', rather than simply a person who engaged in the act of sodomy.⁶ In Foucault's famous line, the homosexual was now a 'species'.⁷ This has not been uncontested, of course, with some historians suggesting medicine was not necessarily central to the construction of the homosexual as a deviant.⁸ Yet this very contestation indicates a need for further investigation, of which this article is only one small contribution.

That mid- to late nineteenth century Western medicine produced a plethora of texts examining the homosexual is undeniable. First, the homosexual could be conceived as a degenerative body, one that was pathological, primitive and deviant. Homosexuality was, then, linked to disease, in particular nervous disorders, and, embodied in Oscar Wilde, the term came to act as shorthand for all forms of degeneration, insanity and the decadence of modernity.⁹ Second (and alternatively, even oppositionally), sexologists read the homosexual as a kind of 'third sex'. Initially the German Karl Ulrichs had constructed the sodomite as a female mind in a man's body. Over time, Edward Carpenter, Magnus Hirschfeld and others developed the idea of a third, intermediate sex.[10] This concept focused less on pathology, and more on difference, with some of the leading sexologists calling for rights for homosexual people. This idea of inversion (where the homosexual took on traits of the opposite sex) was common, and continued to dominate until Freud's focus on the mind, rather than the body, shifted the emphasis to newer, more psychological explanations.[11]

Yet in the Australian colonies, this medical and cultural preoccupation with male homosexuality – that has been seen as one of the defining points of European culture at the turn of the century – was largely absent. There was certainly an outpouring of information on male sexuality in this period. As I have argued elsewhere, the majority of this centred around male sexual excess, with a particular focus on masturbation.[12] Within medical journals, text-books and medical self help guides, auto-eroticism was an ever-present concern, with most local doctors continuing to argue that masturbation was probably medically harmful. There was also frequent medical commentary on other aspects of male sexuality, including rape, sexual excess and nocturnal emissions. Yet in medical writings, there was little on either sodomy or homosexuality. There was plenty of evidence of homosexuality elsewhere – in biographies and memoirs, in low-end rags such as the *Truth*, and of course in legal sources, which have been well mined by a range of historians in Australia. Indeed, doctors were frequently involved in court cases against sodomites, indicating a theoretical and practical understanding amongst some doctors at least.[13] But in sources written by medical men, homosexuality was almost but not quite absent.

This is, in the main, the challenge of even writing on homosexuality and medicine in turn-of-the-century Australia – we are writing on the silences and absences, as much as on empirical evidence. This is probably why Australian historians have focused less on medicine, and more on the law. While scholars such as Denise Thompson have indicated the importance of the medical model in developing and constructing the homosexual in Australia, there has been little attempt to understand how the international literature interacted with the local scene, and how it was read, absorbed, ignored or rejected by Australian doctors. This work, then, feeds into a more general literature that suggests that medicine was not as important in the construction of homosexuality as might be expected. Nonetheless, it is a relationship worthy of further consideration, particularly in the Australian context. This chapter will therefore offer a more detailed examination of the formation (or lack thereof) of concepts of homosexuality in Antipodean medicine. It is, even so, built from a far from sturdy body of literature –

glimpses of the homosexual man in Australian medicine were always brief, but nonetheless tantalising.

The Case Studies

More broadly, in Australian medical literature, heterosexuality was simply assumed, as if there were no options or alternatives. Doctors with a specific interest in sexology may have sought out reading on homosexuality in the international literature and a few grains of knowledge seeped into local publications. For instance, in the maverick George Beaney's *magnum opus*, *The Generative Organs* (1883), there was a brief, oblique mention of male same-sex unions. In a large text devoted to sex, the brevity of the mention is surprising. It was rare of Beaney to shy away from controversy – he was a doctor most famous as a sex writer, and for his controversial involvement with illegal abortions.[14] Yet, here, this sole mention of homosexuality (unnamed) was written only as an aside on lesbianism.[15] In a chapter that details ideas and case studies about 'unnatural feeling in women' Beaney suggests men too could be guilty of same sex desire:

> 'Voltaire, Rabelais and other writers, like Juvenal and Martial under the Roman Empire, make several allusions to these practices [in men], showing that even monarchs – for instance Frederick the Great – were habitually guilty of them, and this proves they must exist to a considerable extent. Evils of such gravity point to a serious want of reverence for Nature, and demand a much more earnest treatment than either jesting allusions, or impotent avoidance of the subject.'
>
> This shows how much the unnatural vice has been, and still is, indulged in by man.[16]

Like Farmer, Beaney appears to want to remain unaware of homosexuality for he cannot bear to think it through. The first part of his commentary is a quote from an unnamed source, and so only the last line is a Beaney's own prose. From a man who wrote extensively on a range of sexual disorders, this is intriguing. Nor does he have the vocabulary to describe homosexuality, nor any kind of framework through which to examine it. Further, Beaney has no clinical cases to back up his thoughts (he does in his examination of lesbians), nor any local evidence. He simply knows it is unnatural, and hence assumes it to be perverse. Beaney really only knows enough to condemn it, even if he is not quite sure what 'it' is.

This research into medical sources uncovered only one other commentary on homosexuality written by an Australian doctor. In 1884, the energetic Sydney doctor-about-town John Springthorpe published a rare article on sexuality in the prestigious local journal *The Australasian Medical Gazette* (the forerunner to the *Medical Journal of Australia*). Springthorpe was not a specialist sexologist, rather he had a wide range of socio-medical interests including various forms of preventative health and hygiene. This article was his attempt to grapple with the new Freudian concepts of sexuality.

In this period, Freud was a marginal, controversial theorist, and few colonial doctors engaged seriously with his frameworks or psychological concepts. Most greeted Freud's theories on sex and life with skepticism and fear, even derision. Yet Springthorpe, though hardly a radical in other ways, engaged rigorously with Freudian concepts, in particular the shocking idea that sex and propagation were central tenants of human existence. The foregrounding of sex was in itself controversial: for the Victorian medical profession, sex was generally something unseemly, unspeakable. In his article, however, Springthorpe found sex worthy of a proper, scientific examination. It was, he suggested, a key to understanding humanity. Yet if sex was central to human existence, this did not render it unproblematic. Rather, suggested Springthorpe, the problems of sex urgently needed both definition and deciphering. Sex, like any other scientific conundrum in the Victorian period, was something to be untangled and resolved, preferably by the appropriate medical authorities.

Most important to Springthorpe and other medics was the idea that sexuality had to be controlled and regulated. If the male body and the male sex initiative was naturally strong and active, the social order required it to be tamed. The Victorian man had to be taught sexual restraint, much as he would learn social and fiscal restraint.[17] Male sexuality, then, was constructed as urgent, impetuous, even volatile – and these functions would have to be curtailed.[18] The challenge for most men was that the Victorian economy demanded late marriage, and hence a long period of (generally theoretical) chastity. If men could not control their urges, Springthorpe claimed that social and psychological disorder would follow. There would be a range of 'terrors for the individual and the race, beginning with masturbation and prostitution, and ending with sodomy, wantonness, birth control and polygamy'.[19]

In Springthorpe's construction of social and sexual deviance, sodomy is but briefly mentioned as one of the possible outcomes of sexual excess. In his understanding, homosexuality is not considered as a form of desire, as a sexual choice, or a sexual identity. Rather sodomy was simply one option, one form of pathology that might overtake a man who allowed himself to indulge. Springthorpe suggested that sodomy was part of a continuum of sexual perversity: beginning with masturbation and prostitution, which would slip, if allowed, into the worst of sexual excesses, including contraception, sodomy and multiple wives. Springthorpe's writing, then, could be read as less a comment about sodomy *per se*, than as a more general diatribe against uncontrollable sexuality. Male-to-male sex was constructed as but one of a number of pathologies, though perhaps at the more serious end.

If Springthorpe's analysis of sodomy was brief and unsatisfying, there was little else written in Australia in this period. Literate, wealthy doctors may have had some access to international books that mentioned homosexuality, including professional journals, guides and jurisprudence texts. Yet rarely were these texts readily available on the local market. One exception was an inexpensive self-help guide, written by an American doctor, M. Lafayette Byrn, from the University of Louisville. His small book was published in Sydney, and hence there is an assumption that he could have been more widely read in Australia. It is not necessarily evidence of a distinct Antipodean thought, but is rather a suggestion of what the colonists may have digested.

Byrn skirted, very tentatively, around the issue of homosexuality:

> It is my belief that naturally – I mean in the state of pure and unperverted nature, but developed, cultivated and refined by education – every man loves womanhood itself, and all women so far as they approximate to his ideal; and that, in the same way, every woman loves manhood, and is attracted and charmed by all its gentle, noble and heroic manifestations.[20]

Thus in this case, homosexuality (un-named of course!) is effectively written out. There is not more than a hint here that there might be other options, that heterosexuality may not be the only choice. While the canny or knowledgeable reader may have been able to interpret his text, for the more naïve, the concept of homosexuality would probably have remained elusive.

Thus in this period, research has so far revealed little Antipodean analysis on homosexuality by the medical profession, in scholarly books, medical journals or self-help texts. If this was a period when concepts of homosexuality were, in Europe, medicalised, pathologised and institutionalised as deviant, the same cannot necessarily be said of Australia. Further there is scant evidence to suggest that wider medical concepts were absorbed (perhaps unconsciously) in the Antipodes, as part of the European intellectual legacy.

The vast majority of publications did not write on sex or desire, nor on same-sex desire.

Nonetheless, evidence of engagement with broader Western models of sexuality appeared in the most improbable of places. In 1900 the *Bulletin*, the masculinist institution of turn-of-the-century Australia, included a surprisingly pithy commentary on Krafft-Ebing's mammoth work on sexual pathology, *Psychopathia Sexualis* (1886). It is possibly true that the *Bulletin* was an eclectic paper which published all manner of unexpected articles, some of which were contradictory. Even so, this article, deeply embedded with European sexology, is unexpected in a journal that was often homosocial, but far from homosexual.[21] In this article, the issue of sex was constructed as 'a subject of paramount importance not only to the English, but to humanity'.[22] Further, the article drew closely on Krafft-Ebing's work, suggesting a familiarity with the specific sexological text and the wider examples of scientific writing on sex. But it was not necessarily quite so pathologising as Krafft-Ebing's chronicle of perversity. It commented most explicitly on homosexuality, and it is worth noting these comments in full:

> The best current hypothesis holds that at the time previous to birth when sex is decided, there is a strife between male and female germ-elements; and though the prepotent [sic] elements gain the victory, the elements of the vanquished sex are only subordinated, never destroyed. Every man has a latent woman in him; every woman has a latent man in her. Individuals are placed at varying points along the sliding-scale of sex. At one end the male victory is complete… at the other the female victory is complete… in the middle there has been a drawn battle, and you have the sex-invert, with the body of one sex, and the inner nature of another.[23]

The newer, less critical, less pathologising concept of inversion had clearly won the day for this anonymous writer. Indeed, while purporting to discuss Krafft-Ebing's work, the author actually relied more heavily on models of inversion and the third sex, developed initially by Karl Heinrich Ulrichs, and refined by sexologists and activists including Magnus Hirschfeld and Havelock Ellis. Within these theories of sexual inversion, homosexuality was constructed as innate and biological, and hence natural and acceptable. This was in direct contrast to Krafft-Ebing, who ultimately viewed homosexuality as degenerative, regressive and hence pathological.[24]

One can only wonder at how the readers received this article, for the peculiarity of such a close reading of medicalised sexological writings in a bush nationalist newspaper cannot be underestimated. And it is difficult to say whether this sole article is representative of a wider understanding of sexological theory. It would seem too optimistic to suggest that *The Bulletin* article is indicative of a wide acceptance of more tolerant theories of homosexuality, or to read this as evidence as a wide cultural shift towards understandings of inversion, rather than pathology. This article, rather, seems to be an anomaly in a society which more generally refused a discursive engagement with homosexuality, even within medicine. For, as we have seen, more generally, doctors, medical writers and popular considerations of health and medicine seem to have knowingly chosen not to write about male-to-male sex. It is clear from medical evidence at trials that many doctors were aware of the possibilities of sodomy. It is clear also in texts on medical jurisprudence.[25] But they were not recording it in general commentaries on sex. The rest of this article is an attempt to explore reasons why this might be so.

Why So Hidden?

As Shirleene Robinson's recent collection on homophobia suggests, there is generally no simple or linear response to homosexuality: there may be multiple levels of fear, ignorance, avoidance, anxiety and (sometimes) tolerance co-existing.[26] It is likely therefore that medicine's avoidance of homosexuality was complex, and here we will examine a number of possible reasons. Perhaps it is all simply a matter of timing: it is possible the Australian doctors were simply running behind the most cutting edge European scholarship. This is likely, given the fact that the British medical profession largely ignored homosexuality in the 1880s.[27] Thus even as other European nations fruitfully engaged with the development of sophisticated scientific theories of sex and gender, colonial doctors probably followed the British model. This is unsurprising, given that most local doctors in this period were still educated in England and Scotland, and were influenced by British journals and training bodies, such as the local branches of the British Medical Association.[28]

Nonetheless, while British doctors became slowly more interested in alternative forms of sexuality, Australian doctors still lagged. There were, in the colonies, only a few doctors writing about sex – and many of these, like Beaney, were not always seen as quite respectable. The specific forms of medical expertise developed in the colonies can begin to explain the avoidance of sodomy in medical discourses. Doctors were still establishing themselves as scientific authorities, slowly but surely, and tended then to prefer areas of work that were respectable, safe and with tangible rewards. Further, there were substantial shortages of medical care in some areas, in particular in regional areas. In Queensland, even as late as 1897 there were only two hundred doctors covering half a million residents.[29] This ensured that doctors were engaged with the most pragmatic work, with only the more elite urban professionals having the time or energy to explore more psychological or philosophical leanings.

So too, even when doctors did write about sex, they focused on the one form of socially respectable sex: the monogamous, heterosexual, married relationship. One of the key anxieties of the late nineteenth century was the declining birth rate.[30] The few local sex guides in this period largely focused on educating citizens to ensure proper propagation, with pleasure coming a very distinct second to obligation. That myriad social, economic, political and medical anxieties coalesced on the importance of reproduction ensured the continued exclusion of alternative sexualities from national and authoritative discourses such as medicine. This resolute focus on reproduction and on the determined continuation of White Australia meant there was little room for discussion of other forms of desire.

It is not surprising then, that Australia produced no major sexologist until Norman Haire in the twentieth century. Nevertheless, there appears to be something rather more cultural in the continuing avoidance of homosexuality. If homosexuality was to some extent 'unspeakable' in England, it was much more so in Australia.[31] The links between our colonial convict past and a fear of homosexuality have been well noted by historians: in the male dominated culture of the early colonies, sodomy appears to have been both common and anxiety producing.[32] For those wanting to build an 'Australia unlimited' at the turn of the century, convictism (and its many evils) was best left far behind: any reminder of a convict heritage was silenced.

Yet colonial society retained at least a partial convict heritage. In particular, it remained a male dominated society, numerically and socially. At the turn into the twentieth century, colonial culture remained ostensibly homosocial. As historians have noted, the key social institutions and symbols of 'Australianness' were united in a theory of mateship. Mateship was predicated, in art and in practice, on the desire for masculine company and on the specific exclusion of women.[33] Unsurprisingly, mateship can be readily linked to the homosocial and the homoerotic: we cannot be sure when the (homoerotic) mateship turns to (homosexual) desire. Yet ironically, the former – homoerotic mateship – seems to have silenced same-sex desire.

In a Derridean conjuring trick, where one effectively negates – yet inherently requires – the other, homosexuality is hidden and silenced behind the broader appeal of mateship. As Australia sought a new and unique national identity before and at Federation in 1901, the emphasis was on the rugged masculinity of white frontier society, and all it had 'achieved'. Again, this stress on a certain kind of masculinity – the bushman, and later the Anzac – unofficially censored other forms of masculinity, including homosexuality. So sodomy was to become great taboo: practiced, yet silent and absent in so many of the sources. The forms of masculinity idealised by the emerging Australian nation did not, could not, celebrate the homoerotic, effectively erasing both sodomy and homosexuality as a potential. It is notable too, that such a taboo was reflected in medicine: science, as always, was culturally informed in deep and often unexamined ways.

Conclusions

Most Australian accounts of sodomy and homosexuality prioritise legal sources. This is not surprising, for it is in the law courts that sodomy is most visible. This article is an attempt to broaden this analysis, to consider the medical understandings of sodomy outside of the courts. This has not been altogether successful – there is so much silence in the texts themselves. The Australian evidence suggests that the concept of homosexuality was not a focus in turn-of-the-century medical knowledge or practice. It is clear that many doctors had some awareness of homosexuality, and some may have had sophisticated understandings. Yet the sources suggest that at least some doctors had only a hazy knowledge of same-sex practices. If in Europe, sexology was key to defining and discussing the homosexual, in Australia medicine was (in this period at least) generally far less voluble.

Endnotes

1 Dr Paul Ward Farmer, *Three Weeks in the Kew Lunatic Asylum*, Melbourne: John J. Halligan, 1900. In his chronicle of his incarceration, Farmer suggested his wife and nurse had conspired to institutionalise him, but it appears more likely that he was declared insane after cutting open a number of quite healthy patients.

2 Farmer, *Three Weeks*, p. 24.

3 Yorick Smaal, 'Coding Desire: The Emergence of a Homosexual Subculture in Queensland, 1890–1914', in Yorick Smaal and Belinda McKay, eds, *Queer Queensland*, Special Edition, *Queensland Review*, vol. 14, no. 2 (2007), pp. 13–28; Clive Moore, 'That Abominable Crime: First Steps Towards a Social History of Male Homosexuals in Colonial Queensland, 1859–1900', in Robert Aldrich, ed., *Gay Perspectives II: More Essays In Australian Gay Culture*, Sydney: Department of Economic History with the Australian Centre for Gay and Lesbian Research, University of Sydney, 1994, pp. 131–

135; Bruce Baskerville, '"Agreed to Without Debate": Silencing Sodomy in Colonial Western Australia', in Robert Aldrich and Garry Wotherspoon, eds, *Gay and Lesbian Perspectives IV: Studies in Australian Culture*, Sydney: Department of Economic History and Australian Centre for Lesbian and Gay Research, University of Sydney, 1998, pp. 95–115.

4 There is some evidence to suggest that homosexuality was widely understood. For example, in court cases uncovered by Jill Bavin-Mizzi, some witnesses showed a clear knowledge of 'buggery' or at least of behaviour they felt to be sexually suspect. Yet Bavin-Mizzi also notes that crimes involving sodomy were often unreported in local presses, with newspapers reluctant to give specific details as they would for heterosexual crimes (though the *Truth* might be an exception here). Certainly oral histories from later in the century suggest at least some men and women did not have even a basic understanding of homosexuality. This debate over public knowledge does deserve further research. See, Jill Bavin-Mizzi, 'An Unnatural Offence: Sodomy in Western Australia from 1880 to 1900', *Studies in Western Australian History*, vol. xiv (1993), pp. 102–120. Oral histories that question non-homosexuals on their knowledge of homosexuality include interviews with Frank Campbell Opie and Dorothy Nosworthy, Mortlock Library of South Australia, J. D. Somerville Oral History Collection, verbatim transcript, 1982, Australia 1938 Oral History Project.

5 Havelock Ellis, 'Preface to the First Edition' [1901], *Studies in the Psychology of Sex: Sexual Inversion*, 2nd edn, Philadelphia: F. A. Davis Company, 1913, p. v.

6 David F. Greenberg, *The Construction of Homosexuality*, Chicago: University of Chicago Press, 1988, pp. 397–433; Jennifer Terry, *An American Obsession: Science, Medicine and Homosexuality in Modern Society*, Chicago: University of Chicago Press, 1999, p. 40; Jonathan Katz, *The Invention of Heterosexuality*, New York: Dutton Books, 1995, p. 82; Jennifer Terry, 'Anxious Slippages between "Us" and "Them": A Brief History of the Scientific Search for Homosexual Bodies', in Jennifer Terry and Jacqueline Urla Bloomington, eds, *Deviant Bodies: Critical Perspectives on Differences in Science and Popular Culture*, Bloomington: Indiana University Press, 1995, p. 130.

7 Michel Foucault, *The History of Sexuality Volume I: An Introduction*, Harmondsworth: Penguin Books, 1987, p. 43.

8 Chauncey suggests, for example, that while 'medical discourse was one of the most powerful anti-gay forces in American culture', it had less influence before the mid-twentieth century. See, George Chauncey, *Gay New York: Gender, Urban Culture, and the Making of the Gay Male World, 1890–1940*, New York: Basic Books, 1995, pp. 5, 125; See also, Joseph Bristow, 'Remapping the Sites of Modern Gay History: Legal Reform, Medico-Legal Thought, Homosexual Scandal, Erotic Geography', *Journal of British Studies*, vol. 46 (2007), pp. 116–142.

9 Terry, 'Anxious Slippages', pp. 131–132; Elaine Showalter, *Sexual Anarchy: Gender and Culture at the Fin de Siècle*, London: Virago, 1992. There is a vast literature on Wilde.

10 Terry, 'Anxious Slippages', pp. 134–135.

11 ibid., p. 135.

12 Lisa Featherstone, 'Pathologising White Male Sexuality in Late Nineteenth Century Australia through the Medical Prism of Excess and Constraint', *Australian Historical Studies*, vol. 41, no. 3 (2010), pp. 337–351.

13 See, on doctors in court cases, Bavin-Mizzi, 'An Unnatural Offence', pp. 108–109, 112; Adam Carr, 'Policing the "Abominable Crime" in Nineteenth Century Victoria', in David L. Phillips and Graham Willett, eds, *Australia's Homosexual Histories: Gay and Lesbian Perspectives V*, Melbourne: Australian Centre for Lesbian and Gay Research and the Australian Lesbian and Gay Archives, 2000, p. 28; Yorick Smaal and Clive

Moore, 'Homophobia in *Fin de Siècle* Colonial Queensland', in Shirleene Robinson, ed., *Homophobia: An Australian History*, Annandale, NSW: The Federation Press, 2008, pp. 76–78.

14   See, Bryan Gandevia, 'James George Beaney', *Australian Dictionary of Biography*, p. 125; C. Craig, 'The Egrarious Dr Beaney of the Beaney Scholarships', *Medical Journal of Australia (MJA)*, vol. 1 (6 May 1950), pp. 593–598.

15   James George Beaney, *The Generative System and its Functions in Health and Disease*, Melbourne: F. F. Bailliere, 1875, pp. 331–332. For analysis of constructions of lesbians in Beaney, see, Lucy Chesser, '"What They Were Doing With Their Clothes Off I Don't Know": Homophobia, Lesbian History and Responses to "Lesbian-Like" Relationships, 1860s–1890s', in Robinson, ed., *Homophobia*, pp. 45–46.

16   Beaney, *The Generative System*, pp. 331–332.

17   See, Ben Barker-Benfield, 'The Spermatic Economy: A Nineteenth Century View of Sexuality', *Feminist Studies*, vol. 1, no. 1 (1972), pp. 45–74.

18   John William Springthorpe, 'On the Psychological Aspect of the Sexual Appetite', *Australasian Medical Gazette (AMG)* (October 1884), p. 9.

19   ibid.

20   Dr M. Lafayette Byrn, *The Book of Nature: A Full and Explicit Explanation of all that can or ought to be known of the Structure and Uses of The Organs of Life and Generation in Man and Woman intended especially for the Married or Those Intending to Marry*, Sydney: The Modern Medical Publishing Company, 1890, p. 44.

21   For broader ideas on this, see, Lisa Featherstone, 'Sex and the Australian Legend: Masculinity and the White Man's Body', in Frank Bongiorno and David Andrew Roberts, eds, *Russel Ward: Reflections on a Legend*, Special Edition, *Journal of Australian Colonial History*, vol. 10, no. 2 (2008), pp. 73–90.

22   'Sex', The Red Page, *Bulletin*, 9 June 1900, p. 33.

23   ibid.

24   For a more detailed discussion of this, see, Terry, *An American Obsession*, pp. 43–47.

25   Bavin-Mizzi, 'An Unnatural Offence', pp. 131, 135.

26   Robinson, ed., *Homophobia*.

27   Lesley A. Hall, *Sex, Gender and Social Change in Britain Since 1880*, Houndsmills: Macmillan Press, 2000, p. 34.

28   T. S. Pensabene, *The Rise of the Medical Practitioner in Victoria*, Canberra: The Australian National University, 1980, p. 57.

29   C. F. Marks, 'Address in Medicine as a Department of State – A Suggestion', *AMG*, February 1897, p. 89.

30   Lisa Featherstone, Breeding and Feeding: A Social History of Mothers and Medicine in Australia, 1880–1925, PhD Thesis, Macquarie University 2004; Neville Hicks, *'This Sin and Scandal': Australia's Population Debate 1891–1911*, Canberra: Australian National University Press, 1978.

31   Harry Cocks, '*Calmus* in Bolton: Spirituality and Homosexual Desire in Late Victorian England', *Gender and History*, vol. 13, no. 2 (2001), p. 191.

32   Including Craig Johnston and Robert Johnston, 'The Making of Homosexual Men', in Verity Burgmann and Jenny Lee, eds, *Staining the Wattle: A People's History of Australia since 1788*, Melbourne: McPhee Gribble, 1988, pp. 90–91; Robert Aldrich, 'Gay and Lesbian History', in Robert Aldrich, ed., *Gay Life and Culture: A World History*, London: Thames and Hudson, 2006, pp. 19–20; Robert Aldrich, *Colonialism and Homosexuality*, London: Routledge, 2003, pp. 218–220.

33 Johnston and Johnston, 'The Making of Homosexual Men', p. 88; Linzi Murrie, 'The Australian Legend: Writing Masculinity/Writing "Australian Masculine"', *Journal of Australian Studies*, vol. 56 (1998), pp. 68–77; Clive Moore, 'The Frontier Makes Strange Bedfellows: Masculinity, Mateship and Homosexuality in Colonial Queensland', in Garry Wotherspoon, ed., *Gay and Lesbian Perspectives III*, Sydney: University of Sydney, 1996, pp. 25–30; Aldrich, *Colonialism and Homosexuality*, pp. 240–241.

'Homosexual Health Hazards'

Public Discourse on Homosexuality and Medicine in Australia, 1973–1984

Emily Wilson

Between 1973 and 1984, there was a prominent public discourse on homosexuality and medicine in Australia. During the 1970s, medical attitudes towards homosexuality were widely debated, and fiercely contested, notably by gay and lesbian activists. In the late 1970s, largely in response to this activism, the medical profession began to withdraw its claims to expertise on the topic, but outside the profession the emphasis placed on medical authority did not necessarily diminish accordingly. The framing of homosexuality as a biomedical issue in the early 1980s is usually seen as a consequence of an increasing awareness of HIV/AIDS in Australia, and certainly the onset of the crisis complicated the relationship between medicine and homosexuality. In fact, though, a tendency to defer to medical expertise on homosexuality was continuously apparent from the late 1970s through to the 1980s. This period thus provides a fascinating insight into the (de-)construction of a biomedical model of homosexuality.[1]

This chapter examines public discourse on homosexuality and medicine in Australia from 1973 to 1984. It utilises the *Medical Journal of Australia* (the dominant national medical periodical during this period) as well as mainstream newspaper sources, drawing comparisons between the two. Discourse in newspapers illuminates a period of unprecedented public debate on homosexuality. Officially, the medical community was abandoning its previous claims to authority on homosexuality, but prejudices about the nature of homosexuality continued to influence biomedical conceptualisations and interpretations of clinical data. At the same time, both journalists and correspondents to newspapers continued to rely on medical authority when discussing homosexuality. This was apparent among those who supported homosexual rights and law reform. It was also apparent among those who opposed these trends, and among this latter group there was a noticeable conflation of medicine and morality, as reflected in the title of this chapter. When a letter from Bishop J. R. Reid to the *Sydney Morning Herald* was given the heading 'Homosexual Health Hazards', there was a clear implication that it was homosexual people themselves who were the hazard, from both a health and a moral point of view. Reid, the chairman of the Social Issues Committee of the Sydney Anglican Diocese, blamed gay men for a rise in sexually transmitted infections (STIs) and argued that chastity was the only 'healthy' solution for this problem.[2]

Background

A number of Australian historians have explored the experiences of gay and lesbian people with the medical profession – particularly regarding treatments aimed at curing homosexuality – most notably Garry Wotherspoon, Graham Willett and Robert Reynolds. Willett and Reynolds in particular have examined how a medical model of homosexuality came to be dominant in Australia, providing invaluable evidence of the way in which medical expertise could be used to reinforce existing prejudices against homosexuality. Reynolds focuses on how these attitudes impacted on the development of a homosexual identity in Australia, while Willett is concerned with activist responses to these attitudes.[3]

Reynolds argues that by the 1960s, Australian understandings of homosexuality were based on a medical model formed primarily in the United States.[4] Medical opinion tended to agree on a number of basic factors: that homosexuality was a neurotic condition or personality disorder; that chances for a cure were far better than was generally believed; and that treatment rather than punishment alone was the most effective strategy for dealing with homosexuality. Articles in medical and psychological journals in Australia during the 1960s indicate a high degree of interest in homosexuality as a potentially curable, or at least treatable, condition[5] and various therapies were practiced to this end.[6] Among those who believed it was possible to cure or at least minimise homosexuality, two main forms of therapy were used.[7] The first was hormone therapy, most commonly the administration of oestrogen to male patients, a treatment which has been described as a form of chemical castration.[8] The second was aversion therapy, in which behavioural modification was sought by the substitution of desirable for undesirable responses. Aversion therapy caused distress to a great number of patients, and also had a dubious success rate; the highest estimate was 20%, but even this was based on studies taken immediately after a course of treatment. There was almost no evidence of long-term change in sexual orientation.[9]

A number of American historians have argued that a medical, and particularly a psychiatric, model was the basis for many negative attitudes towards homosexuals, especially men.[10] The emphasis on male homosexuality, reproduced in Australian sources, was caused by a number of factors, perhaps most importantly the fact that, unlike female homosexuality, it was illegal. A number of patients came to the attention of doctors as a result of criminal proceedings, as sex acts between males were outlawed in all states of Australia until South Australia initiated law reform in 1972. Treatments were therefore undertaken in a climate of legal and social repression. While sex between women was not legally prohibited, lesbians could come to the attention of the law in various ways, primarily through the breakdown of a marriage and in subsequent disputes over custody of children, particularly in the Family Law Court after 1975.[11] The evidence suggests, though, that the majority of patients treated specifically for homosexuality were men: certainly, the medical literature focused on male homosexuality.[12]

By the 1970s, criticism of both legal and medical oppression of homosexuals was greatly increasing. As the gay and lesbian liberation movement gained momentum, those who continued to practice aversion and other therapies were targeted by active and vocal campaigns.[13] At the same time, partly in response to this agitation, mental health professionals began to seriously question the efficacy of treatments. In 1973, the Royal Australian and New Zealand College of Psychiatrists (RANZCP) released a clinical memorandum which supported the idea that homosexuality was 'a developmental anomaly not necessarily or commonly associated with neurotic symptoms'.[14] This memorandum came almost a month before homosexuality was famously, and controversially, removed from the American *Diagnostic and Statistical Manual*. This was a significant step forward in the relationship between the medical and gay communities, although it did not represent a complete acceptance on the medical side that homosexuality was a normal variant of human behaviour. Commentary on the subject frequently drew attention to its controversial nature. In discussing the 1973 memorandum in the *Medical Journal of Australia*, R. F. Barr and M. S. Dalton noted that there was 'no general agreement among psychiatrists on the nature of homosexuality. Professional opinion varies widely, but in recent times has moved away from the view that homosexuality is neurotic'.[15] The authors also claimed that 'the majority of psychiatrists are not prepared to recommend treatment aimed at change in sexual orientation while the patient is not a free agent'.[16]

The emerging homosexual law reform debate was clearly informed by medical interpretations of homosexuality, and a number of medical organisations supported homosexual law reform from a relatively early period.[17] In a 1974 editorial, the *Medical Journal of Australia* argued for law reform, although it acknowledged that homosexuality remained a controversial topic, likely to remain an issue on which the medical profession, and the wider public, would never reach universal agreement.[18] In the same issue, Barr and Dalton recommended law reform as the official view of the RANZCP:

> The psychological adjustment of homosexuals and their psychiatric treatment are made unduly difficult by existing community attitudes. The acceptance of homosexuals by society is slowly increasing, but could and should be facilitated by reform of existing laws against homosexual acts between consenting adults in private.[19]

This apparent support must be critically examined. First, some professionals who espoused tolerance and supported law reform continued to treat homosexual patients with the aim of changing their orientation or at least diminishing their sexual drive. In a 1984 article in *Outrage*, Graeme Brewer documented the history of psychiatric treatments of homosexuality, providing evidence that aversion therapy, in particular, was still being used at least until the late 1970s.[20] Brewer singled out Professor Neil McConaghy as 'Australia's leading aversion therapist practising on homosexuals until the late 1970s'.[21] In 1973, McConaghy had published an article in the *Medical Journal of Australia* in which he discussed what he considered his successful treatment of homosexuality; in the same article, he expressed his support for homosexual law reform.[22] Second, despite the fairly rapid acceptance that homosexuality should no longer be classified as a neurotic disorder, some reluctance remained when it came to completely renouncing medical authority on the issue. Consideration must also be given to any medical support for law reform: it may not have been motivated solely by altruism and there is a sense, at least in part, that the issue concerned territorial claims to a particular area of expertise. Indeed, the rationale for the early support of many medical professionals for law reform was that homosexuality should be treated by doctors rather than punished by the judicial system.[23]

Homosexuality as Health Hazard

By the late 1970s, then, there was a growing belief within the medical community that there was no legitimate reason for medical professionals to be involved in the treatment of homosexuality as a condition in itself. Those doctors who continued to treat patients with the aim of changing their sexual orientation were increasingly a minority. There was, however, a continuing medical-clinical interest in some aspects of homosexual behaviour, particularly when it came to the sexual transmission of disease among homosexual men. During this period, a number of articles in the *Medical Journal of Australia* displayed a distinct emphasis on the promiscuity of gay men. One article on venereal disease suggested that it might be difficult to trace the transmission of the disease in the case of male 'passive' homosexuals, since they 'tend to have bouts of extreme promiscuity and may not be able to give any clues concerning their contacts'.[24] Such an assertion displays a number of assumptions about the nature of homosexuality: that homosexual men were generally promiscuous; that they could be divided into 'active' and 'passive' partners; and that it was the 'passive' partners who were particularly problematic.

Most articles though, simply assumed that all homosexual men were promiscuous despite the active and passive role. The pervasiveness of this belief is apparent in a 1981 article, which attempted to dispel the myth:

> despite much being made of the reported proportions of homosexually acquired syphilis, it must be noted that the total incidence of homosexual syphilis in a major metropolis, such as Sydney or Melbourne, is usually only 100 to 200 cases per year, and that, in terms of the number of male homosexuals, this represents less than 1% of homosexuals.[25]

The 'at-risk' group was therefore only a small sub-section of the gay male population. Nevertheless, in 1983, another article on a similar topic began by stating that: '[h]omosexual men are known to be at a high risk of contracting syphilis'.[26] Later, this second study quoted the first, and pointed out that while it was 'tempting to assume that the results could be applied to all Australian homosexual men, such an assumption may not necessarily be valid'.[27] This qualified discussion sits uneasily with the assertive opening sentence.

These examples are suggestive of the way prejudices, perhaps unconsciously, could affect interpretations of clinical data. Whether or not these examples reflect explicit homophobia, they demonstrate that the lens through which homosexuality was viewed influenced theories developed from clinical data. When the mainstream media reported on these findings, the misunderstandings and misrepresentations, some deliberate, some not, were intensified. For example, in July 1977, the Hobart *Mercury* reported that a rise in venereal disease was linked to homosexual activity, or rather, to homosexuals themselves: 'VD Spread Tied to Homosexuals'.[28] In 1981, Bishop J. R. Reid, blaming gay men for a rise in STIs, argued that promiscuity of homosexuals presented physicians with surgical as well as medical problems. Drawing on medical authority, he went on to explain that the medical literature showed that practising homosexuals were prepared to live with health risks.[29] This supposed willingness to live with health risks was framed as a danger to the rest of the community.

Medical Aspects of Homosexuality: HIV/AIDS in Australia

By the 1980s, there was widespread acceptance that homosexuality *per se* was not a disease or a disorder. The conceptualisation of homosexuality as a disease had, at least within the medical profession, largely been discredited. However, there was some continuing opposition to this new position, and some of this opposition is significant. In 1984, there was widespread support for the decision of the World Health Organization to have homosexuality removed from its listing as a mental disorder.[30] Two branches of the Australian Medical Association opposed its removal, though: the Queensland branch believed it should be kept as a classification for those who were unhappy with their orientation and suffered depression as a result, and the Tasmanian branch opposed it on the grounds of the incidence of disease among homosexuals.[31] The significance of this opposition can perhaps be seen in the fact that these two states were the last in Australia to effect homosexual law reform (Queensland in 1990 and Tasmania in 1997). Such evidence suggests that opinion was far from uniform and that established beliefs – that homosexual behaviour was a legitimate medical concern – persisted to some degree. The linking of homosexual behaviour with disease was, in fact, apparent in both medical literature and wider public discourse in the early 1980s. This nexus was reinforced for many people by the onset of HIV/AIDS in Australia and the persisting mindset on homosexuality and health influenced public discourse on the crisis.

An awareness of HIV/AIDS gathered pace in Australia, at least among gay communities, from 1982 onwards.[32] The first case had been diagnosed in Australia late that year. However, it was not until 1983 that discussion of the disease began appearing in mainstream media sources. This discussion intensified in June that year, when the first Australian death as a result of AIDS occurred. Paul Sendziuk, in *Learning to Trust: Australian Responses to AIDS*, argues that reactions to HIV/AIDS have to be seen in a historically specific context.[33] The response was shaped by the way sex between men had been viewed (from a medical standpoint) in the 1970s, and would not have been the same had the virus emerged at a different historical period.[34] In particular, the main early epidemiological theories about the cause of AIDS linked it directly to homosexual acts.[35] A 1981 study undertaken by the US Centers for Disease Control (US CDC) task force assumed a connection between homosexual behaviour and symptoms of AIDS in homosexual men.[36]

In June 1983, the *Medical Journal of Australia* released an issue dedicated almost entirely to discussion of HIV/AIDS in Australia and the US. The majority of articles simply reported on the findings of the US CDC, although they also stressed the importance of finding a definitive causal agent, given that the virus had not yet been identified as such. Ian Gust and Kenneth Mutton repeated the official CDC definition of AIDS as 'a disease, at least moderately predictive of a defect in cell-mediated immunity, occurring in a person with no known cause for diminished resistance to that disease'.[37] This disease, they said, 'might be associated with passive (receptive) anal intercourse', and 'repeated challenges to the immune system, both infectious... and non-infectious'; for example, drug and spermatozoal antigens 'might progressively paralyse the cellular immune system, allowing latent neoplasms to escape immune control and leaving the host susceptible to opportunistic pathogens'.[38] The authors went on to discuss the apparent epidemiological link between amyl nitrite use and AIDS, linking it to promiscuity: '[d]rug usage... is difficult to separate from total lifestyle. Thus, the use of nitrites correlates with promiscuity, which, in turn, can have associations with particular types of sexual activity, the risk of venereal diseases and the treatment of such infections'.[39]

David Cooper, praising the role of epidemiology in discovering a causal agent, stated that US studies had clearly identified the 'risk factors as the number of male sex partners per year; the passive role in anogenital intercourse with ejaculation of semen by the partner; and a previous history of infections'.[40] Cooper concluded that there was 'an urgent need to identify the causal agent of AIDS… Unless, and until, we identify the cause, even the moral majority could become the victims of AIDS'.[41] Cooper's article was fairly representative of the ambiguity in a great deal of medical reports at this time. Generally, discussion and early theories about the causes and transmission of HIV/AIDS were limited by existing prejudices and beliefs about sex between men; but there was also a genuine desire for objectivity and compassion. The statement that 'even the moral majority could become victims' suggests a willingness to accept that the disease was not bounded by morality; but it also suggests (perhaps unintentionally) that if this happened, it would represent a greater crisis than when the victims were homosexual men and intravenous drug users.

Beliefs about homosexual promiscuity continued to influence theories about the causation and transmission of HIV/AIDS. In 1984, the Sydney AIDS Study Group raised the spectre of the 'overload theory', stating: '[o]ne of the most striking early observations has been that a significant proportion of sufferers from AIDS lead a "fast-lane" lifestyle with multiple sexual partners and regular use of "recreational" drugs'.[42] The immunological overload theory had been widely discredited by this time, as the discovery of a retrovirus as the causal agent was now generally accepted.[43] The Sydney Group did acknowledge that most epidemiological research had been done in the US, and that the results could therefore reflect factors affecting a group following a particular lifestyle, rather than being representative of all gay men.[44] In the same issue, John Armstrong, in a somewhat unfortunate phrase, noted that 'its predilection for promiscuous homosexual men is beyond doubt', although he added that the condition was 'by no means limited' to this group.[45]

In the mainstream media, the medical identification of HIV/AIDS with homosexuality was exaggerated and shorn of its clinical context and qualifications. Seidman argues that, in the US, the media was fascinated with homosexual promiscuity (rather than homosexuality *per se*), so that 'quantitative aspects of homosexual behavior' were breathlessly and endlessly discussed. As he acknowledges, this fascination was partially a result of a medical-clinical preoccupation with the same issue:

> In a sense, the heterosexual media was simply following the pronouncements of the medical establishment. Yet, it is unfortunately not that simple. The medical scenarios, especially through 1983, were

highly tentative, conjectural and often contradictory. The mass media didn't merely report the facts but constructed the very reality of AIDS by drawing selectively on medical data and framing this information in a non-medical interpretive schema. By featuring the number of sex partners as the key causal link without further qualification or contextualization, the heterosexual media was, in fact, offering its own particular image of homosexuality.[46]

Yet this does not give the full picture either; while the media undoubtedly offered its own view of homosexuality, it was not uniform. What was apparent at this time were contradictions and debate about the nature of HIV/AIDS, and the nature of homosexuality.

There was certainly misrepresentation and sensationalising of medical data in Australian newspapers. In 1984, the *Telegraph* reported a 'Shock Find on AIDS Symptoms', claiming that researchers were startled by a new survey which showed that 47% of the subjects (gay men in Sydney) had symptoms of AIDS, while 60% felt at risk.[47] This data, part of a survey conducted by the Sydney AIDS Study Group for the *Medical Journal of Australia*, only encompassed 289 homosexual and bisexual men.[48] The article did eventually mention this small sample size, although essentially as an afterthought. Similarly, the *Courier-Mail* reported in November of the same year that 40% of Australian homosexuals could be carriers, a figure based on the estimate of Dr Peter Harden, the Red Cross Blood Transfusion Service director, rather than actual data.[49]

The causes and consequences of HIV infection were related with hyperbole and described with prurient interest. Notably, there was a fondness for describing the condition as the 'gay plague' or the 'killer sex disease'.[50] An article in the *Sunday Sun* managed to combine both sensationalist titles: 'The Killer Sex Disease Claims its First Life: The Gay Plague Strikes'.[51] The 'gay plague' title was contested in a number of sources;[52] the *Sydney Morning Herald*, for example, pointed out that it was neither gay nor a plague.[53] Nevertheless, the sobriquet proved remarkably persistent, even in unlikely contexts, for example in a somewhat contradictory headline referring to 'Heterosexual "Gay Plague" Victims'.[54]

Contrasting and contested responses to HIV/AIDS could be found within a single source. An early article in the *Bulletin* on the subject began with the sensationalist headline 'US Killer Disease Reaches Aust', although the author, Glennys Bell, was largely balanced and restrained in examining the development and impact of the disease. This was somewhat undermined, though, by the contents of a sidebar, also written by Bell and titled 'Disorders Peculiar to Homosexuals'. In this, she stated categorically that homosexuals were 'prone to certain diseases and disorders which occur far less frequently in the general population', due to their 'sexual proclivities'.[55] She then went on to detail these disorders, as well as the 'proclivities' which led to them, as described at a medical seminar in Sydney given by Dr Dennis M. Greenbaum, based on studies he had carried out at St Vincent's Hospital and Medical Centre in New York. Certain diseases, such as hepatitis, were more common among homosexual men in New York, an observation which was supported by clinical data. Drug overdoses were said to be 'probably more common among homosexuals, although data is lacking', suggesting that assumptions were made about a homosexual 'lifestyle' even in the absence of compelling evidence. Bell also discussed rectal perforation due to fisting, with the aside: '"Fisting" is also practiced in some sections of the Sydney homosexual population in communal steam baths. As one doctor described it, they soap their arms before "fisting"'. This article can be seen as one of the most extreme examples of prurient interest. In addition to the details already mentioned, Bell added that 'homosexual practices also include the insertion of other devices into the rectum', including screws, light bulbs, eggs, torches, and vibrators.

Possibly the most infamous example of sensationalism was the statement of one anonymous source, supposedly a homosexual doctor, who suggested that '[p]erhaps we've needed a situation like this to demonstrate what we've known all along – depravity kills'.[56] This statement was controversially reproduced on the cover of the first issue of the *Medical Journal of Australia* to deal comprehensively with HIV/AIDS in Australia, together with a skull and crossbones and another media grab calling AIDS 'The Black Plague of the Eighties'.

The cover of this issue sparked a fierce debate, both in the mainstream media and in letters to the journal. The cover was publicly criticised by the Health Minister, Neal Blewett, who identified it as an example of the media's 'prejudiced and sensationalist approach' to HIV/AIDS.[57] Dr Kathy King, the editor of the journal, argued that the cover had been an attempt at parodying sensationalist and irresponsible newspaper reports, but this did not prevent some severe criticism from readers. One correspondent congratulated them on the articles on AIDS, but 'was disturbed by the cover', which he found 'judgmental and inflammatory', even if he accepted that it had been an attempted parody.[58] A New South Wales general practitioner, Peter Barker, felt that the cover 'was in very poor taste', lacking in the compassion usually ascribed to medical professionals.[59] Barker continued, 'I may be of very mature vintage and rather "square", but I had felt that, as a profession, doctors had come to accept homosexuality as a simple preference'. This seems to indicate that for this writer, at least, the acceptance of homosexuality as 'a simple preference' was very well established.

Another correspondent, C. J. Dingle, protested against what he saw as the sensationalising of the morality of AIDS displayed on the cover, arguing that other diseases had a 'moral aspect': he singled out cervical cancer and coronary disease.[60] Echoing Barker's sentiments, Dingle also felt that condemnation of homosexuality was contrary to the 'traditional' role of the medical profession: '[n]o doubt we shall one day better understand the moral issues involved in the aetiology of cancer; but the medical profession has traditionally followed the course of trying to help the sick – not throwing stones at them.'[61]

Bob Fonseca, a medical student from the University of Western Australia, found the cover 'offensive and irresponsible', and objected to the final sentence of Cooper's article that suggested the 'moral majority' could become victims of AIDS if a causal agent was not found.[62] He argued that the cover and content, '[b]oth implied that homosexual victims of AIDS have deserved the disease as punishment for their "depraved" and "immoral" behaviour'.[63]

These letters themselves provoked counter-arguments. And while fewer in number they demonstrate the link some still made between homosexual practices and disease. In December 1983, a correspondent complained about the 'moral indignation' expressed over the cover, arguing that there was a call 'for comment, to restore some balance to the discussion about the apparent susceptibility of very promiscuous male homosexuals to contract this frightening and mysterious disease'.[64] He continued:

> It is reasonable and quite compatible with the best principles of objective medical research to examine the practices of male homosexuals to learn whatever lessons we can from their behaviour. While it has long been established that male homosexuals are the principal reservoir of syphilis, and that they suffer repeated attacks of gonorrhoea, herpes genitalis, venereal warts and other common sexually transmitted diseases, it has only recently been recognised that their activities result in a variety of enteric-related diseases which have serious implications from the public health point of view. It is time that the medical aspects of homosexual activity were given more serious consideration by the medical profession.

Another correspondent was even more blunt in his condemnation of the 'unhealthy' nature of homosexuality, and the supposed link between same-sex acts and disease. In February 1984, commenting on the 'recent flurry of letters' on AIDS, John Melov complained that '[v]ery little discussion occurs in the medical press in relation to the social mores of male homosexuals'.[65] He blamed the emergence of AIDS on the promiscuous sexual practices of male homosexuals:

> Thus, with the anal canal being used as a surrogate vagina and trauma being inflicted as a result, it is not difficult to see how immunosuppression may occur in susceptible individuals, e.g., passive, receptor male homosexuals with ano-rectal trauma.[66]

He added that it was well known that homosexual men were more at risk of STIs than heterosexual men. This debate thus reveals the contested nature of homosexuality within the medical community itself, and seemingly confirms statements made a decade earlier in the *Medical Journal of Australia* that any uniformity of medical opinion would not be achieved easily.

Given the nature of HIV/AIDS and the debate which flourished around homosexuality from the early 1970s onwards (both within and outside the medical community), it is perhaps surprising that a number of newspapers were reasonably even-handed in their initial coverage of the disease, cautioning their readers against hysteria. In July 1983, the *Telegraph* told its readers that '[a]ll the work so far indicates that normal, healthy people have little to no chance of contracting the condition. This, of course, includes homosexuals who have a single-partner sex life.'[67]

It satirised those who claimed it was a divine punishment on homosexuals, who had 'so far been unable to explain what God has against haemophiliacs'. The *Australian*, one of the earliest mainstream media sources to report on HIV/AIDS, was also fairly balanced in its reports on the disease in 1983 and early 1984.[68]

This changed dramatically in November 1984, when a gay man in Queensland inadvertently donated infected blood which was responsible for the death of three children. The result of this tragedy was, first, to suggest that this devastating mistake was actually a deliberate desire to infect the population: while most sources acknowledged that the individual involved in this particular case had no such desire, many could not resist suggesting that shadowy 'other' homosexuals had developed a resolution to do so.[69] The second result was an alarming tendency to blame the entire gay community for this attributed vindictiveness and thus to (re)pathologise the homosexual population. Sendziuk traces the way that this idea – that gay men were intentionally donating contaminated blood 'out of spite' – was sensationalised and spread through the Australian media.[70] He points out that the media response can partly be explained by the commercial imperative, but that there were two other crucial factors: 'the belief that AIDS was caused by gays and was originally contained within their ranks, and the conviction that AIDS confirmed that homosexuals were indeed deviant and sick and lived lifestyles that should rightly be avoided'.[71] This chapter does not attempt to replicate Sendziuk's work but rather, it examines the way in which medical authority was conflated with moral condemnation and older prejudices in order to condemn the entire gay community as both unhealthy and immoral during this period.

An editorial in the *Daily Sun*, 'AIDS Kills Babies', blamed the incident on the failure of the gay community to 'regulate' itself:

> A homosexual man has apparently passed on his affliction with the most horrible of results. Homosexuals have no grounds for complaint against the tough legislation introduced last night which will prevent them giving blood. *The shame is that the gay community has not been able to educate and regulate its members more effectively* [emphasis in original]… Three families have suffered deep tragedy because one man refused or neglected to examine the consequences of his lifestyle. It is impossible to believe that his attitude has not been shared by other homosexuals.[72]

The *Daily Sun*'s conflation of HIV/AIDS with homosexuality itself is clear in the opening sentence: the affliction which the man has passed on with 'horrible' consequences appears to be his homosexuality; no mention is made of HIV/AIDS in this context. Furthermore, the infection is explicitly described as a direct consequence of his 'lifestyle'.

The *Telegraph* carried headlines referring to an 'AIDS Blood "Time Bomb"', while Angus Innes, at that time a prominent Queensland Liberal MP, said that homosexuals who gave blood which resulted in deaths should be charged with manslaughter.[73] Another article announced in its headline that 'Donors Give to Spite', attributing this sentiment to a New South Wales Health Department official.[74] In fact, Dr Tony Adams, the official quoted, pointed out that while some homosexuals might donate blood out of spite, the majority did not, and that the man in question in Queensland certainly was not in the first category. Sendziuk also points out that Harden, the director of the Queensland Blood Transfusion Service, was actually quite sympathetic to the man, but that no newspapers printed his comments in full.[75]

The *Australian*, previously one of the more restrained newspapers on the subject, argued that the selfless system of blood donation was in danger, and managed to suggest that homosexuals as a whole were threatening that most cherished of Australian myths, mateship.[76] It called the system of blood donation 'perhaps one of the few real examples of Aussie mateship still left', and in doing so, placed homosexuals outside 'true' Australian society (seemingly ignoring the many non-Australians who donated blood, not to mention the existence of blood donation in numerous other countries). The article warned that it was in the interest of the entire gay community to ensure that no other incidents occurred, and labelled homosexuals who continued to donate blood after advice to the contrary as 'vindictive'. Finally, it stated that the infringement of civil rights was acceptable in this case. It is striking that the article was titled 'The New Plague', given that the *Australian* had strongly disputed the 'gay plague' misnomer.

In Queensland Parliament, during a debate on a proposed amendment to the *Transplantation and Anatomy Act* which would prevent homosexual men from donating blood, Innes united biblical and medical condemnation of homosexuality. He called buggery an 'abominable crime', but claimed to be 'saddened by the thought that there are people with these compulsions'.[77] He questioned the motives of those who might be AIDS carriers who gave blood, arguing that the homosexual community comprised more people with aberrant social patterns who were antisocial or perverse than the heterosexual community, and added that many homosexuals used blood donation as a free check up because donated blood was automatically screened for diseases. He continued:

> It is appalling that innocent people can be so afflicted by a disease with such untoward origins… In my view, in the end result, spreading AIDS is like putting in the boot in a fight or carrying firearms… If the spread of homosexuality is stemmed or even reversed, and the incidence of homosexuality returns to what it once was, the dangers of the spread of the disease will be reduced. If it is a toss-up between indulgence in some selfish lifestyle and protecting innocent people from death, I know which one should be chosen. It is a decision that normal people make a thousand times during their lives.

Innes's rhetoric directly equated the spread of disease with the 'spread' of homosexuality. Indeed, it seemed that a large part of his abhorrence for HIV/AIDS stemmed from its 'untoward origins'. According to Innes, homosexuality was a selfish choice made by abnormal people, and one which had a direct impact on the health of the community. He concluded that, because 'AIDS is a killer disease to which there is no known cure… transmitted by blood', and because the 'infection comes from people who practise homosexuality through anal intercourse', it was clear that homosexuality was the 'root cause' of AIDS. Therefore, the only way to prevent AIDS was to prevent homosexuality itself.

In 1984, Lex Watson, writing in the *Medical Journal of Australia* the month before these developments, pointed out that the mass media was the major source of information about HIV/AIDS for many people, including 'nursing and paramedical personnel, home-care nursing services, work and social contacts of AIDS and LNS suffers, and a substantial section of the homosexual male population'.[78] The consequence of the 'unparalleled media coverage' of the disease was that 'the label "AIDS" is now deeply ingrained in the public mind, and, like no other disease for many years, it has allowed the stigmatisation of a minority group. It is, among other things, a highly political disease'. The attitudes expressed towards homosexuality after a homosexual man was found to have donated infected blood were not only highly political; they also drew on a language of combined medical and moral condemnation, arguing that homosexuality was both immoral and unhygienic. While this link was exacerbated by the outbreak of HIV/AIDS, it was in many ways a continuation of the way homosexuality was considered by some in the late 1970s; a view that was sustained by an appeal to medical authority, even though it was not a link which would have been endorsed by the majority of the medical community at this stage.

Conclusion

Stephen Seidman argues that while HIV/AIDS gave some in the US an excuse for virulent homophobia, it simultaneously allowed 'a far-reaching, perhaps unprecedented, public discussion of homosexuality'.[79] Or, as Watson noted in the *Medical Journal of Australia* in 1984:

> AIDS has also posed quite unusual non-clinical problems. It has provided an opportunity for medical and media enquiry into homosexual men's lives and lifestyles which have not been researched since the 1950s, when medicine was extensively involved in seeking an aetiology of, and a 'cure' for, homosexuality itself… [However] the research has been conducted with that combination of fascination and disapproval that is so often a part of academic enquiry into sexual matters.[80]

The HIV/AIDS crisis in Australia allowed a continuation of a discussion of homosexuality within a medical-scientific framework. In particular, links were made between homosexual behaviour and ill health.

The period from 1973 to 1984 was one of intense debate and the first time that there was sustained public discourse on homosexuality and medicine. During the 1970s, medical views on homosexuality changed rapidly, shifting from disorder, to an accepted, if not precisely normal, variant of personality. There remained those who believed it could and should be treated; and medical interest in homosexuality continued by way of investigation into STIs and homosexual behaviour. In fact, the use of language and appeal to medical authority by those outside the profession continued into the 1980s, when the medical profession moved more definitively away from the idea that it was necessary or desirable to treat homosexuality. The onset of the HIV/AIDS crisis in Australia between 1983 and 1984 strengthened some in their belief that homosexuality was inherently unhealthy and immoral, supported by medical views that homosexual practices were directly linked to causation. From 1984 onwards, medical knowledge about the disease increased exponentially. However, the idea that there was a direct link between homosexuality and disease proved remarkably persistent throughout the period.

Endnotes

1. As this chapter is concerned with public discourse about medicine and homosexuality, particularly during the early years of the HIV/AIDS epidemic in Australia, the focus of the paper will be on male homosexuality. This focus is a consequence of the sources used and the era under examination.
2. (Bishop) J. R. Reid, chairman, Social Issues Committee of the Sydney Diocese, 'Homosexual Health Hazards', letter to editor, *Sydney Morning Herald* (*SMH*), in Greg Weir Collection, Gay Issues 1891–1994: Mainstream Political and Cultural Perspectives; a Comprehensive Archive and Index, Fryer Library, University of Queensland, vol. 6, 155 1981.08.03.
3. Garry Wotherspoon, *'City of the Plain': History of a Gay Sub-culture*, Sydney: Hale and Iremonger, 1991; Robert Reynolds, *From Camp to Queer: Remaking the Australian Homosexual*, Melbourne: Melbourne University Press, 2002; Graham Willett, *Living Out Loud: A History of Gay and Lesbian Activism in Australia*, St Leonards, NSW: Allen and Unwin, 2000.
4. Reynolds, *From Camp to Queer*, p. 14.
5. ibid., p. 18.
6. Graham Willett, 'The Darkest Decade: Homophobia in 1950s Australia', *Australian Historical Studies*, vol. 28, no. 109 (1997), p. 121.
7. For further discussion of medical treatments of homosexuality in Australia during the 1960s and 1970s, see, Emily Wilson '"Someone Who is Sick and in Need of Help":

Medical Attitudes to Homosexuality in Australia, 1960–1979', in Shirleene Robinson, ed., *Homophobia: An Australian History*, Sydney: The Federation Press, 2008, pp. 148–171.
8   Lesley Rogers, 'Hormonal Poofter Bashing', p. 33, in Australian Lesbian and Gay Archives (ALGA), file number 837. An editorial in the gay magazine *Stallion* also described the use of Benperiodol as leading to 'chemical castration' ('Stop This Butchery!', *Stallion*, no. 13, p. 4, ALGA).
9   Rogers, 'Hormonal Poofter Bashing', p. 33; Arnold Veraa, 'Sexual Deviance and Homosexuality: A Social Work Appraisal', *Australian Social Work*, vol. 28, no. 3 (1975), p. 25.
10 Simon LeVay, *Queer Science: The Use and Abuse of Research into Homosexuality*, Cambridge, MA: The MIT Press, 1996, pp. 75–78. See also, Laurie Guy, '"Straightening the Queers": Medical Perspectives on Homosexuality in Mid-twentieth Century New Zealand', *Health and History*, vol. 2, no. 1 (2000), pp. 107–108.
11 Ruth Ford discusses women who came to the attention of the courts in Australia at an earlier period in '"Filthy, Obscene and Mad": Engendering "Homophobia" in Australia, 1940s–1960s', in Robinson, ed., *Homophobia*, pp. 86–112.
12 The history of medicine and female homosexuality in Australia is far less developed than that of male homosexuality. It is likely that lesbians did become the victims of medical and psychiatric interventions: Ford provides one example in '"Filthy, Obscene and Mad"' (p. 87). However, the majority of medical literature focused on male homosexuality, and discussed female homosexuality as an adjunct or afterthought.
13 Willett, *Living Out Loud*, pp. 100–105; Wotherspoon, '*City of the Plain*', pp. 168–169.
14 Australian and New Zealand College of Psychiatrists, Clinical Memorandum: Homosexuality, no. 6, 1973, p. 3.
15 R. F. Barr and M. S. Dalton, 'Homosexuality and Psychological Adjustment', *Medical Journal of Australia* (*MJA*), vol. 1, no. 6 (9 February 1974), p. 187.
16 ibid., p. 189.
17 Reynolds, *From Camp to Queer*, p. 18.
18 'Homosexual Law Reform', editorial, *MJA*, vol. 1, no. 6 (9 February 1974), p. 158.
19 Barr and Dalton, 'Homosexuality and Psychological Adjustment', p. 189.
20 Graeme Brewer, 'Our History on the Couch', *Outrage*, no. 16 (August 1984), pp. 34–35. Brewer's conclusions were based in large part on the work of Lex Watson, particularly his chapter 'Homosexuals', in Erica M. Bates and Paul R. Wilson, eds, *Mental Disorder or Madness: Alternative Theories*, St Lucia: University of Queensland Press, 1979, pp. 134–161.
21 Brewer, 'Our History on the Couch', p. 35.
22 N. McConaghy, 'The Doctor and Homosexuality', *MJA*, vol. 1, no. 2 (13 January 1973), pp. 69–70.
23 John Court, 'Sexual Deviation in Society', *Australian Humanist*, vol. 6 (July 1968), p. 26; McConaghy, 'The Doctor and Homosexuality', p. 70. See also, Reynolds, *From Camp to Queer*, p. 20.
24 'Venereal Disease', *MJA*, vol. 1, no. 6 (10 February 1973), p. 270.
25 Michael W. Ross, 'Attitudes of Male Homosexuals to Venereal Disease Clinics', *MJA*, vol. 2, no. 12–13 (12 December 1981), p. 670.
26 David L. Bradford, 'Syphilis Case-finding in an Australian Men's Sauna Club', *MJA*, vol. 2, no. 11 (26 November 1983), p. 561.
27 ibid., p. 563.

28 'VD Spread Tied to Homosexuals', *Mercury*, 6 July 1977, Weir Collection, vol. 4, 205A 1977.09.13.
29 Reid, 'Homosexal Health Hazards', letter to editor, *SMH*.
30 'Move to Keep "Gay" Listing', *Sunday Mail*, 5 February 1984, Weir Collection, vol. 11, 39A 1984.02.05.
31 ibid.
32 Paul Sendziuk, *Learning To Trust: Australian Responses to AIDS*, Sydney: UNSW Press, 2003, p. 12.
33 ibid., p. 15.
34 ibid., p. 23.
35 Stephen Seidman, 'Transfiguring Sexual Identity: AIDS and the Contemporary Construction of Homosexuality', *Social Text*, vol. 19/20 (1988), p. 190.
36 ibid.
37 Kenneth Mutton and Ian Gust, 'Acquired Immune Deficiency Syndrome', *MJA*, vol. 1, no. 12 (11 June 1983), p. 540.
38 ibid., p. 541.
39 ibid., p. 540.
40 David A. Cooper, 'Epidemic Kaposi's Sarcoma and Opportunistic Infections', *MJA*, vol. 1, no. 12 (11 June 1983), p. 564.
41 ibid., p. 566.
42 Sydney AIDS Study Group, 'The Sydney AIDS Project', p. 569.
43 NHMRC Working Party, 'Acquired Immune Deficiency Syndrome (AIDS): Report of the NHMRC Working Party', *MJA*, vol. 141, no. 9 (27 October 1984), pp. 564–566.
44 Sydney AIDS Study Group, 'The Sydney AIDS Project', p. 570.
45 John A. Armstrong, 'Research Developments in AIDS', *MJA*, vol. 141, no. 9 (27 October 1984), p. 556.
46 Seidman, 'Transfiguring Sexual Identity', p. 191.
47 'Shock Find on AIDS Symptoms', *Telegraph*, 29 October 1984, Weir Collection, vol. 13, 11 1984.10.29.
48 Sydney AIDS Study Group, 'The Sydney AIDS Project', p. 571.
49 'Homosexual Carriers "Could Be 40 Percent"', *Courier-Mail*, 17 November 1984, p. 10, Weir Collection, vol. 13, 36 1984.11.17.
50 '"Gay Plague" Epidemic Sweeping US', *Australian*, 17 July 1982, Weir Collection, vol. 9, 3 1982.07.17.
51 *Sunday Sun*, 10 July 1983, Weir Collection, vol. 9, 46 1983.07.10.
52 In spite of using the term in its headlines, one of the earliest articles in the *Australian* quoted a Sydney general practitioner who pointed out that 'gay plague' was a misnomer (Sue Cook, 'Australia Could Be Next on the List for the "Gay Plague"', *Australian*, 19 July 1982, Weir Collection, vol. 9, 4 1982.07.19). The newspaper challenged the title more directly in an editorial the following year ('No Need for Hysteria', *Australian*, 28 June 1983, Weir Collection, vol. 9, 26 1983.06.28).
53 'The Controversy Over AIDS', *SMH*, 4 July 1983, Weir Collection, vol. 9, 40 1983.07.04.
54 Nicholas Rothwell, 'Heterosexual "Gay Plague" Victims Alarm Doctors', *Australian*, 20 May 1983, Weir Collection, vol. 9, 9 1983.05.20.

55 Glennys Bell, 'US Killer Disease Reaches Aust', *Bulletin*, 10 May 1983, p. 23, Weir Collection, vol. 9, 6 1983.05.10.
56 Michael VerMeulen, 'The Gay Plague', *New York Magazine*, 31 May 1982, p. 61.
57 'AMA Journal's AIDS Report Angers Blewett', *SMH*, 29 June 1983, Weir Collection vol. 9, 27 1983.06.29.
58 Mark A. Barnett, 'AIDS Cover', letter to the editor, *MJA*, vol. 2, no. 8 (15 October 1983), p. 364.
59 Peter Barker, 'AIDS Cover', letter to the editor, *MJA*, vol. 2, no. 8 (15 October 1983), p. 364.
60 C. J. Dingle, 'AIDS Cover', letter to the editor, *MJA*, vol. 2, no. 8 (15 October 1983), p. 364. He claimed that carcinoma of the cervix was 'associated with sexual promiscuity, either of the patient or of her male partner', and that coronary disease could be caused by greed and over-ambition.
61 ibid., p. 364.
62 Bob Fonseca, 'AIDS Cover', letter to the editor, *MJA*, vol. 2, no. 8 (15 October 1983), p. 364.
63 ibid., p. 364.
64 Kevin Hume, 'AIDS', letter to the editor, *MJA*, vol. 2, no. 12 (10/24 December 1983), p. 601.
65 John Melov, 'Pathogenesis of AIDS', letter to the editor, *MJA*, vol. 140, no. 3 (4 February 1984), p. 177.
66 ibid., p. 178.
67 *Telegraph*, 15 July 1983, Weir Collection, vol. 9, 58 1983.07.15.
68 Cook, 'Australia Could Be Next on the List for the "Gay Plague"'.
69 Sendziuk, *Learning to Trust*, p. 61. See, for example 'Donors Give to Spite, Says Official', *Daily Sun*, Weir Collection, vol. 13, 45 1984.11.28.
70 Sendziuk, *Learning to Trust*, pp. 61–63.
71 ibid.
72 'AIDS Kills Babies', *Daily Sun*, 16 November 1984, p. 1, Weir Collection, vol. 13, 25–27, 1984.11.16.
73 'AIDS Blood "Time Bomb"', *Telegraph*, 16 November 1984, p. 1, Weir Collection, vol. 13, 29 1984.11.16. Innes later became the leader of the Liberal Party in Queensland.
74 'Donors Give to Spite, Says Official', *Daily Sun*.
75 Sendziuk, *Learning To Trust*, p. 60.
76 'The New Plague', *Australian*, 17–18 November 1984, p. 24, Weir Collection, vol. 13, 35 1984.11.19.
77 In Weir Collection, vol. 14 1, 16 1984.11.15.
78 Lex Watson, 'Living with AIDS', *MJA*, vol. 141, no. 9 (27 October 1984), p. 559.
79 Seidman, 'Transfiguring Sexual Identity', p. 189.
80 Watson, 'Living with AIDS', p. 560.

HIV/AIDS and Gay Community Print News Media in 1980s Australia

Shirleene Robinson

This chapter analyses the way that Australian gay print news media dealt with HIV/AIDS in the 1980s. It finds that the commercial gay press in Australia was the most effective in the western world in informing a vulnerable community about a major public health epidemic, consistently providing medical information in a non-judgemental way.[1] Australian gay journalists had keenly followed trends in the gay and lesbian liberation movement in America and became aware of HIV/AIDS comparatively early. State AIDS Councils – which featured a number of gay journalists in prominent roles – lobbied federal and state governments for funding and portions of this revenue were used to fund safe sex advertisements in the gay press. This advertising revenue meant that gay periodicals in this country, unlike a number of gay periodicals in America, were not indebted to Sex On Premises Venues (SOPVs) which had a vested interest in promoting casual sex and downplaying the risks of HIV transmission. Furthermore, in states such as Queensland, Western Australia and Tasmania, where the commercial gay press was not always readily available, AIDS Councils produced increasingly sophisticated newsletters which informed and educated the lesbian, gay, bisexual and transgender (LGBT) community about the HIV/AIDS epidemic. Community print media – both commercial and non-commercial – was a central component of Australia's successful response to HIV/AIDS.

The successful Australian public policy response to HIV/AIDS has been adeptly explored by a number of authors. Paul Sendziuk's excellent study,

Learning to Trust is the most detailed exploration of the management of HIV/AIDS in an Australian context.² A number of authors have also explored the way that the mainstream media constructed HIV/AIDS. Deborah Lupton's *Moral Threats and Dangerous Desire* provides a particularly detailed analysis of HIV/AIDS reporting in the mainstream press,³ and while Graham Willett has pointed out that the gay and lesbian press played a vital role in providing the homosexual community with information about HIV/AIDS, it is a topic that has received scant consideration. The treatment of HIV/AIDS in the gay press has received even less attention, with one short article written from a personal perspective and published in the *National AIDS Bulletin* remaining the major piece of work in this field.⁴ This lacuna is not surprising as the role of the gay press in Australia more generally has also been an underexplored topic.⁵

The Emergence of the Gay Press

The earliest gay and lesbian newspapers in Australia were created in the southern states of New South Wales and Victoria. From 1971, the gay liberation group CAMP published a regular newsletter in Sydney under the banner of *Camp Ink*. This newsletter, with its focus on the developing gay rights movement and issues of interest to the LGBT community, marks an important turning point. Technically though, the first commercial gay magazine to be produced in Australia was *William and John*. This magazine was produced in Sydney from 1971 to 1972.⁶ In 1975, *Campaign* magazine was launched and continued publishing until 2000. In 1979, Melbourne's first gay magazine, *Gay Community News*, began production. In 1983, *Gay Community News* was replaced by *OutRage*, which was published for seventeen years until 2000.

The *Sydney Star*, which began life in 1979 as a free gay newspaper, and was later renamed the *Sydney Star Observer*, inspired the later release of similar free queer newspapers across Australia. The *Sydney Star Observer* remains one of the most successful LGBT periodicals to have been produced in Australia. Magazines targeted specifically at a lesbian audience were produced from the late 1980s onwards with varying degrees of success.⁷

HIV/AIDS and the Gay Press

The first newspaper article on HIV/AIDS in America was published in the gay newspaper, the *New York Native*, on 18 May 1981. This article, which measured just under 18 centimeters, was written by Dr Lawrence Mass, and reported that claims of a new 'gay cancer' were largely unfounded.[8] This report preceded the first mainstream coverage on the new disease, which was published by the *Los Angeles Times* on 5 June 1981.[9]

Throughout the 1980s, the *New York Native* continued to provide some of the most comprehensive coverage of HIV/AIDS in the United States. While the newspaper lost many readers in later years by embracing controversial conspiracy theories denying a link between HIV and AIDS, its early coverage was informative and important. The *Washington Blade* newspaper has also been commended by historians for its responsible reporting of HIV/AIDS in the 1980s.[10] Roger Streitmatter has criticised other gay newspapers such as the *San Francisco Sentinel* and *Bay Area Reporter* for not providing better information about safe sexual practices and bathhouses because they feared the loss of advertising revenue from these venues.[11] Randy Shilts, who reported for the mainstream newspaper, the *San Francisco Chronicle*, has stated that:

> San Francisco's newspapers had what every journalistic institution prays for: the opportunity to save lives. It was the one time in history when the gay press could have proven its mettle once and for all. But it performed miserably. The newspapers in the most important gay city in the country sold out to the almighty buck. The men who made that decision will, unquestionably, burn in hell.[12]

Streitmatter has also assessed as inadequate the *Advocate*'s reporting of the crisis.[13]

The mainstream American press has also been criticised for its lack of coverage of HIV/AIDS in the epidemic's early stages and its biased coverage as the 1980s progressed. Roger Myrick has adapted a framework first espoused by Jeffrey Weeks to understand mainstream media representations of HIV/AIDS in the United States during the 1980s. He argues that three main periods may be discerned. During the first period, from 1981–1982, representations focused on anxiety about the affected, the early medical definition and control of AIDS, and an indifferent governmental response. The second period, from 1982–1985, was characterised by a moral panic about the 'gay plague' and the marginalisation of People Living With AIDS (PLWA). From 1985 onwards (the third period), the American government began a preventative campaign which led to more professional educational campaigns.[14] The death of actor Rock Hudson in October 1985 from AIDS-related causes has been credited with a 270% increase in AIDS stories in

American newspapers in that year and motivating the new policy direction of the American government.[15]

Although many of America's gay periodicals were remiss in their coverage of the epidemic, Dennis Altman has argued that the gay press in a number of other countries played a particularly important role during the early years of the HIV/AIDS epidemic. He states that they provided 'much of the available early information on the epidemic, as well as acting as a vital tool in mobilising the community'.[16] Altman singles out the Australian publication, *OutRage*, the Canadian publication, *Body Politic* and the French publication, *Le Gai Pied*, as seeming 'to provide the best explanations for non-specialists of what was painstakingly being reported in the medical press'.[17]

On 3 July 1981, the *Star* newspaper in Sydney became the first newspaper in Australia to mention that gay men in America were suffering from a mysterious new condition.[18] Under the heading 'New Pneumonia Linked to Gay Lifestyle', the newspaper wrote a brief article about five young men in Atlanta, Georgia, who had pneumonia 'which may be linked to some aspect of homosexual lifestyle'.[19] As 1981 continued, other gay publications such as *Campaign* and *Klick!* also included minor stories about HIV/AIDS-related conditions such as Karposi's sarcoma.[20]

Gay Community News was the first Australian gay periodical to devote significant space to HIV/AIDS. In February 1982, the magazine published an article with the headline 'Will We all Die of "Gay Cancer"'? The reference to 'gay cancer' showed just how closely Australian gay journalists were following the language used in the United States. The *Gay Community News* article noted that 'major journals throughout the west have begun reporting what could become known as "gay diseases"' and that 'physicians and gay activists are encouraging homosexuals to practice better hygiene, reduce their sexual contacts and get the names of those they do have sex with'.[21] This information reflected the most up-to-date medical information on transmission that was available at the time. In April 1982, *Gay Community News* carried a further article, by Dr Simon Quest, which was 'about the smattering of news reports about Karposi's sarcoma [which were] appearing in large American and European cities where there [was] a strong gay population'.[22] There were some minor mentions of a potential epidemic in subsequent journal issues and in November 1982, *Gay Community News* published the first major in-depth investigative report on HIV/AIDS in Australia. In a five-page article entitled 'Putting Paid to the "Gay Plague"', journalist Gary Jaynes outlined what was known about the new virus.[23]

The informed early reportage of HIV/AIDS in the gay press in Australia contrasted with the lack of attention the syndrome received in the United States. This can be explained through the more independent nature of the Australian press. As the vast majority of the Australian gay press was not owned by SOPV proprietors, there were no conflicts on reporting on a medical condition many were starting to believe was sexually transmitted. In January 1983, Michael Glynn, the Managing Editor of the *Sydney Star* newspaper, wrote an editorial outlining the independence of that newspaper:

> When I started the *Sydney Star* more than three years ago I was trying to do my bit to make this city better for the gay community in terms of a developing awareness. The *Star* has remained an independent newspaper, not tied to any particular group or business, which enables it to pursue an editorial policy based on integrity and hopefully the good of the community.[24]

A perusal of the advertising in the *Star* in 1982 reveals that the newspaper did manage to attract a diverse selection of business marketing. While SOPVs such as the 253 Club Baths were featured in the newspaper, other companies, such as the Town Hall Hotel, Antonio's Pizza and Restaurant, Astill and Associates Insurance, the Belmore Park Hotel, Numbers Theatre, Stumps Restaurant, the Criterion Hotel, Universal Travel and the Honest Irishman Hotel also took out paid advertisements.[25] Thus, the newspaper could accurately claim to not be indebted to any one type of industry or business.

At the start of 1983, the collective which had published *Gay Community News*, launched its new publication, *OutRage*. Again, this publication was not indebted to larger business interests or any single type of advertiser. Adam Carr, who was appointed assistant editor of the new publication, rapidly became the journalist who wrote the most about HIV/AIDS for a gay audience in the 1980s. Carr remembers that he was galvanised into action by the 'first authentic and undeniable case of AIDS in Australia', involving a Melbourne gay man, who was known to some of the staff of *OutRage*.[26] Carr recalls that this case saw *OutRage* commit to covering 'this AIDS business' and that he 'trotted off to the Melbourne Uni medical library and photocopied everything they had on AIDS: a pile of journal articles about half an inch thick'.[27] Carr's first substantial article on HIV/AIDS was published in the June 1983 edition of *OutRage*. This edition of *OutRage* featured the cover heading 'The AIDS Epidemic: What the Straight Press Won't Tell You'.

Carr, who was also one of the founding members of the Victorian AIDS Action Committee in 1983, continued to provide gay and lesbian readers with frank, open information about HIV/AIDS transmission. Carr's substantial role in informing the homosexual community about the virus cannot be overstated. Bill Rutkin, the President of the Queensland AIDS Council (QuAC) in the 1980s, recalls that Carr appeared to know more about HIV/AIDS than most doctors in this era.[28] Carr also spoke out against homophobic reporting about HIV/AIDS in the mainstream press. He wrote that:

> The Australian media's treatment of AIDS' arrival here has been predictable. Most of the press have been free with discredited phrases like 'the gay plague' and the *Bulletin* [has] excelled itself with a homophobic coverage and offensively irrelevant choice of photograph.[29]

There were a number of homophobic reports about HIV/AIDS from the very start of the epidemic. In November 1982, in the first major piece written about HIV/AIDS in the gay press, Gary Jaynes admonished the mainstream press for 'referring to the "gay plague" in their headlines, a term that is as mischievous as it is inaccurate'.[30] When coverage was not overtly homophobic, it could also be sensationalist and unhelpful. In June 1983, the *Medical Journal of Australia* caused public panic when it printed a cover story on HIV/AIDS, calling it 'The Black Plague of the Eighties' and illustrating the title with grim press headlines and images of death.[31]

By the middle of 1983, the gay press in its entirety was devoting considerable attention to HIV/AIDS. Just as Carr had done, many other journalists suggested readers exercise caution when obtaining information about HIV/AIDS from the mainstream press. On this note, in July 1983, the *Sydney Star* newspaper urged its readers to not 'believe everything you read in the non-gay press. Since when have they had our interest, safety and care at heart'.[32]

As it grew, the LGBT press in Australia also provided a forum to highlight problematic coverage of the AIDS crisis by the mainstream media. Lupton, who has studied the mainstream coverage of HIV/AIDS in detail, has found that there were some consistent themes. First, HIV/AIDS received limited coverage while it appeared to impact predominantly on the gay male community. Second, contradictory, confusing and panic-driven coverage was common. Third, prominent people were able to influence HIV/AIDS coverage. Fourth, HIV/AIDS coverage had been personalised.[33] Lupton notes that the mainstream Australian press included homophobic and xenophobic themes in its coverage, along with imagery of invasion, fear and contamination.[34]

Out of all of Australia's gay periodicals, it was *OutRage* in particular that covered the growing epidemic in detail. *Campaign* magazine also devoted increased space to HIV/AIDS from 1983 onwards. Its coverage and reach did not match that provided by *OutRage* though. *Campaign* did provide direct information about safe sexual practices early though, telling its readers in a June 1983 article that 'the message is clear: avoid the direct exchange of bodily fluids'.[35]

Adam Carr has asserted that the AIDS epidemic prevented *OutRage* from becoming just another commercial advertising avenue selling sex and 'commercial goodies'. He states:

> AIDS gave the magazine a serious agenda to replace the rather stodgy diet of gay liberationist politics it had lived on before 1984. It also created a new market, since many gay men suddenly wanted a forum in which they could read and write about this new and sinister development. The fight against AIDS was the gay male community's great project of the 1980s, and helped forge a new community consciousness of which the gay press was both an agent and a beneficiary.[36]

There were strong links between the Victorian AIDS Council and *OutRage* magazine. The first Committee of the Victorian AIDS Council, which was elected in 1985, included three prominent gay journalists who were involved with *OutRage*: Adam Carr, Jamie Gardiner and Danny Vadasz.[37] Chris Carter, another member of the original Committee, went on to become the first editor of the *Melbourne Voice* and the *Melbourne Star Observer*.[38]

The advertising for safe sex campaigns provided a significant amount of funding to Australia's gay press in the 1980s. As Larry Galbraith, former editor of the *Sydney Star Observer*, remembers:

> In 1985, AIDS Councils began another relationship with the gay press: that of advertising client. As AIDS education became more sophisticated, campaigns were – and are – developed which had gay press advertising as an integral feature.[39]

Carr has also stated that 'more than incidentally, the creation of government-funded AIDS Councils and education campaigns greatly helped [*OutRage*] magazine's finances'. This was also true for the New South Wales publication, the *Sydney Star Observer*, which was able to publish its first full colour glossy cover in May 1986 as part of a campaign with the AIDS Council of New South Wales.

The Grim Reaper Campaign of 1987, which was coordinated by the federal government-funded National Advisory Committee on AIDS (NACAIDS), showed how 'mainstream' HIV/AIDS awareness campaigns had become by this year. This television commercial, which first screened on 5 April 1987, showed a Grim Reaper bowling and knocking over a diverse range of Australians. The camera then panned out to show many more Grim Reapers bowling down other Australians in other ghoulish bowling lanes. While many of individuals who worked at AIDS Councils debated the overall effectiveness of the Grim Reaper campaign, it did cause many Australians to seek out further information on HIV/AIDS from these Councils. The campaign also saw an escalation in the amount of news print that was devoted to HIV/AIDS. State AIDS Councils and gay publications were able to mediate the more homophobic comments and articles that appeared.

Publications by AIDS Councils

AIDS Councils in all Australian states and territories produced newsletters from their formation onwards. While the easy accessibility of a gay press meant that the Victorian AIDS Council newsletter never had to reach the audience that newsletters in states such as Queensland and Western Australia needed to, it still informed its readers that it would provide 'the truth behind the headlines' and an 'in-depth review of the Australian and overseas gay and medical press news and opinions on AIDS'.[40] The Victorian AIDS Council saw its newsletter as providing 'a regular, credible and widely distributed source of accurate information on AIDS and the battles we face'. Phil Carswell, the editor of the newsletter wrote that 'obviously in depth articles continue to be necessary and these will appear in the gay press'.[41] Indeed, the Victorian AIDS Council contracted its media work to Gay Publications Cooperative, the collective responsible for producing *OutRage* since 1985.[42]

In states where male-to-male sexual acts were not decriminalised and where it was not always possible to obtain copies of commercial gay publications, material produced by AIDS Councils played a vital role in mediating the homophobia of the mainstream press and informing the LGBT community about HIV/AIDS. There was often no professionally produced gay media available. The Western Australian AIDS Council, which formed in 1983 and the Queensland and Tasmanian AIDS Councils, which both formed in

1985, all produced their own printed media which informed a marginalised community about HIV/AIDS.

The first edition of *AIDS ACTION*, the newsletter of the Western Australian AIDS Council, was produced by five individuals with the rest of the Council involved in the distribution of the newsletter. It was four pages in length and featured information about fundraising, a support group for people living with HIV/AIDS and medical research updates about HIV/AIDS.[43] Subsequent editions provided open information about condom usage, antibody testing and the importance of safe sex.[44] State and federal funding did assist the Western Australian AIDS Council with its publishing agenda and by May 1988, the newsletter included social photographs and improved production values.[45] The Western Australian AIDS Council also maintained an extensive collection of clippings from national and international publications, both gay and non-gay. In 1990, *AIDS ACTION* affirmed that one of its major roles was in drawing attention to the homophobia of the mainstream media's reporting of HIV/AIDS. Michael Christian wrote:

> when reading the various tabloids, one tends to feel it is a rare day indeed when a balanced view of the issues is presented. It is unlikely anyone would contradict a statement saying that anti-gay sentiments are given far more media space than pro-gay sentiments.[46]

The Tasmanian AIDS Council's newsletter, which was published from 1986 onwards, also reproduced articles from gay newspapers, including the *Sydney Star Observer*, as well as homophobic articles from the mainstream media. By doing so, the Council created a sense of community, while also drawing attention to the prejudices surrounding HIV/AIDS. The newsletter also included features on regional events, support for volunteers and information about medical and social developments pertaining to HIV/AIDS.

The Queensland publication, *Duck News*, which was produced in a particularly difficult political climate, was one of the most professional of all publications and served as a substitute gay publication in a state governed by the conservative and reactionary Bjelke-Petersen government.[47] Queensland had no homosexual press and the periodicals that provided a voice for gay people in southern states were banned from public sale in the state.[48] These difficulties were compounded by the active use of homophobia as a political tool by conservative ministers. Historian Clive Moore points out that while Queensland's gay and lesbian culture is 'quintessentially Australian', the 'gerrymandered, rural/reactionary rule of the National/Liberal and National

Party government' during the Bjelke-Petersen era meant that mainstream Queensland was slower to embrace homosexual reform than other states.[49]

Duck News, which was published from 1985 to 1991, was produced in an A4 format with its initial length only two pages. By the next year, it was averaging at least 10 pages per edition. It was distributed freely in bars and gay venues and via the offices of QuAC. It was also possible to subscribe to the publication. *Duck News* assumed particular importance in Queensland, not only as a result of Bjelke-Petersen's government neglecting to inform gay men about safe sexual practices, but also because other homosexual media was not freely available to members of the broader gay community in the state.[50]

The volunteers involved in producing *Duck News* subscribed to international gay publications and reproduced relevant medical information for Queensland readers. In 1988, committee member Dr Malcolm McCamish noted that during the early 1980s, the gay magazine, the *New York Native*, had been 'the major source of medical information on AIDS and physicians treating patients would subscribe to it rather than to the more established journals for the most up-to-date information'. McCamish recognised the role that gay community printed media could play in informing this community about safer sex practices in a way they would understand. McCamish himself was an academic chemist, employed at the University of Queensland, and served as a scientific consultant for *Duck News*.[51]

Although some Queenslanders would have also subscribed to national periodicals such as *OutRage*, QuAC's publication, *Duck News*, probably reached more gay and lesbian individuals in that state. Until 1987, *Duck News* was produced by volunteer Cory Prickett, who was aged around 16 years at the time and had access to a printing press through a family connection. Prickett, along with his team of other young volunteers 'initiated' the magazine and 'devoted countless hours to its production', as well as assisting in welfare-related activities. *Duck News* informed both QuAC workers and the broader community about safe sex, community events and many other pieces of important information. By March 1986, due to its popularity, members of the organisation increased the numbers of copies of *Duck News* being produced from 500 to 680 per month.[52] It is also likely that many more copies than the number produced were read, as *Duck News* was distributed in venues such as gay bars, where issues would have been read by multiple people. QuAC also agreed to lodge copies of the publication in the National Library, as they believed this would help

QuAC to receive more recognition.[53] In October 1987, the national gay periodical *OutRage* referred to *Duck News* as 'the most interesting and informative AIDS Council newsletter in the country'.[54] Certainly, until the decriminalisation of male-to-male homosexuality in Queensland in 1990, *Duck News* played a unique and crucial role in HIV/AIDS education and prevention.

The arrival of HIV/AIDS significantly exacerbated the homophobic rhetoric that was espoused by members of the Bjelke-Petersen government.[55] In July 1984, the media reported that 30 recipients had received blood contaminated with the HIV virus. This was modified the next day to 26. The reporting of this event was not handled with any degree of sensitivity. Fears of an AIDS epidemic, however, increased significantly in November. In this month, Brian Austin, the Minister for Health, announced that three babies had died after they received transfusions of blood contaminated with HIV/AIDS. The blood had been donated by a 27-year-old homosexual Brisbane man. The *Courier-Mail* and *Daily Sun* both devoted their front page to comments from the father of one of the dead babies. The father of the baby not only referred to homosexuality as 'this degenerate trend' but also urged the donor of the contaminated blood to commit suicide.[56]

In August 1984, when concern over contaminated blood was mounting, Bjelke-Petersen described homosexual people as 'insulting evil animals who should go back to New South Wales and Victoria where they came from in the first place'.[57] Bjelke-Petersen also took the opportunity to declare that the New South Wales Labor Premier, Neville Wran, 'should hang his head in shame for legalising homosexuality in New South Wales'.[58]

The arrival of HIV/AIDS in Queensland caused considerable public fear. The legislative response of the Bjelke-Petersen government appears highly reactionary. It quickly introduced amendments to the *Transplantation and Anatomy Act*, allowing for a $10,000 penalty or two years' imprisonment for those who knowingly gave false information in respect of body tissue used for transplant or transfusion. The introduction of this legislation helped to convey the impression that homosexual blood donors might have knowingly donated infected blood.

When introducing the amendments, Austin continued with the rhetoric that had been expressed by Bjelke-Petersen, associating the Labor Party with homosexuality and HIV/AIDS with both. Austin stated that the children who had died as a result of receiving contaminated blood:

appear to be the innocent victims of the permissive society Australia is becoming. It distresses the Queensland government to see how some other states and Canberra support legalised homosexuality.[59]

The conflation between HIV/AIDS and homosexuality was part of conservative political discourse in the 1980s but it was particularly marked in Queensland.

As the HIV/AIDS crisis continued, the Bjelke-Petersen government steadfastly refused to open discussions with the activists involved in promoting safe-sex campaigns. Bjelke-Petersen also refused to allow condom machines to be installed in public facilities and did not allow for non-judgemental discussions of safe sex or indeed any sexual education in Queensland schools. While other states set up testing and treatment facilities and funded AIDS Action Councils, the Queensland state government refused to fund such facilities.[60]

Despite a lack of support from the Queensland government, QuAC pushed ahead with its educational aims from the outset. This was particularly important because, as Roger Myrick has pointed out, gay community organisations have a proven track record of effectively being able to convey safe sex messages within their community.[61] Carr has also argued that campaigns within the gay community were a major factor in Australia managing to successfully contain the epidemic.[62] By mid-December 1984, QuAC had designed cards explaining safe and unsafe sex practices and these were being distributed in beats and bars. In July 1985, the Council rented a house and had a telephone connected so that concerned individuals would easily be able to access support. Later, in 1987, during the Grim Reaper advertising campaign era, this phone-line operated 24 hours a day, responding to increasing mainstream community concerns about the epidemic.[63] The first advertising campaign that was mounted by QuAC in August 1985 saw 30 Brisbane City Council buses carrying large side-panel advertisements with the contact telephone number for the AIDS Council.[64]

This contrasts heavily with the educational stance adopted by the Bjelke-Petersen government during this era. As Paul Sendziuk points out, throughout 1985 the Queensland Department of Health provided two pieces of material about HIV/AIDS. One had been compiled by David Pennington's Task Force and was entitled *AIDS: The Facts*. The other was a booklet entitled *AIDS: Acquired Immune Deficiency Syndrome: Information for Physicians*.[65] No material had been designed to target the male homosexual community, nor were condoms suggested as a preventative measure. Furthermore, material about HIV/AIDS was not promoted or highly visible, leading Bill Rutkin to note that you 'have to know about it before you ask about it'.[66]

Conclusion

By the 1990s, new combination therapies greatly extended the life expectancies of many people living with HIV/AIDS. While AIDS Councils still exist in all Australian states and territories, their role has shifted slightly to encompass broader LGBT health. In tandem with this, as Adam Carr has pointed out with some irony, the publicity surrounding HIV/AIDS in the 1980s and the growth of AIDS Councils, Mardi Gras and commercial elements and the expense of activist organisations actually served to hasten the 'mainstreaming' of gay life. He states:

> The gay commercial sector throve and prospered. Gay men and lesbians became increasingly prominent and increasingly open in the arts and public life generally. What used to be called the 'gay ghetto' was disappearing, and the role of what had begun as a 'ghetto press' was in question.[67]

The rapid growth of the internet also significantly altered the way members of the LGBT community communicated and shared information. In 2000, as a reaction to these changes and a depleted readership, both of Australia's main gay magazines, *Campaign* and *OutRage*, ceased publication. Free and regional LGBT newspapers are still published across the country.

Australia's response to HIV/AIDS is widely regarded as one of the most effective in the western world. The Australian Federal Government has rightfully received acknowledgement for empowering and working in conjunction with marginalised communities to contain the epidemic. The role of the LGBT community in promoting safe sex strategies, devising educational campaigns and developing a strong and active press that allowed for the provision of vital information, support and a platform to refute homophobia was also crucial to the management of this epidemic. Printed gay news media was central to Australia's successful management of HIV/AIDS.

Endnotes

1. Roger Streitmatter, *Unspeakable: The Rise of the Gay and Lesbian Press in America*, Boston: Faber and Faber, 1995, p. 245.
2. Paul Sendziuk, *Learning to Trust: Australian Responses to AIDS*, Sydney: University of New South Wales Press, 2004.

3   Deborah Lupton, *Moral Threats and Dangerous Desires: AIDS in the News Media*, London: Taylor and Francis, 1994.
4   L. Galbraith, 'AIDS: How the Gay Press Told the Story', *National AIDS Bulletin*, vol. 6, no. 6 (1992), pp. 18–21.
5   See, Shirleene Robinson, 'On the Frontline: The Queer Press and the Fight Against Homophobia' in Shirleene Robinson, ed., *Homophobia: An Australian History*, Annandale, NSW: The Federation Press, 2008, pp. 193–217; Martyn Goddard, 'The Whole Truth: Limits on Gay and Lesbian Journalism', in Garry Wotherspoon, ed., *Gay and Lesbian Perspectives III*, Sydney: Department of Economic History, University of Sydney, 1996, pp. 1–16; Anne Scahill, 'Queer(ed) Media', in Craig Johnston and Paul van Reyk, eds, *Queer City: Gay and Lesbian Politics in Sydney*, Sydney: Pluto Press, 2001, pp. 179–192; Rob Cover, 'Engaging Sexualities: Lesbian/Gay Print Journalism, Community, Belonging, Social Space and Physical Place', *Pacific Journalism Review*, vol. 11, no. 1 (April 2005), pp. 113–132; and, Shirleene Robinson, 'Queensland's Queer Press', in Yorick Smaal and Belinda McKay, eds, *Queer Queensland*, Special Edition, *Queensland Review*, vol. 14, no. 2 (2007), pp. 59–78.
6   Garry Wotherspoon, *'City of the Plain': History of a Gay Sub-culture*, Sydney: Hale and Iremonger, 1991, p. 175.
7   Dennis Altman, 'Homosexuality', in Richard Nile, ed., *Australian Civilisation*, Melbourne: Oxford University Press, 1994, p. 114.
8   Larry P. Gross, *Up from Invisibility: Lesbians, Gay Men and the Media in America*, New York: Columbia University Press, 2001.
9   ibid.
10 Streitmatter, *Unspeakable*, p. 243.
11 ibid., p. 245.
12 ibid.
13 ibid.
14 Roger Myrick, *AIDS, Communication and Empowerment: Gay Male Identity and the Politics of Public Health Messages*, New York: Harrington Park Press, 1996, p. 43.
15 Edward Alwood, *Straight News: Gays, Lesbians and the News Media*, New York: Columbia University Press, 1996, p. 234.
16 Dennis Altman, *Power and Community: Organizational and Cultural Responses to AIDS*, London: Taylor and Francis, 1994, p. 21.
17 ibid.
18 O'Donnell, 'Star Wars: Patterns of Change in Community Journalism at the *Sydney Star Observer*', p. 148.
19 Galbraith, 'AIDS: How the Gay Press Told the Story', p. 18.
20 ibid.
21 *Gay Community News*, ibid., vol. 4, no. 1 (February 1982), p. 5.
22 ibid., vol. 4, no. 3 (April 1982), p. 39.
23 ibid., vol. 4, no. 9 (November 1982), pp. 17–19, 24–25.
24 *Sydney Star*, 3 July 1981, p. 2.
25 See, for example, *Sydney Star*, vol. 4, no. 4 (10 September 1982).
26 Adam Carr, 'When We Were Very Young: The Early Years of the HIV/AIDS Epidemic in Victoria', *National AIDS Bulletin*, vol. 6, no. 6 (July 1992), p. 15.
27 ibid.

28 William Rutkin, interview with Shirleene Robinson, Brisbane, 5 February 2010.
29 *OutRage*, no. 3 (June 1983), p. 3.
30 *Gay Community News*, vol. 4, no. 9 (November 1982), pp. 17–19, 24–25.
31 *Medical Journal of Australia*, 11 June 1983.
32 *Sydney Star*, vol. 4, no. 24 (1 July 1983), p. 4.
33 Lupton, *Moral Threats and Dangerous Desires*, p. 21.
34 ibid.
35 *Campaign*, vol. 4, no. 22 (3 June 1983), pp. 7–8.
36 'OutRage at 15 or the Rise and Fall of Practically Everyone', Adam Carr website, available at, http://www.adam-carr.net/003.html, date accessed 16 July 2010.
37 Adam Carr, *A Dangerous Decade: Ten Years of the Victorian AIDS Council 1983–1993*, Melbourne: Victorian AIDS Council, 1993, p. 5.
38 Carr, 'When We Were Very Young', p. 17.
39 Galbraith, 'AIDS: How the Gay Press Told the Story', p. 21.
40 *Victorian AIDS Action Committee News*, no. 2 (March 1984), p. 4.
41 *AIDS ACTION: A Newsletter from the Victorian AIDS Council* (15 February 1985), p. 1.
42 ibid., no. 4 (June 1985), p. 1.
43 *AIDS ACTION: Western Australian AIDS Council Newsletter*, no. 1 (August 1985), p. 1.
44 ibid., no. 5 (December 1985 – January 1986), p. 3.
45 ibid., no. 18 (May 1988), pp. 11–12.
46 ibid., no. 25 (September 1990), p. 11.
47 Shirleene Robinson, 'Responding to Homophobia: HIV/AIDS, Homosexual Community Formation and Identity in Queensland, 1983–1990', *Australian Historical Studies*, vol. 41, no. 2 (2010), pp. 181–197.
48 Robinson, 'Queensland's Queer Press', pp. 59–78.
49 Clive Moore, *Sunshine and Rainbows: The Development of Gay and Lesbian Culture in Queensland*, St Lucia, Qld: University of Queensland Press, 2001, p. 213.
50 Robinson, 'Queensland's Queer Press', pp. 59–78.
51 *Duck News*, August 1987, p. 20.
52 Minutes of the Queensland AIDS Committee Meeting Held on 4 February 1986, Malcolm McCamish Collection, Fryer Library, University of Queensland, UQFL335.
53 ibid.
54 *Duck News*, November 1987, p. 7.
55 P. Thornton, 'Is the Old Right Now New? The State, the Family and Sexual Repression in Queensland', *Social Alternatives*, no. 5 (1987), p. 8.
56 *Daily Sun* (Brisbane), 3 December 1984, p. 1.
57 *Australian*, 31 August 1984, p. 3.
58 *Weekend Australian*, 17–18 November 1984, p. 1.
59 ibid.
60 ibid.
61 Myrick, *AIDS, Communication and Empowerment*, p. 79.
62 Adam Carr, 'What is AIDS?', in Eric Timewell et al., eds, *AIDS in Australia*, New York; Sydney: Prentice-Hall, 1992, p. 17.
63 William Rutkin, interview with Shirleene Robinson, 26 August 2009.

64 Media Release, 'Queensland's First AIDS Information and Phone Counselling Service Launched in Brisbane', 11 August 1985, Queensland Association for Healthy Communities Archives.
65 Sendziuk, *Learning to Trust*, p. 121.
66 William Rutkin, interview with Shirleene Robinson, 26 August 2009.
67 '*OutRage* at 15 or the Rise and Fall of Practically Everyone'.

Australian HIV/AIDS Life Writing

The Human and the Historic

Geoff Allshorn

> There is a point, somewhere, usually in the future of a piece of writing, in its rediscovery as something other than what it first was, where memoir, recollection or diary turns into history...
>
> – Stephen J. Williams.[1]

In 1988, US journalist Randy Shilts stunned the world with his seminal study, *And The Band Played On*, a monograph which documented the rise during the late 1970s and early 1980s of a deadly new world pandemic, and included biographical material on several afflicted individuals, particularly gay men in the USA. His writing marked the rise of a new genre: AIDS life writing. Australian authors would soon contribute to this emerging genre, which would later evolve into HIV life writings. This study will explore how these narratives document the lives and culture of Australians affected by AIDS during earlier times, and the social and medical transformation for those with HIV in more recent years. US academic Marita Sturken suggests the importance of cultural memories: '[t]he collective remembering of a specific culture... both defines a culture and is the means by which its divisions and conflicting agendas are revealed'.[2] Such material constitutes part of our collective memory, which contributes to both the individual and national identities we construct in the present.

In recent decades, according to US academic Thomas R. Smith, 'traditional' biographies have been defined as novel-length linear narratives written by white males – with all other authors or forms of life writing slotting into a second biographical category ('other'). Smith suggests that such categories are not 'satisfactory' because life writings do not often fit rigidly within established structures.[3] Sociologist Ken Plummer expands the concept of 'life writing' to include a variety of human 'documents of life',[4] such as auto/biographies, letters, pictures, web sites, films and tombstones.

In Australia, AIDS life documents encompass a variety of forms and narrative styles, including quilt panels, interviews, articles by people living with HIV and AIDS, diaries, photographs and documentary films – as well as art, music and fiction. This study will only document and analyse a fraction of these materials, focusing on public life writings. The texts examined here are mainly 'traditional' book-length life narratives, supplemented by one documentary film and two diaries. Other materials, including collections of interviews and shorter biographical works on people with HIV/AIDS, have not been included except when they directly contribute to the discourse as part of an emerging pattern during the last decade.

Literary Context

Life writings show how the universal is exemplified in individual stories. For example, Australian politician Rodney Cavalier proposes that diaries (such as those by Eric Michaels and Charles Roberts, discussed below) reduce the unfathomably big-picture to an individual reality which we can grasp: '[d]iaries serve history by providing a narrative of the day. Diaries are the record of an individual life. They record a life as lived'[5] (and in this context, we could add: 'and as died'). By extension, we can study such writings as narratives which are not only the product of their time, but also a time capsule. Cavalier was referring specifically to political narratives, but his principles apply equally to other life texts; in implicit connection, Australian academic John Wiltshire suggests that AIDS writings are 'political and social statements',[6] while Dennis Altman explains AIDS as 'a very political epidemic'.[7]

Life writings also show how individual stories reveal wider human experiences. AIDS life narratives can comprise what US academic Joseph Cady describes as 'immersive' texts, in that they immerse the reader into the full-blown horror of AIDS and thereby challenge public denial or avoidance of the ordeal.[8] Similarly, Ken Plummer suggests that life narratives present the individual as part of a larger grouping of 'collective stories'[9] which portray a community of 'auto/ethnographies'.[10] Australian AIDS 'auto/

ethnographies' are soon likely to be the only evidence of early AIDS experiences available in the public domain, because most of the protagonists within the early narratives are dead and the memories of surviving friends and families are growing dim. These texts deserve recognition because they allow the general public immediate, personal access to the lives and losses – and to the humanity and courage – of people belonging to this marginalised group. Reviewer Stephen J. Williams, whose quote prefaced this study, suggested that one such writing (*Take Me to Paris, Johnny* by John Foster) was history as much as memoir.

Historical Context

In Australia, AIDS arrived in the early 1980s as a largely feared and misunderstood phenomenon. It was contextualised as a doubly-stigmatised problem: a debilitating medical affliction which caused people to suffer from a range of dreadful and usually fatal diseases; and it was linked to homosexuality, which still faced stigma and some legal sanctions across Australia. (One early biographical account, published in the gay magazine *OutRage*, reveals that stigma prevented one young man from disclosing his homosexuality to his doctors, contributing to a delay in his diagnosis and probably hastening his death.)[11] AIDS was later recognised as endangering other people as well as gay men, including haemophiliacs and other blood transfusion recipients; this led to transmission of AIDS being commonly perceived in terms of the social dichotomy of 'guilty' versus 'innocent'.

A wave of AIDS hysteria swept Australia during the 1980s. A national scandal, involving Queensland babies being fatally exposed to HIV through blood transfusions, led to a call for the gay blood donor to face execution or suicide.[12] The Grim Reaper infamously appeared on television community service announcements, as a cowled personification of death, to warn that AIDS was a personal threat to every Australian.[13] People feared contagion through mosquito bites and swimming pools, from sitting on toilets or kissing, and from sharing food or water or communion cups.[14] A child with HIV was banned from her kindergarten, and her family migrated to New Zealand to escape the prejudice.[15] Gay men faced harassment or dismissal from their jobs regardless of their HIV status;[16] others, including those presumed to be gay, faced the threat of 'poofter bashers'.[17] It is this context which shaped the HIV stigma that still persists, albeit covertly, in Australia to this day.

By the late 1990s, new medical treatments challenged the inevitability of illness and death. The death rate from AIDS began a steep decline and people with HIV generally began to live much longer, healthier lives. Subsequently, domestic HIV/AIDS largely disappeared from public discourse, even though new HIV infections remained a concern to public health.

The Evolution of HIV/AIDS Life Writings

Early AIDS life writings take the form of 'pathographies' – stories of lives contextualised by disease. John Wiltshire described AIDS pathographies in 1994 as 'the (literally) dying protest of individualism… taking courage to speak of its experience only within the narrative of illness and death'.[18] This study will show that pathographies form only the first two stages of a four-stage evolution of HIV/AIDS life writings, beginning during the times of horror and evolving into the calmer writings of modern-day long-term survival with HIV in Australia.[19] The first AIDS pathographies, predominantly featuring gay men, were followed by a second wave of pathographies featuring those with medically-acquired AIDS. A third, transitional phase, featured people with HIV/AIDS whose stories were reflective of improving medical treatments and an emerging political activism. The final stage is the current era of 'living with HIV' in which long-term survivors reflect a new reality. Taken chronologically, these writings tend to fall neatly within these categories, demonstrating both their contemporary social context and their contribution to that narrative. In presenting this progression, these texts conform to the 'generational' nature of life writings[20] – although they have evolved through a number of distinct 'generations' within a single lifetime, reflecting the frenetic development of HIV/AIDS within those few short years.

The people within these writings have not always disclosed the full details of their private lives. However, of those who have disclosed this information, gay men form the majority of writers or subjects. Following them, HIV-positive heterosexual women constitute the other early grouping of people within these narratives, possibly implying some underlying connection of disadvantage between these two traditionally-disempowered groups. Haemophiliacs and blood recipients appear later in this chronology. Conversely, although many lesbians worked to help their gay brothers during the crisis years,[21] there appears to be no comprehensive history documenting their contribution. Further cohorts of people, including those deemed to be potentially at high risk, are either poorly represented in these texts or do not appear at all. This may reflect the relatively low infection rates in Australia outside of the gay male community, and the fact that such writing is not always the preferred option of some people who may prefer more orally nuanced shorter forms of writing. It is also possible that people from other backgrounds may remain reluctant to publicly disclose their HIV status.

In the Beginning

No significant AIDS life writing narratives were publicly available in Australia until the end of the 1980s. This silence during almost the entire first decade of AIDS in Australia was reflective of the homophobia and AIDSphobia which were endemic throughout society, as well as a societal reluctance to mention sexual matters.

During much of this decade, the Australian gay community shared information about their friends who were suffering and dying, but this material remained largely hidden from the general public. Ken Plummer observes that '[m]emories may be more than just the properties of individuals. There is also social memory',[22] and one of the very first public instances was the collaboration of Maria Pallotta-Chiarolli with members of the Adelaide gay community in the early 1990s to write an AIDS biography of a deceased gay friend; her gay advisers encouraged her, as a 'safe' heterosexual person, to disseminate this information into wider society.[23] AIDS life writing thus became an extension of a gay tradition: a 'coming out' story, not just for individuals, but for a whole community.[24]

The first known public AIDS life narrative was exceptional in this chronology: it was not a book but a TV documentary,[25] telecast a few weeks after the infamous Grim Reaper TV campaign, with the potential to reduce (or possibly heighten) community fears. This documentary did not feature a gay man nor express the common societal disapproval of such people; it featured a heterosexual woman.

The remainder of this paper presents a typology of narratives from each era, including an annotated listing of writings and a thematic summary of their pertinent themes.

Pathographies – Predominantly Gay Men (Late 1980s to Late 1990s)

The initial years were times of fear and confusion as gay men were struck down by this unknown agent, seemingly at random; and other people were also afflicted – though often more covertly. Even after confirmation of the causative virus, HIV, and the development of an HIV-antibody blood test, the medical community struggled to develop effective medical treatments.

- **Suzi's Story** (Ian Gillespie), Sydney: Suzi Lovegrove Family Trust with Pro-Image Studios Limited and United Telecasters Sydney Limited, CEL Home Video, 1987.

  US-born Suzi Lovegrove was a young wife and mother who had been exposed to HIV during a previous heterosexual relationship; both she and her infant son, Troy, developed AIDS. The film documented her last weeks of life.

- **Unbecoming: An AIDS Diary** (Eric Michaels), Sydney: Empress Publishing, 1990 [reissued by Duke University Press, 1997].

  Eric Michaels was a gay US academic who arrived in Australia in 1982 before being diagnosed with AIDS. He kept a diary during the last year of his life, and it was published posthumously.[26]

- **Someone You Know: A Friend's Farewell** (Maria Pallotta-Chiarolli), Adelaide: Wakefield Press, 1991, 2002.

  Jon was a young school teacher working in Adelaide during the 1980s until he was struck down with AIDS. He asked his friend, Maria, to speak out about AIDS after he died, and she subsequently wrote this tribute.

- **Take Me to Paris, Johnny** (John Foster), Port Melbourne, Vic.: Minerva, 1993 [reissued by Black Inc., 2002].

  John Foster's memoir focuses on the life and death of his lover, Juan Céspedes, a Cuban refugee and US émigré.

- **Infected Queer: Notes of an Activist** (Charles Roberts), Melbourne: Nosukumo, 1994 [limited edition].

  US-born long-term survivor, Charles Roberts, wrote a set of unstructured diary entries which presented his life and thoughts as an AIDS activist. Although not a traditionally-structured autobiography, it incorporated many contemporaneous responses to the AIDS pandemic.

- **Holding the Man** (Timothy Conigrave), Melbourne: McPhee Gribble, 1995; Ringwood, Vic.: Penguin, 2007, 2009; also adapted into a successful stage play by Tommy Murphy.[27]

  Melbourne schoolboy Timothy Conigrave fell in love with his school's football captain, John Caleo, and they lived together for fifteen years until they succumbed to AIDS.

- How Far is it to London Bridge? A Journey through AIDS with My Daughter (Joan Hurley), Alexandria, NSW: Millennium Books, 1996.

    Joan Hurley recalled the life and death of her young adult daughter, Caroline.

Summary of this Period

All of these pathographies focus upon the suffering and death of their protagonists and/or others around them, and these people face their fate with the same courage and dignity that are evident in their willingness to challenge social stigma simply by going public.

Suzi Lovegrove's status as a heterosexual woman begs the question of why Australia's first public AIDS life discourse does not feature our nation's most-afflicted AIDS grouping: gay men. (Similarly, the last narrative during this period concerns Caroline Hurley, another heterosexual woman.) Furthermore, Maria Pallotta-Chiarolli – whose book is the first Australian AIDS life text to be accepted by a major publishing company – also wonders, 'if I was a gay/bisexual man, would my book have been published?' Nevertheless, the appearance of such material encourages others to follow – and it challenges prejudice: Maria receives hate mail from some Christians, and letters of appreciation from some parents who, having been estranged from their gay sons with AIDS, are led to effect reconciliation. While some schools invite Maria to be a guest speaker, a small number of parents ring her own school to complain that their sons may have been exposed to AIDS through their classroom contact with Jon.

In detailing the pain and frustration for people with AIDS, these life writings serve as a call for compassion: Suzi Lovegrove's 'life advice' to her husband, Vincent, is to 'forgive'; John Foster describes the loss of grace, strength and dignity for ballet dancer Juan Céspedes while Timothy Conigrave does the same for footballer John Caleo; Maria Pallotta-Chiarolli is unable to use Jon's surname in her narrative.

These texts also evoke great intimacy, tenderness and inspiration in the midst of their tragedy. In John Foster's narrative, Juan's deathbed scene transforms a life of decline and despair into a story that Robert Dessaix describes as 'something of unutterable beauty'[28] and inspires Peter Craven to call Foster's book 'unparalleled in Australian letters'.[29] The book testifies to the redemptive power of love, a conviction shared by Timothy Conigrave and Maria-Pallotta-Chiarolli, but a concept which many Australians would consider anathema to their views about gay relationships during the 1980s and 1990s.

The texts also contain open expressions of anger.[30] Charles Roberts' writing testifies to the motivational power behind strong emotion: 'I am a rebel; I am antinomian. Antinomy keeps me among the living, keeps me living, alone with anger, rage and a few other "good" things in my life'.[31] John Foster is outraged at the Grim Reaper, who has attacked the dignity and humanity of his dying partner. Eric Michaels' anger inspires a partial parallel which arises from his knowledge of some indigenous Australian customs: '[u]pon death, an individual's property, image, even name, must be obliterated',[32] implying that, although such silence may occur within some traditions, social obliteration is abhorrent to other cultures, including his own. His book, like all writings in this collection, is an attempt to oppose such erasure; ironically, it is now long out of print in his adopted home of Australia.

Pathographies – Medically-Acquired AIDS (Mid- to Late 1990s)

Although many haemophiliacs and others with medically-acquired AIDS became infected in the early 1980s, their life narratives were not published until the 1990s.

- **A Kid Called Troy** (Vincent Lovegrove), Sydney: ABC Books, 1993.

    Infected through paediatric transmission from his mother (see Suzi's Story), young Troy Lovegrove was immortalised by his father, Vincent, in both a written and film narrative.

- **April Fools' Day** (Bryce Courtenay), Melbourne: William Heinemann, 1993 [various reprints].[33]

    A memoir written by prominent writer Bryce Courtenay about his adult son, Damon, who died after receiving an HIV-contaminated blood transfusion.

- **Beyond Heartbreak: The True Story of Lorraine Cibilic** (Christopher Smith), Kenthurst, NSW: Kangaroo Press, 1995.

    Lorraine Cibilic was a housewife infected with HIV following a blood transfusion, and she campaigned to secure compensation for hundreds of people in NSW with medically-acquired AIDS.

- **Pink Balloons: The Story of a Young AIDS Sufferer** (Beverley McGregor), Sydney: Ashton Scholastic, 1995.

    A biography of Skye Bussenschutt, exposed to HIV through a blood transfusion, who died as a young girl.

Summary of this Period

People infected through medical accident evidently feel more isolated and stigmatised than some gay men, and this might explain why testimonies about their lives do not start to appear until later in the pandemic. Bryce Courtenay's text remains the only major Australian life writing to publicly acknowledge that AIDS has spread to heterosexual and haemophiliac men, and he acknowledges its related stigma: '[f]or the first time haemophilia has become something to hide'.[34]

The two adult stories in this category express overt or implicit rage, while the narratives about children express no such anger – for example, young Skye Bussenschutt hopes that her blood donor will receive medicine to help him get better. Lorraine Cibilic's efforts to establish 'innocence' and compensation for those with medically-acquired AIDS, but not for others, demonstrates the complexities posed by HIV/AIDS for some people from CALD backgounds.

The Transitional Phase (late 1990s)

In his second (1996) study of these texts, John Wiltshire redefined AIDS pathographies as 'critical patient narratives', that is, texts which allowed patients to present viewpoints and critical analysis beyond their medical compartmentalisation.[35] His redefinition reflected the progression of AIDS life writings in Australia, particularly during this transitional stage.

These writings represent a reversal of perspective: while early autobiographers had presented their lives within the context of AIDS, autobiographers of the late 1990s presented AIDS within the context of their lives. This decade included the rise of the activist protest group, ACTUP, and the arrival of new drug treatments which began to prolong lives. Many people defiantly adopted an attitudinal change from 'dying with AIDS' to 'living with HIV', even though the protagonists of these texts would still ultimately succumb to the condition.

- **The Boy from Oz: The Peter Allen Story** (Stephen Maclean), Milsons Point, NSW: Random House Australia, 1996.

Australian entertainer Peter Allen was the subject of a 1995 ABC TV documentary. Later, this biography was adapted into the successful stage musical of the same name by Nick Enright.[36]

- **Screw Loose: Uncalled-for Memoirs** (Peter Blazey), Sydney: Picador, 1997.

  The life and experiences of political activist and journalist Peter Blazey were typical of the way Australian society moved from the straight-laced 1950s to the bohemian experimentation of the 1970s, which included Gay Liberation and Mardi Gras.

- **Desire Lines: An Unusual Family Memoir** (Peter and Richard Wherrett), Sydney: Hodder Headline/Sceptre, 1997.

- **The Floor of Heaven: My Life in Theatre** (Richard Wherrett), Sydney: Hodder Headline/Sceptre, 2000.

  Richard Wherrett discussed his life and career in the Australian theatre, and AIDS comprise merely one portion of his life in these accounts.

- **John Hargreaves, A Celebration: An Actor's Life as He Saw It** (Tony Watts and Genevieve Picot, comp.), Newport, Vic.: Parrot Books, 2000.

  AIDS brought the final curtain call to the life of actor John Hargreaves. However, it was not the main focus of this book, which celebrated his life and works.

Summary of this Period

Although these narratives still feature illness and imminent death, they also show defiant self-empowerment and cautious optimism. Richard Wherrett reports little serious medical difficulty except for a bout of cryptococcal meningitis.[37] John Hargreaves does not see his HIV diagnosis as an omen of immediate physical decline: '[i]n fact, when I found out that I had it I stopped smoking and drinking, and ate well, and I was probably healthier than I'd ever been in my adult life'.[38] A slogan from the AIDS activist group ACTUP during the 1990s was 'Silence = Death', and these texts are evidence of this change of outlook.

Living with HIV (early 2000s onwards)

By the end of the 1990s, new medical treatments had transformed HIV into a more manageable medical condition enabling many 'People Living

With HIV' to live longer. This enhanced the feeling of relative optimism which had developed during the earlier transition period, and this optimism was also reflected in the life narratives: formerly literary obituaries, AIDS autobiographies became testimonies to life written by long-term survivors with HIV. The small number of professional publications in this category suggests either that the Australian public now considers HIV/AIDS to be of little concern, or that continuing stigma perpetuates social invisibility.[39] This stigma is being challenged by community groups such as those from Victoria which are listed below.

- **Legends: Positive and Proud, a Victorian Perspective** (PLWHA Vic.), 2001.[40]

    A booklet compilation of photographs and biographies of gay men, a positive woman and an Indigenous Australian who were lost to AIDS, many of whom were community leaders and activists.

- **Blood Ties: The Stories of Five Positive Women** (Sally Trathen, ed.), Lane Cove, NSW: Finch Publishing, 2001.

    The autobiographical stories of five HIV-positive women confront the fact that heterosexual women (and their male partners) are also at risk of HIV.

- **Positive** (David Menadue), Crows Nest, NSW: Allen and Unwin, 2002; soon to be reprinted and available as print on demand.

    Activist and teacher David Menadue became one of Australia's longest-term survivors after being diagnosed with HIV in 1984. His book presents AIDS and activism within the context of his overall life.

- **Lessons Learnt** (Robert Newey), self published, 2005.

    Another long-term survivor, Robert Newey, produced a life writing which spanned some decades and included the early days of AIDS. His text is raw, and evocative of the savage impact of AIDS upon the lives of ordinary people in earlier decades. He recalls the illness and deaths of friends – but he also suggests that his experiences taught him many significant 'lessons learnt'.

- **Speaker Biographies** (PLWHA Victoria Inc.), c. 2006, Available at http://www.plwhavictoria.org.au/downloads/Speaker_Bios_Tes timonials.pdf, date accessed 20 February 2010.

A small, autobiographical list of positive speakers who are available for community speeches, including men and one woman. This is evidence of the dissemination of such material in new forms, such as the internet.

- **The Gay Hello: Stories from www.stayingnegative.com.au** (Max McLean, ed.), Victorian AIDS Council/Gay Men's Health Centre, n. d. [possibly 2009] with accompanying 2009 calendar.

  A booklet collection of life narratives featuring HIV-negative gay men discussing how to avoid HIV.

- **Closer** (Max Niggl, Project Supervisor), PLWHA Victoria Inc., launched 31 March 2010; along with

- **Changing Voices: Stories of Living with HIV** (Jo Pearson, Prod.), PLWHA Victoria, 2010.

  This booklet and accompanying DVD feature autobiographical narratives of speakers from the PLWHA Victoria Speakers' Bureau.

Summary of this Period

David Menadue exemplifies the optimism characterising this new period: '[w]hile I don't subscribe to the view that you can defeat something like AIDS with affirmative thought alone, taking an optimistic view about your prognosis is an important ingredient in your survival'.[41]

David Menadue has wondered whether his autobiography would be relevant in a new era of AIDS invisibility. 'Is it too late?', he asks. The public response to his writing confirms that survival stories are important. Newly-infected HIV-positive readers tell him that they have learnt from both his good and bad experiences, and David considers this kind of public disclosure by people with HIV/AIDS to be an important step in fighting social invisibility: '[p]eople need to tell their stories'.[42] Although Robert Newey's text is grittier than David Menadue's writing, he also offers a reversal from earlier perceptions of AIDS. While revisiting the tragedies of earlier times, his writing suggests both community and individual resilience.

The shorter texts from this era also serve an educational role. Sally Trathen's collection includes stories of HIV and disclosure in heterosexual families, fighting stigma by helping to 'normalise' AIDS in the public context. The speakers' biographies from PLWHA Victoria serve a similar function, particularly by presenting HIV among people from diverse backgrounds; Max McLean's material extends this educative role by overturning the traditional context of HIV/AIDS life writings and using narratives of HIV-negative gay men as a tool to promote safe sex harm reduction.

Conclusions

The life writings explored here chart the evolution of HIV/AIDS in Australian society and enable readers to share the journeys of people, past and present, who have been affected by this epidemic. Such material evokes the question of whether or not those affected by HIV/AIDS, who were once openly marginalised, may now have been more readily assimilated within society. By reigniting diverse recollections, emotions and responses to HIV/AIDS, a process Marita Sturken calls the 'technology of memory';[43] these texts allow readers to construct a collective cognisance which provides a basis for our continuing cultural development.

Over the short life of this genre, these narratives have swung radically from suffering and death, towards empowerment and life – and they offer a call for acceptance and equality. Maria Pallotta-Chiarolli spoke optimistically at her 1991 book launch: '[o]ut of the AIDS pandemic may come greater social justice and understanding of human diversity'. Decades later, the latest HIV life writings offer the same challenge.

Sadly, our departed AIDS heroes suffer a new form of stigma: their removal from our folklore. Related life tributes – AIDS quilts, newspaper stories, arts and music, and candlelight vigils – have largely faded from public discourse. Fortunately, their life writings remain a valuable resource for our 'social and collective'[44] or 'cultural memory'.[45] Other people – those who live with HIV today – also deserve recognition as heroes in the ongoing struggle. Early AIDS autobiographer Eric Michaels challenged the Gay, Lesbian, Bisexual, and Transgender community to claim their place in history – at a time that would turn out to be the very dawn of the epidemic: '[w]e need to take some responsibility for our own history, for conveying it to our young. It is not nostalgia. If one is going to go to all the trouble to be gay, one ought to do a more interesting and useful job of it. [Role] models exist in our very recent past. They should be recalled'.[46] By the time his words were published, Michaels and many others had succumbed to AIDS. His call to gay people had symbolically become a wider rallying cry for those with HIV/AIDS, one which still resonates today.

Acknowledgements

Special thanks go to Dr Maria Pallotta-Chiarolli and David Menadue for being willing to be interviewed for this study; and to Dr Mirna Cicioni and Dr Michael Hurley for their assistance. Thanks also to Dr Graham Willett, Robert Newey, Charles Roberts, Kate Doolan, and the staffs of Positive Women Victoria, PLWHA Victoria, and the Australian Lesbian and Gay Archives.

Endnotes

1. Stephen J. Williams, 'The Personal Will Be History, One Day', *Overland*, no. 136 (1994), p. 84.
2. Marita Sturken, *Tangled Memories: The Vietnam War, the AIDS Epidemic and the Politics of Remembering*, Berkeley: University of California Press, 1997, p. 1.
3. Thomas R. Smith, 'Generating Selves: Issues of Self-Representation', *a/b: Auto/Biography Studies*, vol. 19, nos 1 and 2 (2004), pp. 59–60.
4. Ken Plummer, *Documents of Life 2: An Invitation To A Critical Humanism*, London: SAGE Publications, 2001, p. 17.
5. Rod Cavalier, 'A Consideration of the Value of Diaries with Occasional Reference to the Efforts of Mark Latham', *AQ (Australian Quarterly)*, vol. 77, (September–October 2008), p. 4.
6. John Wiltshire, 'A Narrative Quilt: Australian Pathographies of AIDS Criticism', *Meridian*, vol. 13, no. 1 (1994), p. 59.
7. Dennis Altman, *AIDS and the New Puritanism*, London; Sydney: Pluto Press, 1986, ch. 2.
8. Joseph Cady, 'Immersive and Counterimmersive Writing About AIDS: The Achievement of Paul Monette's *Love Alone*', in Timothy Murphy and Suzanne Poirier, eds, *Writing AIDS: Gay Literature, Language and Analysis*, New York: Columbia University Press, 1993, pp. 244–245.
9. Plummer, *Documents of Life 2*, p. 30.
10. ibid., pp. 34–35.
11. 'I Want to Construct Something Positive from the Death of Someone I Loved', *OutRage* (March 1985), pp. 20–21.
12. 'The Parents' Plight – by AIDS Baby's Father', *Courier-Mail*, 3 December 1984, p. 3; 'Die, You Deviate', *Midweek Truth*, 8 December 1984, pp. 1–2.
13. John Tulloch and Deborah Lupton, *Television, AIDS and Risk: A Cultural Approach to Health Communication*, St Leonards, NSW: Allen and Unwin, 1997, pp. 85–88.
14. Derryn Hinch, *AIDS: Most of the Questions, Some of the Answers*, Melbourne: Bay Street Publishing, 1987, p. 24.
15. 'Girl Taught All A Lesson', *Herald Sun*, 22 November 1993, p. 11.
16. Jo McKenna, 'AIDS Scare: Our Jobs Go, Say Gays', *Herald*, 11 February 1985, p. 15.
17. David Buchbinder, *Masculinities and Identities*, Melbourne: Melbourne University Press, 1994, p. 56; 'Gays Bashed in AIDS Hysteria', *Sun*, 26 November 1985. For a detailed analysis which places AIDS attacks within the wider context of anti-gay

violence in Australia, see, Stephen Tomsen, *Hatred, Murder and Male Honour: Anti-Homosexual Homicides in New South Wales, 1980–2000*, Canberra: Australian Institute of Criminology, 2002.
18 Wiltshire, 'A Narrative Quilt', p. 49.
19 For a detailed examination of the dichotomy of distinction between HIV and AIDS, see, Michael Hurley, 'When HIV is Endemic Amongst Gay Men', in this volume.
20 Smith, 'Generating Selves', p. 59.
21 For example, see, 'ACON: Commemorating 25 Years: Lemon AIDS', *Lesbians on the Loose*, August 2010, p. 41 (back pages supplement, p. 4).
22 Ken Plummer, *Telling Sexual Stories: Power, Change and Social Worlds*, London; New York: Routledge, 1995, p. 41.
23 Maria Pallotta-Chiarolli, interview with Geoff Allshorn, Melbourne, 5 February 2010. Other references to Maria or her book, where not clearly identified as coming from her text, are taken from this interview or her supplied notes.
24 Plummer, *Telling Sexual Stories*, p. 50.
25 I have been advised that there was an auto/biographical TV documentary featuring a gay man which was produced around 1987, but have been unable to track down a copy from the TV station. This highlights the difficulty of securing such material as an historical resource.
26 Paul Foss, 'Foreword', in Eric Michaels, *Unbecoming: An AIDS Diary*, Durham, NC: Duke University Press, 1997, p. xiv.
27 Tommy Murphy, *Strangers in Between/Holding the Man: Two Plays by Tommy Murphy*, Sydney: Currency Press, 2006.
28 Robert Dessaix, 'The Dark Rose', *Meanjin*, vol. 53, no. 1 (1994), p. 170.
29 Peter Craven, 'A Rare Thing', *Voices*, vol. IV, no. 2 (1994), p. 118.
30 Wiltshire, 'A Narrative Quilt', p. 55.
31 Charles Roberts, *Infected Queer: Notes Of An Activist*, Melbourne: Nosukumo Press, 1994, p. 15.
32 Eric Michaels, *Unbecoming: An AIDS Diary*, Sydney: EmPress Publishing, 1990, pp. 31–32.
33 At the time of writing, this book is among the 'Top 100' books on sale in a prominent chain of Australian bookshops.
34 Bryce Courtenay, *April Fools' Day*, Melbourne: William Heinemann, 1993, p. 166.
35 John Wiltshire, 'Decompositions: Some Narratives of AIDS Criticisms', *Mattoid*, no. 50 (1996), pp. 107–119.
36 *The Boy From Oz* (theatrical program booklet), Playbill, NSW, n. d.
37 Richard Wherrett, *The Floor of Heaven: My Life in Theatre*, Sydney: Hodder Headline/Sceptre, 2000, p. 303.
38 Tony Watts and Genevieve Picot, comp., *John Hargreaves, A Celebration: An Actor's Life As He Saw It*, Newport, Vic.: Parrot Books, 2000, p. 283.
39 For material on HIV stigma in Australia, see, David Menadue, 'Are You Clean?', *Positive Living: A Magazine for People with HIV* (March 2010), pp. 6–7; and Daniel Tarantola, 'Stigmatisation, Discrimination: A Health and Human Rights Perspective', *HIV Australia*, vol. 7, no. 3 (2009), p. 10.
40 David Menadue was the author of this booklet but he was not credited in the publication.
41 David Menadue, *Positive*, Crows Nest, NSW: Allen and Unwin, 2002, p. 1.

42 David Menadue, interview with Geoff Allshorn, Melbourne, 2 February 2010; subsequent information also provided by David.
43 Sturken, *Tangled Memories*, p. 12.
44 Sidonie Smith and Julie Watson, *Reading Autobiography: A Guide for Interpreting Life Narratives*, Minneapolis: University of Minnesota Press, 2001, p. 21.
45 Plummer, *Documents of Life 2*, p. 235.
46 Michaels, *Unbecoming* (1990), p. 192.

When HIV is Endemic amongst Gay Men

Michael Hurley

New and dramatic medical events like AIDS take decades or longer to run their historical course to prevention and cure.

– Cindy Patton[1]

While we might wish we could reach a point when no new infections occur among gay men in a single year, we know that once a disease becomes endemic to a population – as HIV has become endemic to American gay men – it requires radical interventions, such as vaccines or new technologies, to eliminate.

– Eric Rofes[2]

The biomedical and social relations between HIV and AIDS in Australia have been changing for the last 15 years. In this essay, I describe and analyse these changes and discuss some of their implications for HIV education and prevention amongst gay men.[3]

It took about four years for the distinction between HIV and AIDS to be firmly established after the initial reports of an outbreak of rare opportunistic infections and cancers amongst American gay men in 1981. In the year following, the same diseases were documented amongst injecting drug users and Haitians. The diseases resulted in rapid bodily deterioration and a rapidly increasing number of deaths. The cause of the diseases was at first unclear. Some scientists attributed them to 'GRID' – Gay Related Immune Deficiency. At this point, gay activists began to invent safe sex. They thought it likely that whatever was causing the diseases was sexually transmitted, and recommended the use of condoms. In 1983 Gay Men's Health Crisis in New York City published Berkowitz and Callen's *How to Have Sex in an Epidemic*. About a year later it was confirmed that the diseases were caused by the Human Immunodeficiency Virus (HIV). HIV attacked the immune system, and was spread through body fluids such as blood and semen, mostly through anal intercourse.[4] The diseases associated with this viral infection became known collectively as Acquired Immune Deficiency Syndrome (AIDS). However, the scientific distinction between HIV infection and AIDS was blurred initially because, in terms of illness and the effects of epidemic, HIV and AIDS were synonymous. AIDS was largely untreatable – gay men, Haitians, intravenous drug users and soon people with haemophilia were dying at an alarming rate and though affected communities were responding to the epidemic in an extraordinary fashion, they were also reeling under its effects.[5] Even so, over time, people with HIV and AIDS began to speak of living with the virus and its effects, rather than dying of AIDS. They resisted the notion that they were 'victims'.

The distinction between HIV and AIDS is still frequently confused in Australia and other western countries. One of the reasons for this is that media coverage of local HIV epidemics has fallen substantially, and has been replaced by coverage of HIV/AIDS epidemics in countries where there are generally much higher levels of HIV prevalence, substantial continuing AIDS epidemics and limited rollout of successful antiviral treatments.[6] In those countries HIV and AIDS are often still synonymous. A second reason is that much Australian population health based HIV research and associated prevention recommendations still proceed implicitly on the assumption that both HIV infection and an AIDS diagnosis are fatal. As a result, 'prevention' is officially configured through a no-risk lens ('a condom every time') that to a degree sidelines both the social contexts of sexual behaviour and desires for intimacy and pleasure, and those who practice risk reduction, especially sero-sorting. The theoretical efficacy of biomedical technologies, procedures and practices (for example, condom use under every circumstance, circumcision) is prioritised over consideration of the likely ongoing social *effectiveness* of prevention techniques and strategies.[7]

Historically, community-driven HIV education around safe sex was never *only* about condom use and behaviour change. It was a social apparatus organised around what would work.[8] It included respect for the sexual and social practices of the affected populations: sex positivity,[9] community mobilisation, the likelihood of particular kinds of behaviour change,[10] harm reduction – needle and syringe programmes – and a concept of communal education that involved information provision, but was not reduced to it. This was highly effective amongst gay men. We now know that HIV infection rates fell dramatically in Australia after 1986. It is very likely that the changes which produced the lower infection rate can be attributed to a fear of death, reinforced by mass exposure to some of the bodily effects of AIDS. For many gay men now, neither of these is often the case, and has not been for some time.

The change in circumstances has produced considerable disquiet and a variety of responses in Australia and elsewhere. Much has stayed the same, especially sexual moralism. However, as Douglas Crimp put it in 2004,

> [s]ometimes the déjà vu seems more like a nightmare from which we cannot awake... however there has been a drastic change, but it is a psychic change, a change in the way we think about AIDS, or rather a change that consists in our inability to continue thinking about AIDS.[11]

Crimp's remark was made in the context of ongoing conservative hostility to funding safe sex education for gay men in the USA. In that context, it was perhaps difficult for Crimp to see the implications of a diminishing AIDS epidemic. Eric Rofes had a somewhat different take on the varieties of political moralism involved. Shortly before he died in 2006, Rofes wrote about how gay men in the USA were being demonised and pathologised by aspects of the ongoing response to increased HIV infection. He saw this as coming from Lesbian, Gay, Bisexual, Transgender (LGBT) organisations, and more liberal commentators, as well as from the political right. From his point of view they were denying the evidence of gay men's commitment to safe sex, their resilience and creativity in the face of HIV, and the reality that HIV infection was endemic amongst gay men.[12] This chapter is a reflection on some of the implications of Rofes' argument in the Australian situation.

In what follows, I first discuss HIV and AIDS epidemics, and some of the differences between them. I then suggest some implications of these differences. I am aware that for many of us some of what I have to say touches on deeply painful matters. The years between 1983 and 1996 were those of increasing horror, and many of us were and are still deeply affected by what occurred. The number of deaths amongst men rose annually from 200 in 1988 to a peak of almost 700 in 1994 alone. The figures do not describe the individual pain and trauma, the multiple hospitalisations, the despair, the courage, the bedside care by volunteers, the funerals or the endurance required of those involved. I have not forgotten those who died, or those still living whose lives and health have been deeply affected by HIV and AIDS, or their partners, friends, families and sexual networks. I am also very aware that the situation is different in many other countries where AIDS is still rampant, treatment options are limited and discrimination is rife. The Australian context is a reminder that there are many HIV epidemics, not just one.

HIV and AIDS

The discussion here is framed by the following figure from the 2009 annual surveillance data reported by the National Centre in HIV Epidemiology and Clinical Research (NCHECR) at the University of New South Wales.

In this figure the lower line tracks the number of new AIDS diagnoses annually in Australia between 1981 and 2007. The upper line tracks new HIV diagnoses in the same period. AIDS diagnoses are not the same as HIV diagnoses. When AIDS occurs, it does so subsequent to an HIV infection. As the AIDS epidemic progressed, the period between an HIV infection and the onset of AIDS began to increase. Also, an HIV infection can occur well before it is diagnosed, and as a result the number of new HIV *diagnoses* in a given year is always larger than the number of new *infections* in any given year. This figure charts historical trends in new diagnoses of HIV and AIDS. It does *not* specifically chart newly acquired HIV infections according to the year in which the infection occurred, as distinct from when the diagnosis occurred.

The two lines in the figure meet coincidentally in 1994, and subsequently diverge. As it happens, 1994 was also the peak year for both the number of new AIDS diagnoses and of deaths from AIDS. Historically, over 90% of the people who made up the numbers represented by these two lines were gay men and included gay community connected Indigenous Australians and men from culturally and linguistically diverse backgrounds.[13]

While graphs such as this are important, to non-researchers they often seem dry and too detached from the stories embodied within them. That is their strength. They enable analysis. We use them to track epidemics. But the analysis requires that we know what occurred to the individuals, to the communities in which they lived and died, and what has changed. If we do not know these histories then we misinterpret what the data mean, especially if we assume they provide statistical norms against which we can assess what is occurring in the present.

After new treatments options became widely available from 1996 on, some of us spoke cautiously of improvised optimism, of a breathing space. There is a risk in hope. It can disappoint. In this case it paid off. In hindsight we now know how dramatically social relations and individual lives changed. Between 1994 and 2008 both AIDS diagnoses and AIDS deaths fell by about 90%. These were momentous, extraordinary changes. Further, since 2001, amongst people living with HIV, 'estimated deaths from causes other than AIDS have exceeded AIDS deaths in Australia'.[14]

Even so, though the number of deaths annually is much lower, there are still people being diagnosed with AIDS. Many of the current AIDS diagnoses appear to occur as a result of late HIV diagnosis, are often from culturally and linguistically diverse populations and are usually somewhat less likely to be amongst gay men. Lower numbers do not mean these diagnoses do not matter. They matter to the individuals involved and their social networks – partners, friends, families. They also affect how medical and hospital care and other support resources are distributed and rearranged. People are still hospitalised and some do still die. While AIDS as an epidemic has largely faded, compared with the period between 1984 and 1994, we need to take into account what it means now to live with and manage an HIV infection, as we do for those with AIDS.

The HIV Futures Study conducted by the Australian Research Centre in Sex, Health and Society at La Trobe University and other research continues to indicate that people with HIV are generally living much longer, healthier lives than they were before highly active retroviral therapy became available.[15] The average age for new HIV infections is 38, and though people who contracted HIV more recently are unlikely to have an HIV-related illness until they have lived with the virus for much longer, nearly 30% of people with HIV in Australia are now aged over 50. This proportion will keep rising, consequently over time there will be more and more older people living with HIV. Living longer with HIV makes you prone to earlier onset of age related conditions.[16] It also contributes to an increase in the prevalence of HIV in Australia.

Even given all that, however, Elizabeth Pisani was pretty well right when she said in the *Guardian* in 2009 that treatments have meant that AIDS as distinct from HIV infection is largely a thing of the past in most western countries.[17] At a population level in Australia, it is possible to suggest that socially we no longer have an AIDS epidemic. I am coming at this from a somewhat different angle to that taken by Gary Dowsett and David McInnes when they conceptualised 'post-AIDS' in 1995–1996, but it sits well with their analysis and its subsequent elaboration in the work of people like Eric Rofes, and myself.[18] The post-AIDS discussion concerned the constantly changing social contexts of prevention education, and the multiple ways gay men, irrespective of serostatus, were responding to HIV in their sexual practices.

The research evidence base says that most gay men still practice safe sex most of the time, and about half do so all of the time. Analysis of survey data and interviews from the recent Pleasure and Sexual Health (PASH) study in which I am involved indicates continuing support for safe sex, but again makes it clear that many gay men now use condoms under sufferance.[19] They do not like them. They use them because they have to, but if HIV were not a factor they would not. This is the case irrespective of both HIV status and their preferences in relation to condom use and risk reduction. A considerable proportion of unprotected anal sex in casual contexts is occasional and not the result of an intention present before the event. What is also clear, however, is that many men also use strategies to avoid condoms where they can, whether by negotiating 'safety' within relationships, or by choosing casual sex partners whom they know or believe have the same HIV status as themselves (sero-sorting). The PASH study indicates that,

> those men who consciously seek opportunities to forego condom use are almost entirely those men who are fairly unconcerned about HIV, or even those who are 'over' HIV and think that it is no longer sufficiently serious to warrant sacrifices of their sexual pleasure.[20]

Many of the men also appear to engage sometimes or more frequently in various forms of risk reduction while also seeking to maximise sexual pleasure and intimacy. That is, the unprotected anal sex in casual contexts is accompanied by sero-sorting, withdrawal and less often, strategic positioning (only 'topping' or 'bottoming'). The men universally value not transmitting HIV or becoming infected. In that sense, a general ethical and attitudinal consensus around safe sex is accompanied by a circumstantial practical ethics. The difficulties here include that in many circumstances the men cannot or do not properly know the status of their partners, that risk reduction is precisely what it says – reduced risk not risk elimination – and they often do not adhere to their own risk reduction practices. These result in new infection.

Not surprisingly, if we return to the upper line in the figure, what we see in Australia is an epidemic of HIV. The National Center in HIV Epidemiology and Clinical Research reports that '[t]he annual number of diagnoses of newly acquired HIV infection increased from 171 in 1999 to 308 in 2006 and declined to 281 in 2008.'[21] Eighty-two per cent of those new HIV infections occurred amongst gay men. What the upper line indicates is that HIV is endemic amongst gay men, and that it has been since 1984. No news there, you may think, and in one way that is true, but the situation has changed. Since 1995, the HIV epidemic has been decreasingly accompanied by deaths from AIDS. That is, HIV incidence has risen, while diagnoses of AIDS have fallen. For the past 10 years, it has been very difficult to get the implications of this onto the table for discussion, much less keep them there in full view. It simply was not politically possible during a period of sustained rises in new HIV infections.

Put bluntly, gay men are not now living on ground zero and have not been for the past 15 years. However, it took several years for some of the implications to become apparent. Mostly, because any deviation from safe sex was represented in various ways as 'dancing with death'.[22] That is not true, and it is a very unhelpful metaphor through which to understand effective HIV education. Once new treatments came into the picture the meaning of an HIV infection changed. (There is no longer an almost automatic progression to AIDS following an infection.) Not surprisingly, so did the social relations between gay men, condom use, anal sex and risk taking. The rate of new HIV infections rose. We cannot proceed any longer by assuming that a continuously falling rate of new HIV infection is either the norm or sustainable. As important as the achievements of the first 15 years of the epidemic were in the establishment of a safe sex culture, the 1984 to 1999 section of the upper line in the figure presented earlier now has limited relevance for HIV prevention – unless your primary purpose is to maintain fear of disease and AIDS.

If the purpose of HIV prevention is fear then it has already succeeded. Many gay men, especially those who are HIV negative, are still highly fearful of HIV, yet, as the PASH study reports,

> the main feature that characterises the men who retain this deeply-felt fear of HIV is that they are often men who claim to have *never* engaged in sexual risk behaviour such as UAIC [unprotected anal sex in casual contexts]. For many who remain so deeply fearful of HIV, their fears are both abstracted from knowledge and veer toward phobia. They often have relatively limited gay friendship and sexual networks, and limited contact with HIV-positive gay men.[23]

For these men anal sex itself is often problematic, and condom use is accompanied by fear (reliability, fear of breakage). This undermines the confidence required for ongoing ease in condom use.

We have not been able to face the implications of an HIV epidemic largely separated from AIDS, and responses based in fear of HIV and AIDS with any ease in a decade of rising HIV infection. Between 2000 and 2006, rises in new HIV infection produced a public health panic that foreclosed much discussion of how to do risk reduction in prevention education, and was not helped by political conservatism, and increasing criminalisation of HIV. Yet Australia still has one of the lowest HIV prevalence levels in the world. I am not complacent about that, but we do need a sense of proportion about these matters, even as we pay attention to how risk reduction is being done.

We do and will remember what came before, but as I have suggested, if we do not take into account that in this country we are no longer in an AIDS epidemic, we remember badly. *The conditions that produced a constant decrease in new infections no longer hold.* I am glad those conditions characteristic of an AIDS epidemic (high rates of morbidity and mortality, community crisis) no longer apply, even though I recognise that this shift creates challenges for prevention education. It is a situation further complicated by health funding streams that often, but not always, require gay men be represented in terms of deficit.

Deficit accounts of gay men primarily speak of them, in Rofes' terms, as variously 'damaged and dangerous'. Their 'sexual practices, patterns of socializing, and cultural norms' are represented as 'troubling'.[24] This is not to deny there are sometimes uneven health outcomes for gay men or other sexual minorities. Rather it is a refusal to construct the cultures involved *only* in reference to health disparities and disease. As Pitts et al. showed in the national *Private Lives* study: 'despite health inequalities, it is also clear that most gays, lesbians, bisexuals, transgender and intersex people live happy and fulfilled lives'.[25]

This sense of fulfillment clearly matters to the people involved. However we refer to it – as social resilience, resistance, creative problem solving, social agency, community, the development of personal repertoires – we are describing an active capacity to live meaningfully. One part of the explanation is to be found in social connection: '[t]he strength and stability of relationships and friendships within GLBTI communities and the value placed on these things indicates a real capacity in our participants to live optimistically and well'.[26] Deficit accounts reproduce queers as socially and politically marginal and sick in ways that do not recognise political achievement, social capacity or the strengths of their sexual cultures.[27] While there are aspects of those cultures that can be challenged, any challenges need to be based on social respect and consideration of what will enable sustained change. There are mental health issues for some gay men, but as Dowsett has recently argued, unprotected sex is not primarily about relapse or low self esteem.[28] Not only is much unprotected sex safe – negotiated safety, successful sero-sorting amongst HIV negative men and between HIV positive men – much depends also on the contextual prevalence of HIV.

The most recent seroconversion study indicates that while the men in that study are those who took risks and did seroconvert and have taken responsibility for that, they are also in many ways similar to the men who have not seroconverted, but have also occasionally or more frequently practiced unprotected anal sex in casual contexts. They have similar educational backgrounds, are knowledgeable about safe sex, are older, are strongly community connected, are sexually adventurous and play in similar contexts.[29] Social research tells us that seroconversion is circumstantial and contextual. It is not caused by moral failure or complacency. This is not a discussion about good and bad gay men. It is about what it means to be sexually active in a situation of endemic HIV.

Implications for HIV Education and Prevention

Short of a vaccine or a cure, it appears we are highly unlikely to see a sustained fall in the number of new HIV infections. HIV is endemic because there are no preventative vaccines and it is quite possible there will not be for a long time, if ever. I first heard an imminent vaccine trumpeted in 1987. We now know that it is very hard scientifically to create a vaccine.[30] In terms of both managing living with HIV and doing HIV prevention, the closest thing to a cure appears to be undetectable viral load amongst people living with HIV.

I anticipate that what we will see over time is a series of rises, hopefully small, and falls in the annual number of new infections. New HIV infections have remained stable in New South Wales and Victoria for the past two years. The plateau, however, is at a higher level than it was in 1999. For many this is a politically unpalatable scenario. For other people it is shocking. From my perspective as a researcher, it is to be expected, irrespective of what I might feel about it personally.

Like it or not, what we see on the upper line in the figure post-1999 is a much more realistic representation of what is statistically normal now than what occurred before. If condom use between 1984 and 1996 marked a community-based response fed by the fear of an almost untreatable virus, constantly rising AIDS deaths and considerable social hostility, it now only partly does so. While the general commitment to infection prevention remains, the context has changed. Even in the earlier context, however, the Sustaining Safe Sex survey in the early 1990s indicated that men were practicing negotiated safety well before it was named or officially promoted in the mid-1990s.[31] We see a similar time lag between 1996 and 1999. Organisations responded somewhat cautiously to the relatively rapid changes in gay men's sexual behaviour and sexual cultures. When rates of sexually transmitted infections rose and then new HIV infections increased in the 2000s, behaviour changed again. That appears to be what happens, at least in the medium term, when you no longer have an AIDS epidemic. Education and information provision still work, and in the case of Sexually Transmitted Infections (STIs) the curative effects of treatments are well known amongst the more experienced.

Endemic HIV epidemics in the absence of AIDS appear to be characterised by increasing HIV prevalence, marked variations in HIV incidence, increasing sexual adventurousness and risk taking including unprotected anal intercourse in casual sex contexts and substantially diluted knowledge amongst non-HIV positive gay men of what it is like now to live with and manage an HIV infection. While the majority of men in PASH agreed that HIV is no longer a death sentence and nearly a third believed it is a less serious threat than it was in the past, only about half believed that rates of HIV infection were increasing in the area where they lived.

Safe sex was invented by gay men under extraordinary circumstances. In the space of about 12 years somewhere between a third to a half of my generation of gay identifying men and a smaller number of lesbians died. I am still enormously relieved that subsequent generations of gay men, and many gay men in general, now know less and less of what it means to live in an AIDS epidemic, even though this makes HIV prevention more difficult. I wish more knew the history, but I am glad they did not experience it. There is more to life than fear of disease and death. In the PASH study, 'over half knew no one who had died of AIDS, almost a half spent no time with PLHIV [People Living with HIV] and only a small minority knew anyone diagnosed with HIV in the previous year'.[32] I also wish, however, they knew more about what is involved now in managing HIV infection over a lifetime, and how best to respond to a friend disclosing their HIV positive status. Those involved in the response to an endemic HIV epidemic will live with the associated frustrations and sorrows until the HIV epidemic is also over, but the operative word here is live.

Our task is to contain new infection as best we can, until something happens to radically affect the picture. There are three things we can do in relation to keeping HIV contained. The first is to *sustain* current HIV and STI testing rates amongst gay men, in particular by advocating for the introduction of easily accessible rapid HIV testing. There was substantial support for this amongst the men in the PASH study. Second, not all gay men relate to sexual risk taking in the same way. We can support those gay men who use risk reduction to sustain those risk reduction practices, rather than simply position them as problematic. Those doing risk reduction, whether episodically or frequently, need to be included in a long term conversation, spoken with, not just spoken to, or spoken about.[33] That is beginning to happen, but the process is slow.

Third, we need to rethink what we are doing when we speak about risk, accept that we are working in a new situation and advocate around this with policy makers and politicians. This is a moment to be brave. State and federal elections will affect what community organisations and health departments can do. Yes the politics are difficult, but if community leaderships are driven only by caution in their relations with funders, and their reputations, the more benign, sanitised and ultimately irrelevant the health promotion resources produced will be. Official responses driven only by caution may well involve the men most able to have an effect on new HIV and STI infections increasingly detaching from what the organisations are saying. They need to be supported with practical, relevant information on how to stick with risk reduction, particularly at those moments when pleasure undercuts care of the self. HIV policy infrastructures have a major role here in brokering this at state and Commonwealth levels. The zero tolerance approach to sexual risk taking that characterises some STI and HIV research and much of the prevention in Australia has the potential to increase resistance to testing. Goodwill and professionalism require that testing occur without sexual moralism.

Endemic HIV in these circumstances involves, to use that quaint 1990s term, a paradigm shift. We still need medium to long term thinking separate from National AIDS Strategies, changes of government, funding arrangements and moral panics. Think tank style activities can play a major role here.

I recall the economist Ernest Mandel counselling a young revolutionary in the 1970s to remember that it took 600 years to overthrow feudalism. As you see, I also tend to the longer view. What is remarkable, from my point of view, is the creativity involved in how gay men respond to reducing the risk of infections, after 25 years, and the relative smallness of the numbers involved in the increases in new infections. Most gay men are not living with an HIV infection. Nor will they.

Endnotes

1   Cindy Patton, *Sex and Germs: The Politics of AIDS*, Boston: South End Press, 1985.
2   Eric Rofes, 'Gay Bodies, Gay Selves: Understanding the Gay Men's Health Movement', *White Crane*, 2005, available at, http://www.ericrofes.com/books/gay_bodies_gay_selves.pdf, date accessed 26 April 2010. Over time, Rofes had strongly advocated for an 'assets-based' approach to gay men's health, taking a lead role in the formation of a multi-issue, multicultural gay men's health movement that included HIV and AIDS, but was not defined by them. He came to this position after a long history of early gay activism, substantial involvement in HIV and AIDS organisations, and careful consideration of both the effects of HIV on gay communities and the benefits of the treatments that emerged in 1996 and later. In two of his books, *Reviving the Tribe* (1996) and *Dry Bones Breathe* (1998) he argued fiercely for recognition of wider perspectives on the communal, life-affirming nature of gay communities and sexual subcultures.
3   I thank Ross Duffin, Bill O'Loughlin and Graham Willett for comments on various drafts of this chapter. They bear no responsibility for the argument within it.
4   Because this article is primarily about gay men, I have not referred here to mother-to-child transmission through breast milk or *in vitro* infection or vaginal intercourse, each of which has its own discovery histories.
5   See, Dennis Altman, *AIDS and the New Puritanism*, London; Sydney: Pluto Press, 1986; Douglas Crimp, 'Mourning and Militancy', *October*, vol. 51 (1989), pp. 3–18.
6   See, Nilanjana Bardhan, 'Transnational AIDS-HIV News Narratives: A Critical Exploration of Overarching Frames', *Mass Communication and Society*, vol. 4, no. 3 (2001), pp. 283–309; Michael Hurley et al., 'Mainstream Print Media Reporting of HIV Increases 2000–2003', *HIV Australia*, December 2003 – February 2004.
7   'The concept of "risk" itself poses a challenge. In public health, we typically look at issues such as HIV and other STIs as posing a "risk", with the presumption that our task is to eliminate or minimise that risk. This is the position of rational actors, who make decisions

based on a "risk-calculation" to minimise potential harms (firstly to themselves and secondarily to others) while maximising potential rewards. However, this perspective is usually founded on the premise that individuals will primarily be concerned with the first half of this calculation (to minimise harms), and the maximising of rewards is only secondary, if it is given any real consideration at all. This may not necessarily be the way everyone approaches such calculations', Garret Prestage et al., *Pleasure and Sexual Health: The PASH Study, 2009* Sydney: National Centre in HIV Epidemiology and Clinical Research, 2010, p. 16.

8   'Anal intercourse is one of the central practices in the gay/bisexual repertoire… for considerable numbers of men it has been experienced as a central part of being gay… It is hardly surprising that statements of the personal importance of anal sex are consistently and strongly associated with frequency of practice. From this point of view, insisting on a total safe sex regime may be counter-productive. Over-rigid rules are impractical and invite blowouts: the net effect may be greater risk than a more moderate regime from the start', Susan Kippax et al., *Sustaining Safe Sex: Gay Communities Respond to AIDS*, London: Falmer, 1993, p. 77. See also the reflections on the first 10 years of safe sex in, E. King, *Safety in Numbers: Safer Sex and Gay Men*, London; New York: Cassell 1993; and, Bruce Parnell, 'Changing Behaviour', in Eric Timewell et al., eds, *AIDS in Australia*, Sydney: Prentice Hall, 1993, pp. 185–205.

9   '[T]he key to this approach is modifying what you do – not how often you do it nor with how many partners', Berkowitz and Callen, *How to Have Sex in an Epidemic, One Approach*, News from The Front Publications, 1983, p. 3. See also, Douglas Crimp, *How to Have Promiscuity in an Epidemic*, Cambridge, MA: The MIT Press, 1987; and, Simon Watney, *Policing Desire: Pornography, AIDS and the Media*, London: Comedia, 1987.

10 See, Parnell, 'Changing Behaviour'; Kippax et al., *Sustaining Safe Sex*; and, Gary Dowsett, *Practicing Desire: Homosexual Sex in the Age of AIDS*, Stanford: Stanford University Press, 1996.

11 Douglas Crimp, *Melancholia and Moralism: Essays on AIDS and Queer Politics*, Cambridge, MA: The MIT Press, 2004, p. 17.

12 Rofes was an invited keynote speaker at the first Australian national lesbian, gay, transgender and bisexual health conference, Health in Difference, organised by the Australian Federation of AIDS Organisations in 1996. There have always been substantial differences in the Australian and US responses to AIDS and HIV, much of it due to America's lack of a public health system, more limited government support for a community-based response, and a more puritan sex culture. Even so, there have also been important crossovers at the level of how gay men, lesbians, their allies and friends have built strong cultures in the face of social hostility and disease, and have celebrated communal life and sexual pleasure. See, Juliet Richters et al., *Health in Difference: Proceedings of the First National Lesbian, Gay, Transgender and Bisexual Health Conference, Sydney, 3–5 October 1996*, Sydney: Australian Centre for Lesbian and Gay Research, 1997.

13 In 2009, new HIV infections amongst Indigenous Australians occurred at the same per capita rate as in non-Indigenous populations; however, rates of other sexually transmitted infections were considerably higher. Amongst CALD populations, 'the *per capita* rate of HIV diagnosis in Australia in 2006–2008 was at more than eight times higher among people born in countries in sub-Saharan Africa than among Australian born people'. See, National Centre in HIV Epidemiology and Clinical Research 2009, pp. 7–8.

14 J. Murray et al., 'Rapidly Aging HIV Epidemic Among Men Who Have Sex With Men in Australia', *Sexual Health*, vol. 6, no. 1 (2009), pp. 83–86.

15   Jeffrey Grierson et al., *HIV Futures 6: Making Positive Lives Count*, monograph series no. 74, Melbourne: Australian Research Centre in Sex, Health and Society, Latrobe University, 2009; The Antiretroviral Therapy Cohort Collaboration, 'Life Expectancy of Individuals on Combination Antiretroviral Therapy in High-Income Countries: A Collaborative Analysis of 14 Cohort Studies', *The Lancet*, vol. 372, no. 9635 (26 July 2008), pp. 293–299.

16   See, Ross Duffin, 'Ageing with HIV', *Talkabout*, November 2009, available at, http://positivelife.org.au/talkabout/2009/oct-nov/ageing-hiv, date accessed April 2010.

17   Elizabeth Pisani, 'HIV Doesn't Always Kill', *Guardian*, 9 September 2009, p. 34. See also her 'One HIV Test, But Two Results', *Guardian*, 23 February 2010, p. 30.

18   See, Gary Dowsett and David McInnes, 'Gay Community, AIDS Agencies and the HIV Epidemic in Adelaide: Theorising "post-AIDS"', *Social Alternatives*, vol. 15, no. 4 (1996), pp. 29–32; Eric Rofes, *Dry Bones Breathe: Gay Men Creating Post-AIDS Identities and Cultures*, Binghamton, NY: Haworth Press, 1998; and, Michael Hurley, *Then and Now: Gay Men and HIV*, monograph series no. 46, Melbourne: Australian Research Centre in Sex, Health and Society, La Trobe University, 2003.

19   Part of this can be explained by the tension inherent in the differing economies of desire involved in anal sex for gay men: 'There are two different but related domains of desire at work here. The first involves wanting to avoid infection, and what makes that possible. It is constituted around disease, condom use and risk, and a desire for no disease, no risk and no need for condoms. The second involves what counts as sexually desirable, and how that desire may be satisfied. It is constituted around pleasure. These two domains are potentially present when sex is negotiated circumstantially. Both are involved in care of the self and others. The practical challenges in negotiating the tensions between the desire to stay HIV-negative or to not transmit HIV, condom use and sexual desire and pleasure are ongoing', Prestage et al., *Pleasure and Sexual Health*, p. 5.

20   ibid., p. 157.

21   National Centre in HIV Epidemiology and Clinical Research, *2009 Annual Surveillance Report. HIV/AIDS, Viral Hepatitis and Sexually Transmissible Infections in Australia*, Sydney, p. 7.

22   See, Michael Hurley and S. Croy, *HIV Infection, Gay Men, the Media, and the Law*, forthcoming; and, Hurley, *Then and Now*. For a different view, see, Steve Dow, *Gay*, Altona, Vic.: Common Ground, 2001.

23   Prestage et al., *Pleasure and Sexual Health*, p. 155.

24   Rofes, 'Gay Bodies, Gay Selves'.

25   Marian Pitts et al., *Private Lives: A Report on the Health and Wellbeing of GLBTI Australians*, monograph series no. 57, Melbourne: Australian Research Centre in Sex, Health and Society, La Trobe University, 2006.

26   ibid., p. 62.

27   These issues have been taken up in recent social health research. See, Lynne Hillier et al., 'Guest Editorial: Mental Health and LGBT Communities', *Gay and Lesbian Issues and Psychology Review*, vol. 4, no. 2 (2009), p. 65. See also, Michael Hurley, 'Who's on Whose Margins', in Marian Pitts and Anthony Smith, eds, *Researching the Margins*, London: Palgrave Macmillan, 2007, pp. 160–189; and, Graham Willett, *Living Out Loud: A History of Gay and Lesbian Activism in Australia*, Sydney: Allen and Unwin, 2000.

28   Gary Dowsett, 'Dangerous Desires and Post-Queer HIV Prevention: Rethinking Community, Incitement and Intervention', *Social Theory and Health*, vol. 7 (2009), pp. 218–240.

29. Garrett Prestage et al., *HIV Seroconversion Study: Newly Diagnosed Men in Australia 2007–2009*, Sydney: National Center in Clinical Research and HIV Epidemiology, University of New South Wales, 2009.
30. For some of the science involved, see, Kendall Smith, 'The HIV Vaccine Saga', *Medical Immunology*, vol. 2, no. 1 (2003), available at, www.medimmunol.com/content/2/1/1, date accessed April 2010.
31. See, Kippax et al., *Sustaining Safe Sex*; and, Dowsett, *Practicing Desire*, 1996.
32. Prestage et al., *Pleasure and Sexual Health*, p. 6.
33. See, Tony Valenzuela, 'Men Who Bareback Should Be Made Partners in Health Promotion, Not Banished', 10 August 2009, available at, www.trevorhoppe.com/blog/archives/2009/08/men_who_bareback.html, date accessed April 2010.

Australian Lesbian Artists of the Early Twentieth Century

Peter Di Sciascio

Women were virtually invisible in Australian art in the nineteenth century, but went on to become leaders in the Australian Modern Art movement between the wars. Here, we shall look at some of the changing social conditions and events that enabled women, who were mostly from the upper classes and unmarried, to forge successful artistic careers. These women had the ability or inclination to avoid the traditional female role in society and this chapter proposes one method of examination which reveals that lesbians were disproportionately represented in this cohort of successful artists.

Women Artists in the Nineteenth Century

The social conditions for women in nineteenth century Australia led inexorably to their entrapment into the roles of wives, mothers and homemakers. This locked most women into the domestic sphere and prevented the pursuit of any career, let alone one in art. However, for those with a creative bent, and time and money, craft in the domestic environment[1] and art, were available as genteel pursuits for young ladies.[2] Unlike other areas of public endeavour (politics, university, professions, and trades) there were no institutional or legal barriers to women's involvement in art.

To demonstrate that women were actively involved in formal art education, Graph 1 shows the male and female enrolments in the National Gallery School's (NGS) Painting Class between the years 1886 and 1914.

The NGS in Melbourne was Australia's premier art school. The graph shows that women far outnumbered men during this period.

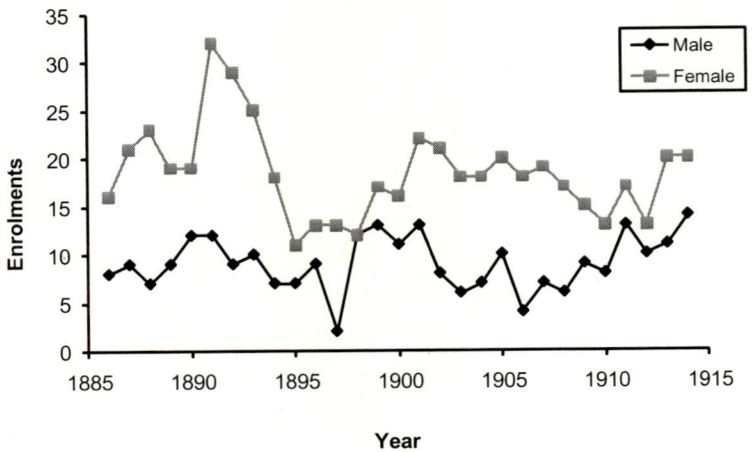

Graph 1: National Gallery School Enrolments in the Painting Class[3]

Further, during Frederick McCubbin's years as drawing master at the NGS (1886 to 1917) three quarters of his 2000 students were women.[4] This pattern was repeated in the Art Schools, Mechanics Institutes and Schools of Mines in towns and regional centres around Australia where art and craft were taught.[5]

If women were actively engaging in art training did this translate into artistic output and professional careers? In 1906 the Royal Art Society of New South Wales exhibited 'The Hundred Best Pictures of the Royal Art Society', 83 were by males, and only 17 were by females.[6] Anyone with a basic knowledge of nineteenth century Australian art will have male artists in mind when thinking of the period. While recent research has uncovered the depth and breadth women's artistic pursuits in the nineteenth century,[7] very few women achieved the success and notability of male artists of the time. This was apparent when I visited the Ian Potter Centre at the National Gallery of Victoria (NGV) and surveyed the hang in the nineteenth century Australian art galleries and noted the gender of the artist for each work of art on display. The results of my findings appear in Graph 2. The category of 'paintings' includes oils, watercolours and drawings. The category of 'objects' includes sculpture, silverware and furniture.

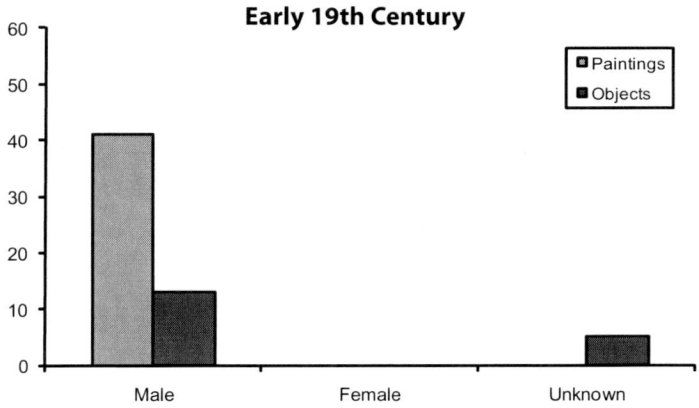

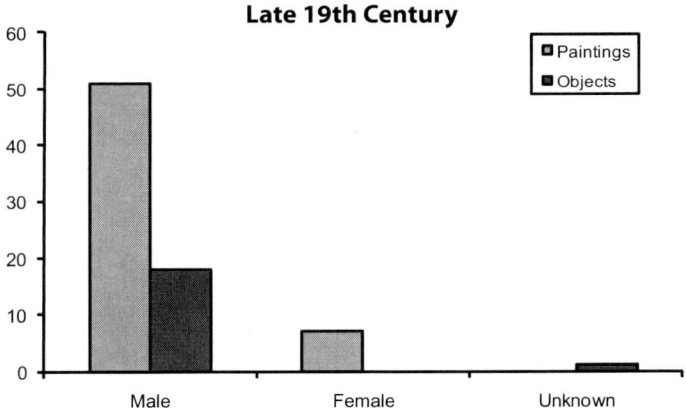

Graph 2: Current Hang at the NGV, Nineteenth Century Australian Art [8]

The data reveal that no women are represented in the early nineteenth century gallery,[9] and only a small number (six works by Emma Boyd, Jane Sutherland and Clara Southern) appear in the late nineteenth century gallery. What the research suggests is that the training that women were receiving in premier art schools was not translating into artistic output worthy of collection and display in one of Australia's foremost art galleries.

Events at the Turn of the Century

Events at the turn of the century resulted in some social changes in Australia that benefited women in both the private (reduced marriage and birth rates, for example) and public spheres (Federation prosperity and white women achieved the vote, for example).[10]

The next major part of the story of Australian women's art is the Arts and Crafts Movement. This was a decorative arts movement that emanated from Britain in the 1860s, inspired by the teachings of William Morris and John Ruskin. Its hallmarks were the hand-crafting of items, the use of plant and animal motifs and the merging of art, craft, design and architecture. The movement hit Australia in the 1890s and really took off in the first decade of the twentieth century with the formation of a number of Arts and Crafts Societies; Tasmania in 1903, New South Wales in 1906, and Victoria in 1908, to name just three.[11] While interest in the Arts and Crafts Movement came from both men and women, a closer look at the histories of these societies shows that women were particularly prominent.[12] Arguably this interest stems from the movement's connection with craft and its applications to the domestic environment, a point that has been made by Anthea Callen.[13] Women's creativity, for years locked away in domestic craft, now had an open, public and legitimate artistic forum. The flood gates had been opened. The Arts and Crafts movement successfully gave women an *entré* into the art world via craft where they were already well established.

While women continued to participate in mixed Arts Societies with mixed success, specific women's arts societies formed which provided opportunities for mutual support: Sydney's Society of Women Painters was formed in 1910, and the Melbourne Society of Women Painters and Sculptors in 1902.[14]

Then there was the Women's Work Exhibition of 1907. Held at the Exhibition Buildings in Melbourne, it was the brainchild of the Governor General's wife Lady Northcote. A quarter of a million people attended the exhibition. The exhibition contained 16,000 works spread across a broad range of categories, both competitive and non-competitive. The largest section was needlework, with 7000 entries. The second largest section was fine and applied arts, with 5000 entries.[15]

In the same year, William Moore wrote an article for a women's magazine specifically describing the potential for art as a career for women.[16] He provided advice on training, the genres of art where money could be made, and included many examples of successful role models. Moore's article was the last of a series on 'Careers for Australasian Girls' published in *The New Idea*.[17] While a subsequent comprehensive publication about women's work opportunities in Victoria excluded art or artistic pursuits, with the exception of *Black and White Art* for fashion and advertisement drawing,[18] artist

George Taylor, in 1919, called for men to 'give women equal opportunities and acknowledgement in Art'.[19]

New art magazines of the period featured women artists and craftswomen. First, *Art and Architecture* (published from 1905 to 1912), which later became *The Salon* (1912 to 1916), and then *Art in Australia* magazine (published from 1916 to 1942) were especially influential. The editor of *Art in Australia*, Sydney Ure Smith, was a key figure in the art world at the time.[20] He somehow managed to straddle the demands of the conservatives and the modernists, both male and female. This journal, as well as another he edited, *The Home: The Australian Journal of Quality* (published from 1920 to 1942), were great vehicles for exposing the public to women's art. Margaret Preston was the most featured artist in *Art in Australia*.[21]

Women to the Fore between the Wars

By World War I women had started to establish themselves amongst (male) career artists. The tide had turned for women in art. But who was in this wave and what distinguished them? Upper class women were prominent and most of the successful women artists never married. Lesbians were disproportionately represented.[22] What these women shared was an ability or inclination to avoid the traditional female role in society; they could devote the time and money needed for a successful career in art.[23] For those who could afford it, travel to major capitals such as London and Paris, and elsewhere in Europe and Japan, provided wider exposure to art, culture and worldly experience.[24]

Women, much more than men embraced modernism and introduced it to Australia.[25] Grace Cossington Smith's 1915 work *The Sock Knitter* is believed to be the first fully post-impressionist painting to be exhibited in Australia.[26] Dorrit Black, Grace Crowley and Anne Dangar were notable amongst the few Australian artists to dabble in cubism. With a small number of exceptions, male art at the time remained vehemently conservative, stuck in the impressionist style typified by the Heidelberg School, or, as Jeanette Hoorn describes it 'Pastoral Painting'.[27] This was reflected in the acquisition patterns of many of the state galleries which did not collect Australian women's art until well after the 1940s.[28]

Consumerism exploded with the rise of the middle classes. Art, design and decorative arts were in demand and the buyers were mostly women.[29] Approximately three women for every one man frequented art exhibitions.[30] Sydney Ure Smith commented in 1937 that women were the principal supporters of the visual arts and 'if artists had to depend on the men folk, there would not be much art'.[31] Mass media burgeoned in the early twentieth century, with women artists producing images and covers for art and women's magazines,[32] which appealed to the stylish, consumer woman who was interested in art and design. Women were also prominent in the resurgence of printmaking that occurred in Australia in the 1920s.[33] They pioneered coloured woodblock prints (Violet Teague) and revolutionised coloured linocut printing (Eveline Syme, Ethel Spowers and Dorrit Black). They were not afraid of new techniques and styles.

The 1920s also saw the emergence of the 'new woman'. This international western phenomenon was characterised by working, independent females; they smoked, were less inclined to marriage and children, were better educated and more likely to use contraception.[34] One argument often put to explain women's artistic success between the wars was the absence or death of a generation of young male artists due to World War I.[35] I refer to this as the 'void theory', that is, the idea that women filled the artistic void. I do not subscribe to this argument. Not only is this premise too convenient for a later, very patriarchal art world to use, suggesting that second-rate female artists only got up due to the lack of men, but if it was the case then a similar trend should be observable in the years after World War II, which it is not. Also, if women were just filling the void then they could have done it by continuing the traditional impressionist/landscape territory set out by the men. But they did not. Women became innovators and expanded the boundaries of art more than men.

A more feasible argument is that there was a general absence of a generation of men after World War I, which reduced the pressure to marry and that the necessity for women to live and work independently that occurred during the War carried over in part, to the following decades.[36] Indeed, Caroline Ambrus suggests that these women were still empowered by the first wave of feminism that occurred at the turn of the century, although it became less resonate with later generations of women at and beyond World War II.[37]

The answer, I believe, can be found in the presence of the constellation of factors that I have described thus far (some international, some unique to Australia). Together, they provided the right conditions for women's success, and for once, male action (or inaction) had nothing to do with it.

The Emergence of the Lesbian Artist

Having described the conditions that allowed the emergence of the woman artist, it is now appropriate to examine lesbian artists more specifically and attempt to explain why the time was also ripe for female artists who desired the physical and social company of other women. Travel, especially travel to Paris, forms a significant part of that explanation.

Paris is now regarded as having been a lesbian Mecca during the *belle époque* (1900–1930s). It was certainly a key destination for artists for several centuries[38] and the twentieth century saw the development of a significant lesbian community in Paris.[39] Some maintain that the 'simple' Australian artists visiting at the time did not engage with such things: 'few… demonstrated even a mild interest in overstepping the conventional cultural prescriptions of their time'.[40] However, I believe that the prevalence of lesbians and their influence in artistic and literary Parisian life would make this assumption naïve. Certainly, more recent writings acknowledge the interaction between Australian artists and the diverse society presented in Paris.[41]

Bertha Harris provides a colourful description of lesbian society in Paris:

> They were American and English and French but mostly American, but with the father's nationality in effect wiped out by the more profound nationality of their lesbianism. From the turn of the century and into the twenties, they escaped the American Gothic with huge hunks of papa's fortune stuffed in their pockets.[42]

Harris saw that community as being vehemently upper class. Shari Benstock challenges this view to some degree, reminding us that female homosexual practice was evident in all levels of society but that women would have experienced it differently according to class.[43] She does confirm that by 1900 Paris had an international reputation as the capital of same-sex love among women and was designated 'Paris-Lesbos': 'Same-sex love was part of the "mad gaiety" of *belle époque* life, where men and women alike sought new and exotic pleasures.'[44] In regard to a lesbian community, Benstock goes on to say that 'it would seem that the commitment to art represented a common bond of experience at least as strong as sexual orientation'.[45]

Australian women artists were entering a Paris not just full of art, but coincidentally, full of sexual freedom. I believe it is reasonable to suggest that many woman artists in Paris at the time would have encountered the lesbian community, and if they were so inclined or interested, engaged with it.

This chapter is about Australian lesbian artists and so far I have stuck to the word 'lesbian', but some space should be devoted to the term itself. Here, Adrienne Rich's discussion of 'compulsory heterosexuality' is useful.[46] The assumption is always that a woman is heterosexual unless there is significant evidence otherwise. In investigating various women artists' lives, I often encountered the response 'it's important not to over-interpret or read too much into these relationships' and even suggestions that these female artists forwent intimate or sexual relationships for their art; asexuality is clearly the next safest thing to heterosexuality. Given the circumstances of these women's lives and the systematic silencing of homosexual history, this chapter casts a wide net and errs on 'our side' for a change. I believe that relationships with other women, that is, lesbian relationships, were a real possibility for these women. If they had not worked that out in the back blocks of the Western District or the suburbs of Melbourne then the possibilities would have become apparent once they visited Paris. Marriage and childbirth were definitely considered as barriers to an artistic career and these women were young, wealthy and intelligent, with the world at their feet. There is evidence that they experimented with sexuality and 'unconventional lives'.

Rich also discusses the idea of the 'lesbian continuum'. She argues that lesbianism can include a range of woman-identified experience, 'not simply the fact that a woman has had or consciously desired genital sexual experience with another woman'.[47] It can be expanded 'to embrace many more forms of primary intensity between and among women', she explains, 'including the sharing of a rich inner life, the bonding against male tyranny, the giving and receiving of practical and political support'.[48] It is in this sense that I have used the term 'lesbian' in this chapter, not to try and define the term, or draw more women into the term, but to remove or blur the line already drawn by compulsory heterosexuality. It is a question of creating a framework to allow visibility in an art history that has made women (let alone lesbians) invisible. Erica Rand provides interesting discussion on this and, in fact, disagrees with Rich's view, but she acknowledges that hers is just a different strategy for the examination of art history.[49] Late twentieth century feminism has done much to recover and celebrate women's art history. However, as Elizabeth Ashburn points out '[l]esbian artists are not only absent from standard surveys of art history, they are also missing from many accounts of feminist art'.[50]

Having set such a playing field, I will present six examples of Australian women artists that might be considered in this framework.

Agnes Goodsir (1864–1939)

Agnes Goodsir was born into a wealthy family in Portland, western Victoria. Soon after her birth the family moved to Melbourne, eventually settling in Brunswick at 'Lyndhurst Hall' in Albert Street. The Goodsirs had connections with Bendigo and in 1898–1899, Agnes studied art at the Bendigo School of Mines under Arthur T. Woodward. Woodward's reputation attracted students to the school and the curriculum was based on that of the Parisian art schools. In 1899, with her father's support and Woodward's encouragement, Agnes departed for Paris to pursue studies in art. She stayed there until 1905 and then returned to Australia for six months. Agnes then returned to Europe, this time settling in London.[51]

While in London during the war, Agnes was close friends with Bernard Roelvink and his American wife Rachel. Rachel subsequently divorced Roelvink and her name reverted to Mrs Rachel Dunn, with the nickname 'Cherry' used among friends and close associates. Cherry became Agnes' artist's model, close companion and the dominant subject of later works.[52] Agnes and Cherry settled in Paris. Agnes' career developed, especially in portraiture. In 1926 she was the third Australian to be elected to the *Salon Nationale des Beaux Arts* (after Rupert Bunny and Bessie Davidson), an important accolade. In 1927 Agnes returned to Australia for nine months to much fanfare and at the peak of her career.[53] She then went back to Paris where she remained for the rest of her life with her beloved Cherry. Agnes died in 1939, Rachel in 1950. They are buried in the same grave outside Paris.

The bulk of Agnes' work was commissioned portraits, for which she was in demand. Otherwise, she produced still life, and *Portraits Intérieur*, a style popular at the time where women (often Cherry) were depicted in soft and elegant interiors with gentle poses and beautiful fabrics and furnishings. Agnes also captured the 'new woman' or 'Latin type'[54] of the mid-1920s as evident in her 1924 painting, *The Parisienne*.[55] The sitter is dressed in masculine attire with a cigarette in her elongated fingers. The hair is short. The effect, while masculine, is elegant.

Janet Cumbrae Stuart (1883–1960)

Janet Cumbrae Stewart was born in middle-class Brighton, Melbourne, in 1883. As early as the age of 15 she is known to have attended drawing classes. Between 1902 and 1907 Janet studied drawing and painting at the National Gallery School. She was awarded a number of prizes in her time at the School.

Janet established a successful career as a pastellist and figure painter in Melbourne during the years 1909 to 1922 which included being a full member of the Australian Artists Association, something usually conferred on elite male artists. She was the subject of a handsome monograph in 1921.[56]

In 1922 Janet moved to London where her success continued with exhibitions in London and Paris. Periodically, she sent works to commercial galleries in Australia. After extensive travel throughout Europe between 1923 and 1931, she settled in Alassio, Italy with her companion Miss Argemore Farrington Bellairs (Billy Bellairs). Billy also acted as Janet's publicist and business manager. She was a distinctive and enterprising woman of independent means who dressed in masculine attire. Janet and Billy travelled to Melbourne to visit family in 1939. The outbreak of war turned the visit into a permanent move. Janet continued her successful art career well into the 1950s. She and Billy divided their time between their homes in Hurstbridge and South Yarra. Janet died in 1960, survived by her partner Billy.[57]

While Janet's *oeuvre* includes some still life, townscapes and 'straight' portraits, she is mostly known for her sensitive and evocative female nudes. Drawing the female nude in an intimate and feminine domain was a new and controversial subject for a woman artist.[58] In 1921 John Shirlow (artist and soon-to-be NGV trustee) said of Janet: '[t]hough telling the secrets of the boudoir, she never descended to the indelicate or vulgar'.[59]

Margaret Preston (1875–1963)

Margaret Rose McPherson was born in Adelaide in 1875. By 1888 she had decided to study art and had won a prize for china painting at a local show.[60] From this point on, her desire to make a career of her art would be untamed. Margaret became one of Australia's leading artists with her innovative modernism and her use of Aboriginal motifs as inspiration for a distinctly Australian modern art.

Until her marriage in 1919, she was known variously as Margaret or Rose, McPherson, MacPherson or Macpherson.[61] Once married in 1919 to Bill Preston, she took the unusual step for a woman artist and changed her name to Margaret Preston. She set up married life in Sydney and appeared to turn her back on her earlier life. This extended to re-signing some of her earlier works.[62]

What lurked in those earlier years were two significant relationships with women that have been largely ignored in official and conservative biographies. The first relationship was with Bessie Davidson, another artist, and a pupil four years her junior. They travelled and studied extensively together, largely on Davidson's allowance, between 1904 and 1910. Margaret gave Bessie a late nineteenth century book of poetry.[63] The book is scattered with hand drawn images of roses, lovers, butterflies, and other figures – and inscribed '[i]t was roses, roses all the way... Love the book and me together' (Margaret Preston's middle name was Rose and in her early years that was her preferred first name).[64] After their relationship ended, Margaret returned home and set up a studio with Gladys Reynell, who became Margaret's intimate companion until about 1919 when Margaret married. Bill Preston later recalled that he 'broke up the twosome'.[65]

At the time of her marriage Margaret was 44, but recorded her age on the marriage certificate as 36,[66] a lie that many believed until her death. The motivation for this is unknown. Was it vanity? Did she want to appear closer to her husband's age? (He was six years younger than her.) Or was she hiding from her husband the fact that she was probably past child-bearing age? Bill Preston was described by arts writer Leon Gellert as '[t]he all-time dream husband of women artists... the handsome and worshipful Bill seemed to regard it as his national duty to keep his beloved Margaret happy and artistically productive'.[67] In a discussion of the two relationships with women, Butel puts them on equal footing with the marriage,[68] although it was not until 2005 that they were considered as lesbian relationships, albeit confined to footnotes.[69] The *Age* picked up on this and effectively 'outed' Margaret in the same year.[70]

If you are wondering what happened to Bessie Davidson, she returned to France and lived the rest of her life as an artist with her 'patron' and 'beloved companion' Marguerite Le Roy, also known as Dauphine. They were buried in the same grave. In her book of Davidson's life, Penelope Little concluded that the friendship was platonic,[71] a statement which led to some criticism by reviewers.[72] Gladys Reynell married George Osborne, a returned solider and gardener 12 years her junior in 1922. Much of their creative years were spent developing their pottery until George contracted lead poisoning.[73]

It is useful to reflect upon Preston's three relationships. Butel says that 'Preston does seem to have thrived on an intimate, supportive relationship, firstly with her two close women friends and later with her husband'.[74] In all three, Margaret was older and relied on the partner for professional, financial as well as personal support. We should not underestimate the value of financial support to single women at the time. Most successful single women came from wealthy families and had allowances (Davidson and Reynell, for example). Margaret relied on those allowances and on the wealth of Bill Preston. Arguably, it is no coincidence that Preston's marriage came after child-bearing age.

Mary Cockburn Mercer (1882–1963)

Another artist with a fascinating life story is Mary Cockburn Mercer. She came from a wealthy family of pioneer settlers in the Western District of Victoria. In her early teens her mother took her to Florence and London to 'finish' her education. At the age of 17 she ran away to join the bohemian life of artists in the Montparnasse district of Paris.[75]

In the early 1920s she lived in France with her male partner, American artist Alexander Robinson, and together they built an idyllic home on the Mediterranean coast at Cassis near Marseilles. Mary then spent time on the island of Capri, amongst the fashionable lesbian set epitomised in Compton Mackenzie's 1928 satire *Extraordinary Women*.[76] She then fell in love with a male German photographer and they settled in Spain until the Spanish Civil War and German conscription separated them.

Mary returned to Australia in 1938, with a couple of years in Tahiti along the way. Upon her return to Melbourne, she enrolled for several months at George Bell's Art School to take advantage of the available life models. Fellow student, Jack Courier, remembered her as 'an exciting and forceful woman who wore "mannish" tweed suits and talked of Europe'.[77] During the war years she exhibited with the Contemporary Art Society in Melbourne, her 'decadent' female nudes often hung behind the gallery doors.[78] In Melbourne, Mercer had a second affair with Janet Cumbrae Stewart (the first in Paris)[79] and cultivated a circle of artist friends including Ian Fairwether, William Frater, Arnold Shore, Lina Bryons (who was a beneficiary of her will) and Colin McCahon. In 1952 Mary returned to her house at Cassis in France. There she remained until severe arthritis forced an end to her art and a move to a nearby apartment. For stimulation she learnt Russian, already being fluent in French and Italian. Mary died in 1963 aged 81.

The NGV holds a beautiful example of her work from c.1940, which depicts two women in relaxed intimacy on a bed.[80] It has broad luminous washes of watercolour that reveal a lightness of touch resulting in a suggestive rather than explicit image. The untitled work is referred to as *Two Women* but the alternate title of this work used by the gallery staff is *The Lesbians*.[81]

Grace Crowley (1890–1979)

Grace Crowley, also known as 'Smudge', is believed to have been in a relationship with Anne Dangar between about 1915 and 1929. Anne Dangar studied and then taught at Julian Ashton's Sydney Art School, at the same time as Grace Crowley. The two went to France together in 1926 where they studied painting for several years, including at the influential cubist school *Académie Lhote*. Dangar returned to Australia in 1928, Crowley in 1930. Dangar travelled back to France in 1930 and settled at Albert Gleize's Art Colony, Moly-Sabata, in southern France where she immersed herself in pottery, for which she became most famous. She remained there for the rest of her life.

In his review of Dangar's life, Bruce Adams describes Crowley and Dangar as physically and temperamentally complementing each other. Dangar's niece, Norah Singleton, recalled their parodies of conventional gender roles both in private conversation and their public appearances. Her observations about their coded behaviour never became an open issue, certainly not in the family circle.[82] Dangar's dependency on Crowley did not diminish after their separation, and a remarkable collection of letters express deep affection and physical longing for her friend's feminine presence.[83]

Grace appears to have had short-lived artistic and/or personal relationships in Sydney with Dorrit Black and Rah Fizelle, eventually settling into a lasting relationship with Ralph Balson.[84] All of Grace's relationships were with artists, and the professional aspect was clearly important. Grace had her own income and had no real need for a husband or anyone to support her financially.

Grace's artistic career is extraordinary. While she is known to have destroyed her works at various times, approximately 50 extant works show a remarkable development from post-impressionist to cubist and then to abstract art. Grace and Balson were leaders in the colour-abstract field in the 1940s. They were then very much 'on their own' in Australian art. Her painting, *Les Baigneuses* of 1928 depicts two naked female bathers, unusually and notably with pubic hair, in the geometricised cubist style she learned from André Lhote.[85]

Kathleen O'Connor (1876–1968)

Kathleen O'Connor was born in New Zealand in 1876 but grew up largely in Western Australia. She showed early talent as an artist. This, combined with her independent and determined personality, and her upper-class background, set the foundation for a life-long career as an artist, unmarried and childless. Kathleen's forte was portraiture and still life. She disliked Western Australia and spent a large part of her life, almost 50 years, overseas. She was most at home in Paris.

Reading through Julie Lewis' biography, what is noticeable is the stark absence of any significant relationships despite a vibrant and eventful life. Life was either very lonely or there are gaps in the biography. Kathleen decided by the age of 24 to never marry despite her popularity and a number of male suitors. She was never tempted to marry for convenience or material security. She was a hoarder of the ephemera of life, so there is a substantial archive of her activities, but nothing to illuminate the inner Kathleen. She kept her inner thoughts to herself. Throughout her long life she seldom gave away any personal information.[86]

While there were friendships with other female artists such as Frances Hodgkins, and a patron Harriet Stewart Dawson (later Princess Radziwill), and hints at relationships with male artists such as painter Isaac Israels and sculptor José Clara, Kathleen was always very evasive about personal relationships, deflecting questions with responses such as 'that would be telling' or 'wouldn't you like to know!'[87] Janda Gooding concludes that there is little evidence to support relationships with men or women and that either is possible (a refreshing rejection of the compulsory heterosexuality discussed earlier). For Kathleen, lifestyle, and by implication her sexual orientation, was not important to an understanding of her art.[88] Again, confined to a footnote we find the most direct comment: 'O'Connor's social background and the *mores* of Australian culture at the time may well have induced her to conceal any sexual relationships she might have had with women'.[89] Kathleen is one woman artist that we will never totally understand. Lewis begins her biography with a telling statement: 'In many ways she remains an enigma. She would have liked that. She enjoyed keeping people guessing'.[90]

Conclusion

A woman's art does not always give an insight into her sexuality. Often, femininity can be read in the art but a sense of sexuality is not necessarily apparent. Arguable exceptions to this would be Janet Cumbrae Stewart and Mary Cockburn Mercer whose female nudes crossed into what was conventionally male artists' territory.[91] There was no specific backlash against lesbians during the period under examination here. Rather, there is a pervasive historical 'silence' about any actual or possible lesbian presence in society, perhaps helped by the lack of criminal sanctions to lesbianism and a belief that if it was ignored, it will go away.[92] In artistic and upper-class circles, female relationships were discretely pursued and largely ignored by others.

A very conservative white male art hierarchy in Australia was very much against Modernism and women in art, rather than lesbians *per se*. Notable amongst these were Lionel Lindsay (artist, writer, critic), J. S. MacDonald (Director of the NGV) and Robert Menzies (politician). In 1934 in the *Bulletin*, J. S. MacDonald wrote and argued against modernism and largely blamed it on women. He abandoned any restraint in voicing his prejudice against women artists and while overlooking lesbians as a group, he got stuck into male homosexuals:

> This development [modern art] has led to the emergence in numbers of what the Americans call 'pansies'; and fine allies they make. These beings can trim a hat or tie a bow with any girl. Both can talk Art… though neither think nor express themselves… in anything but *in*significant form. They rule the world of art today, and unless real painters speak up for themselves and right art, the women and their near men abettors will ruin both.[93]

Unfortunately, the tide turned against women artists after World War II. Australian male artists regained their prominence at the cutting edge of art; women seemed to be banished back into their homes and kitchens with the conservatism of the post-war era.[94] Lesbian artists of the period remained overseas, married, or settled into quiet lives as couples or spinsters, their sexuality now morbidified by the sexologists and medicine.[95]

In 1993, Jo Derbyshire noted that 'many Australian women artists had primary relationships with each other that are now only being taken seriously'.[96] Research conducted for this chapter leads me to be more pessimistic. The grand silence and denial still exists and it comes mostly from women and their sense of compulsory heterosexuality. There is a perceived reluctance or danger of reading biography from an image: 'I'm just interested in The Art', one (male) Gallery Director told me, complaining about the feminist takeover of Australian women artists; needless to say I did not mention the 'L' word. But as Jo Darbyshire explains, '[s]ometimes… this becomes a positive strategy, opening possibilities beyond hegemonic heterosexual readings that dominate art history.'[97] In 2010, polite art history considers these women as heterosexual at the slightest whiff of a man, or ascribes them an asexual identity; women who (safely) sacrificed their innermost self for their art. At best, more direct conjecture is still relegated to obscure endnotes. Embracing the speculative nature of the material, it is time to accept the often scant evidence when it is there, acknowledge the circumstances where they existed, and where there is no clear answer (as for Kathleen O'Connor), at least acknowledge the possibilities. After all, if women wanted to hide their relationships or sexual liaisons, common sense would tell us that lesbian relationships would be hidden before heterosexual ones, even if they were extra-marital. Hopefully, this chapter is the first of many, that will move this information out of the endnotes and into the text!

It took the women's movement and the gay liberation movement to allow women and lesbians back into the artistic world, although this time the liberation was not confined to a particular class. We saw the emergence of openly lesbian artists as well as women artists who happened to be lesbian.[98] Unfortunately, gender stills plays a part in the success of artists, and the art world is still male dominated.[99] To this extent, the development of niche lesbian art or a more general lesbian presence in the art world is hindered. For historians of homosexuality, those with a 'cultivated sensitivity to a "hidden Agenda"',[100] the early part of the twentieth century provides a rich period for the discovery of the unique individuals who were the Australian lesbian artists of the time.

Endnotes

1   Andrew Montana, *The Art Movement in Australia: Design, Taste and Society 1875–1900*, Melbourne: Melbourne University Press, 2000, pp. 19–28.
2   Linda Nochlin, 'Why Have There Been No Great Women Artists?', in Thomas B. Hess and Elizabeth C. Baker, eds, *Art and Sexual Politics*, New York: Collier Books, 1973, pp. 27–29.
3   These data come from Helen Topliss, *Modernism and Feminism: Australian Women Artists 1900–1940*, Sydney: Craftsman House, 1996, p. 204.
4   Alan McCulloch et al., *The New McCulloch's Encyclopedia of Australian Art*, Fitzroy: AUS Art Editions, 2006, p. 1037.
5   Caroline Miley, *The Arts Among the Handicrafts: The Arts and Crafts Movement in Victoria 1889–1929*, Banyule, Vic.: St Lawrence Press, 2001, p. 73.
6   Caroline Ambrus, *Australian Women Artists: First Fleet to 1945: History, Hearsay and Her Say*, Woden, ACT: Irrepressible Press, 1992, p. 98.
7   For the colonial period, see, Caroline Jordan, *Picturesque Pursuits: Colonial Women Artists and the Amateur Tradition*, Melbourne: Melbourne University Press, 2005. For the Heidelberg era, see, Victoria Hammond and Juliet Peers, *Completing the Picture: Women Artists and the Heidelberg Era*, Melbourne: Artmoves, 1992.
8   Research by the author, August 2009.
9   Although colonial women artists did exist, see, Jordan, *Picturesque Pursuits*.

10 A perspective on the effect of female suffrage for women artists is briefly given in Topliss, *Modernism and Feminism*, pp. 44–47.

11 Caroline Miley, *Beautiful and Useful: The Arts and Crafts Movement in Tasmania*, Launceston, Tas: Queen Victoria Museum and Art Gallery, 1987, p. 13; Nonie McFarlane and Judy Mackinolty, eds, *A History of The Society of Arts and Crafts of New South Wales 1906–1991*, Sydney: The Society of Arts and Crafts of New South Wales, 1991, pp. 1–3; Miley, *The Arts Among the Handicrafts*, pp. 87–107. For a New Zealand perspective, see, Ann Calhoun, *The Arts and Crafts Movement in New Zealand 1870–1940: Women Making their Mark*, Auckland: Auckland University Press, 2000.

12 See, McFarlane and Mackinolty, *A History of The Society of Arts and Crafts*, p. xiv. All but one of the presidents between 1906 and 1991 were women. See also, Jennifer Isaacs, *The Gentle Arts: 200 Years of Australian Women's Domestic and Decorative Arts*, Sydney: Lansdowne, 1987, pp. 168–171; Eveline W. Syme, 'Women and Art', in Frances Fraser and Nettie Palmer, eds, *Centenary Gift Book*, Melbourne: Robertson and Mullens, 1934, p. 86.

13 Anthea Callen, *Women Artists of the Arts and Crafts Movement 1870–1914*, New York: Pantheon Books, 1979, p. 218.

14 Ambrus, *Australian Women Artists*, pp. 57–60. Also see, Heather Johnson, *The Sydney Art Patronage System 1890–1940*, Sydney: Bungoona Technologies, 1997, pp. 44–48; Juliet Peers, *More than Just Gumtrees: A Personal, Social and Artistic History of the Melbourne Society of Women Painters and Sculptors*, Melbourne: Dawn Revival Press, 1993.

15 *Portrait of an Exhibition: Centenary Celebration of the First Australian Exhibition of Women's Work 1907*, exhibition catalogue, Castlemaine: Castlemaine Art Gallery and Historical Museum, 2007.

16 William Moore, 'What the Artist's Life Offers', *The New Idea*, 6 December 1907, pp. 848–849. Moore later published the important two volume study, *The Story of Art in Australia*, in 1934.

17 Other careers in the series were nursing (6 February 1907), p. 173; dentistry (6 April 1907), p. 303; typewriting (6 May 1907), p. 371 and (6 June 1907), p. 508; law (6 August 1907), pp. 562–563; massage (6 September 1907), p. 631; and, millinery (6 October 1907), pp. 697, 743.

18 Henrietta C. McGowan, *Woman's Work*, Melbourne: Thomas Lothian, 1913, pp. 142–143.

19 George A. Taylor, *Art and the Woman: A Plea for Better Recognition*, Sydney: Society of Women Painters of NSW, 1919, p. 3.

20 Michael Bogle, *Design in Australia 1880–1970*, Sydney: Craftsman House, 1998, pp. 58–66; Anne-Marie Willis, *Illusions of Identity: The Art of Nation*, Sydney: Hale and Iremonger, 1993, p. 145; Nancy D. H. Underhill, *Making Australian Art 1916–49: Sydney Ure Smith, Patron and Publisher*, Melbourne: Oxford University Press, 1991.

21 Willis, *Illusions of Identity*, p. 149.

22 For an insightful exploration, see, Janine Burke, *Australian Women Artists 1840–1940*, Collingwood, Vic.: Greenhouse Publications, 1980, pp. 37–57. Lesbians are discussed in Burke, *Australian Women Artists*, pp. 58–61; and, Topliss, *Modernism and Feminism*, p. 25.

23 Ambrus, *Australian Women Artists*, pp. 61–83.

24 This is most evident in Jane Hylton, *South Australian Women Artists: Paintings From the 1890s to the 1940s*, Adelaide: Art Gallery Board of South Australia, 1994, with its large chapter on 'The Call of Europe', pp. 8–29, and much smaller chapter, 'Those Who Stayed at Home', pp. 30–34. See also, Topliss, *Modernism and Feminism*, pp. 34–37, 57–79; Jane Hylton, *Modern Australian Women: Paintings and Prints 1925–1945*, Adelaide: Art Gallery of South Australia, 2004, 'Paris and London: The Call of Life and Study Abroad', pp. 29–43.

25 Topliss, *Modernism and Feminism*, pp. 15–27.
26 Grace Cossington Smith, *The Sock Knitter*, 1915, oil on canvas, 61.6 cm x 50.7 cm, Art Gallery of New South Wales (AGNSW), purchased 1960, accession no. OA18.1960. Also available at, AGNSW website, http://www.artgallery.nsw.gov.au/work/oa18-1960+the-sock-knitter, date accessed 5 October 2010; and, Burke, *Australian Women Artists*, p. 43.
27 Jeanette Hoorn, 'Misogyny and Modernist Painting in Australia: How Male Critics Made Modernism their Own', *Journal of Australian Studies*, vol. 16, no. 32 (1992), p. 7.
28 Jennifer Phipps, *Creators and Inventors: Australian Women's Art in the National Gallery of Victoria*, Melbourne: National Gallery of Victoria, 1993. See also, Pam James, '"No Thank You but do you have any Fan Decorations?": Modernist Women Artists and Gatekeepers of Culture', in Maryanne Dever, ed., *Wallflowers and Witches: Women and Culture in Australia 1910–1945*, St Lucia, Qld: University of Queensland Press, 1994.
29 For an exploration on the nexus between consumerism and modern art, see, Martin Pumphrey, 'The Flapper, the Housewife, and the Making of Modernity', *Journal of Cultural Studies*, vol. 1, no. 2 (1987), pp. 179–194.
30 Ambrus, *Australian Women Artists*, p. 104.
31 ibid.
32 Robert Holden, *Cover Up: The Art of Magazine Covers in Australia*, Sydney: Hodder and Stoughton, 1995, pp. 78–117.
33 Kirsten McKay, *Women Printmakers 1910 to 1940 in the Castlemaine Art Gallery and Historical Museum*, exhibition catalogue, Castlemaine: Castlemaine Art Gallery and Historical Museum, 1995; 'Woodcuts and Linocuts Mainly of the 20s and 30s', in *Outlines of Australian Printmaking*, exhibition catalogue, Ballarat: Ballarat Fine Art Gallery, 1976; Peers, *More than Just Gumtrees*, pp. 49–56.
34 For an art perspective, see, Pamela Niehoff, 'The New Woman and the Politics of Identity', in Jeanette Hoorn, ed., *Strange Women: Essays in Art and Gender*, Carlton: Melbourne University Press, 1994, pp. 38–52. For a lesbian perspective of the 'new woman', see, Emmanuel Cooper, *The Sexual Perspective: Homosexuality and Art in the Last 100 Years in the West*, London: Routledge and Kegan Paul, 1986, pp. 156–182.
35 Bernard Smith, *Australian Painting 1788–1960*, Melbourne: Oxford University Press, 1962, p. 199.
36 Taylor specifically relates this to art, Taylor, *Art and the Woman*, p. 16.
37 Caroline Ambrus, *The Ladies' Picture Show: Sources on a Century of Australian Women Artists*, Sydney: Hale and Iremonger, 1984, pp. 24–25.
38 While London was also a key destination for Australian artists, it was far less bohemian or tolerant of homosexuality, see, Diana Souhami, *Wild Girls, Paris, Sappho and Art: The Lives and Loves of Natalie Barney and Romaine Brooks*, London: Weidenfeld and Nicholson, 2004, pp. 144–145.
39 Florence Tamagne, *A History of Homosexuality in Europe: Berlin, London, Paris, 1919–1939*, vol. 1, New York: Algora Publishing, 2004, pp. 20–21.
40 Mary Eagle, 'Australian Painters in France 1890s to 1920s', in Anne-Marie Nisbet and Maurice Blackman, eds, *The French-Australian Cultural Connection*, Sydney: University of New South Wales, 1984, pp. 197–198.
41 Juliette Peers, 'I Love Paris Every Moment: the Women Artists', in Karen Quinlan, ed., *The Long Weekend: Australian Artists in France 1918–1939*, exhibition catalogue, Bendigo: Bendigo Art Gallery, 2007, pp. 46–47.

42 Bertha Harris, 'The More Profound Nationality of their Lesbianism: Lesbian Society in Paris in the 1920s', in Phyllis Birkby et al., eds, *Amazon Expedition: A Lesbian Feminist Anthology*, Washington, NJ: Time Change Press, 1973, p. 79.
43 Shari Benstock, *Women of the Left Bank: Paris, 1900–1940*, London: Virago Press, 1987, pp. 47, 174.
44 ibid., p. 47.
45 ibid., p. 175.
46 Adrienne Rich, 'Compulsory Heterosexuality and Lesbian Existence', in Ann Snitow et al., eds, *Powers of Desire: The Politics of Sexuality*, New York: Monthly Review Press, 1983, pp. 177–205.
47 ibid., pp. 192–193.
48 ibid.
49 Erica Rand, 'Women and Other Women: One Feminist Focus for Art History', *Art Journal*, vol. 50, no. 2, (1991), pp. 29–31, 34 fn 17.
50 Elizabeth Ashburn, *Lesbian Art: An Encounter with Power*, Sydney: Craftsman House, 1996, p. 13, in the chapter titled *Fighting Invisibility*.
51 Karen Quinlan, *In a Picture Over the Sea: Agnes Goodsir 1864–1939*, exhibition catalogue, Bendigo: Bendigo Art Gallery, 1998, pp. 22–29.
52 ibid., p. 33.
53 ibid., pp. 12–16.
54 Referring to the Latin-quarter in Paris.
55 Agnes Goodsir, *The Parisienne*, c. 1924 (Paris), oil on canvas, 61.0 cm x 50.1 cm, National Gallery of Australia, purchased 1993, accession no NGA 93.5, available at, http://artsearch.nga.gov.au/Detail.cfm?IRN=169716, date accessed 20 October 2010.
56 Janet Cumbrae Stewart, *The Pastels of Cumbrae Stewart*, Melbourne: Alexander McCubbin, 1921.
57 *Janet Cumbrae Stewart: The Perfect Touch*, exhibition catalogue, Mornington: Mornington Peninsular Regional Gallery, 2003.
58 Pamela Gerrish Nunn, 'A View of One's Own: Female Artists and the Nude', *Australian and New Zealand Journal of Art*, vol. 1, no. 1 (2000), pp. 66–67.
59 Cumbrae Stewart, *The Pastels of Cumbrae Stewart*.
60 Roger Butler, *The Prints of Margaret Preston: A Catalogue Raisonné*, Canberra: National Gallery of Australia, 2005, p. 1.
61 ibid., p. 36 fn 3.
62 For an example, see, *Summer* 1915, in Elizabeth Butel, *Margaret Preston: The Art of Constant Rearrangement*, Melbourne: Viking in Association with the Art Gallery of New South Wales, 1986, p. 4; Deborah Edwards, *Margaret Preston*, Sydney: Art Gallery of New South Wales, 2005, p. 49.
63 Eric Mackay, *Love Letters of a Violinist, and Other Poems*, London: Walter Scott, 1893.
64 Edwards, *Margaret Preston*, p. 288 fn 31.
65 Butler, *The Prints of Margaret Preston*, p. 14.
66 Butel, *Margaret Preston*, pp. 21–22.
67 Janet Hawley, 'Thoroughly Modern Maggie', *Age (Good Weekend)*, 4 June 2005, p. 27.
68 Butel, *Margaret Preston*, p. 12.

69. Butler refers to it as 'rumour' and 'by no means certain'; see, Butler, *The Prints of Margaret Preston*, p. 36 fn 26. Edwards is more positive on the notion of Margaret and Bessie being lovers, see, Edwards, *Margaret Preston*, p. 288 fn 31.
70. Hawley, 'Thoroughly Modern Maggie', pp. 24–29.
71. Penelope Little, *A Studio in Montparnasse: Bessie Davidson, An Australian Artist in Paris*, Melbourne: Craftsman House, 2003, p. 78.
72. Sarah Thomas, 'Bessie in Paris', *Australian Book Review*, March 2004, p. 16.
73. Joan Kerr, ed., *Heritage: The National Women's Art Book, 500 Works by 500 Australian Women Artists from Colonial Times to 1955*, Sydney: Art and Australia, 1995, pp. 435–436.
74. Butel, *Margaret Preston*, p. 12.
75. Anne McDonald, 'Mary Cockburn-Mercer: The Epitome of the Modern Australian Woman', *Artonview*, vol. 26 (2001), p. 15.
76. Compton Mackenzie, *Extraordinary Women: Theme and Variations*, London: Martin Secker, 1928. Margaret was said to have lived next door to Compton with a character in the book being modelled on her.
77. McDonald, 'Mary Cockburn-Mercer', p. 16.
78. Mary Eagle and Jan Minchin, *The George Bell School: Students, Friends, Influences*, Melbourne: Deutscher Art Publications, 1981, p. 206.
79. Kerr, ed., *Heritage*, p. 405.
80. Mary Cockburn Mercer, *Two Women*, c. 1940, watercolour over pencil on buff paper, 23.8 cm x 27.0 cm, National Gallery of Victoria (NGV), Joseph Brown Collection, presented through the NGV Foundation by Dr Joseph Brown AO, OBE, Honorary life benefactor, 2004.
81. Unfortunately there is no web image for this painting but it is reproduced in, Kirsty Grant et al., *The Joseph Brown Collection at NGV Australia*, Melbourne: National Gallery of Victoria, 2004, p. 140.
82. Bruce Adams, *Rustic Cubism: Anne Dangar and the Art Colony at Moly-Sabata*, Chicago; London: University of Chicago Press, 2004, p. 15.
83. Helen Topliss, ed., *Earth, Fire, Water, Air: Anne Dangar's Letters to Grace Crowley, 1930–1951*, Sydney: Allen and Unwin, 2000.
84. Elena Taylor, *Grace Crowley: Being Modern*, Canberra: National Gallery of Australia, 2006, pp. 32–53.
85. Grace Crowley, *Les Baigneuses*, 1928 (Paris), oil on canvas on composition board, 45.2 cm x 64.2 cm, National Gallery of Australia, Gift of the artist 1979, Accession no. NGA 79.1272. The painting is available at, http://artsearch.nga.gov.au/Detail.cfm?IRN=57137, date accessed 21 October 2010.
86. Julie Lewis, 'A Biographical Study', in P. AE. Hutchings and Julie Lewis, eds, *Kathleen O'Connor: Artist in Exile*, Fremantle: Fremantle Arts Centre Press, 1987, pp. 22, 30, 28, 53.
87. ibid., pp. 42–46, 53–54, 60, 73, 90.
88. Janda Gooding, *Chasing Shadows: The Art of Kathleen O'Connor*, Perth: Art and Australia in Association with the Art Gallery of Western Australia, 1996, p. 8.
89. ibid., p. 118 fn 2.
90. Lewis, 'A Biographical Study', p. 13.
91. For a discussion of the lesbian influence on the nude, see, Nunn, 'A View of One's Own', pp. 71–77.

92　This was exemplified in 1921 when the UK Parliament attempted to criminalise lesbianism. See, *Parliamentary Debates*, House of Commons, 5th Series, vol. 145 (4 August 1921), pp. 1799, 1808; House of Lords, vol. 43, (15 August 1921), cc 567–577.
93　J. S. MacDonald, 'Feminism in Art', *The Bulletin*, 55, no. 2815, 24 January 1934, p. 5.
94　Cooper, *The Sexual Perspective*, p. 182; Ambrus, *Australian Women Artists*, pp. 150–152.
95　Martha Vicinus, 'Distance and Desire: English Boarding-School Friendships', *Journal of Women in Culture and Society*, vol. 9, no. 4 (1984), pp. 600–601.
96　Jo Darbyshire, 'Crushes, Kisses and Crossdressers: A Historical Positioning of Lesbian Artists', *Art Reading Material*, no. 9 (1993), p. 11.
97　Jo Darbyshire, Lesbian Community in Modernist Discourse, Graduate Diploma of Arts Thesis, Canberra Institute of the Arts, 1990, p. 6.
98　See, 'Lesbian Art and Artists', *Heresies: A Feminist Publication on Art and Politics*, no. 3 (1977), a ground breaking special edition devoted to *Lesbian Art and Artists*.
99　Melissa Miles, 'Whose Art Counts', *Art Monthly Australia*, no. 224 (October 2009), pp. 5–8.
100　Darbyshire, 'Lesbian Community in Modernist Discourse', p. 6.

The Bois of King Vic

Roberta Foster

In *The Drag King Book*, Del LaGrace Volcano investigates female-to-male (FTM) drag king scenes – which concern the gender performance of female-bodied people assuming masculine attire[1] – outside American and English centres. That Australia does not bear mention on his list reveals the understated position of local drag king culture within the international context. The following chapter pays critical attention to this imbalance and focuses upon the thriving drag king scene of Melbourne where it largely plays out at King Victoria (King Vic) drag nights.[2] This paper begins by considering some historical perspectives: it explores some Australian cases of gender play in order to locate a queer lineage from which contemporary drag kinging may draw influence. Informed by a series of oral interviews and king performances, the central thrust of the argument provides a theoretical investigation of the contemporary setting of drag king performance as a central component of Melbourne's lesbian community. The exchange of desire from audience to performer is situated as a powerful relationship that spurs important considerations of bodies, space and identity,[3] and international frameworks on gender performativity are applied to the Melbourne drag king scene in order to facilitate a critical awareness of these local subversive acts. The Melbourne drag king scene is a place where queer performances consolidate translesbian[4] subjectivity and where translesbian communities, in turn, develop and strengthen the queer agenda – a scene, certainly, that warrants exploration.

A Place in History

Surveying the existence of gender play and lesbian forums in local histories reveals not only a historical foundation for current drag king expression, but also the importance of such scenes in the development of community. While the documentation of FTM drag in the early to mid-twentieth century is scant, it can be uncovered. Male impersonators such as Ella Shields visually epitomise early twentieth century gender play and her presence at the Tivoli (along with other impersonators such as Nellie Cole) reveals a history of parodic gender performativity in Australia.[5] Certainly, for some, the conception of drag through the fifties, sixties and seventies took on an intimate form less concerned with conscious gender play than identity. For Jan Hillier (organiser in the 1970s of Pokey's gay bar), dressing in men's clothing was a 'fashion trend'[6] integrated into her self-identification as butch. For others, like Noel Tovey, dragging up was 'the ultimate gesture of defiance against the police'.[7] For these people, the drag act existed as a challenging gesture disconnected from identity politics. While motivating factors may be diverse, these expressions provide a structure of gender play from which contemporary drag kings might draw influence and with which they can construct a history.

Before going any further, it is important to acknowledge one problem with this kind of construction: that there is a danger of surveying history from a contemporary vantage point which harbours its own values and motivations. Certainly, the historicising of events and biographies from the past has resulted in certain perspectives or meanings being exalted, and others lost. However, in talking about gender play in Australia and its relationship to contemporary drag expression, I do not aim to introduce these stories or moments into a drag lineage and make them static within this constructed history. Nor do I not wish to reinscribe contemporary meanings upon these histories. Rather, I simply draw them into focus to illustrate how the contemporary drag king world may identify with earlier models and draw strength from their existence. Surveying moments of gender play in Australia within such a framework functions to create a space for biographies and events that are excluded from dominant modes of Australia's history telling.

Continuing the historical exploration, it is also important to acknowledge the colonial ties of Australia and Australia's permeability as a colonial nation. The historical documentations of gender play, as expressed by Shields, Cole and Hillier are, of course, indebted to the canonical English images of the Dandy and the 'mannish lesbian' or New Woman of the eighteenth and nineteenth centuries.[8] In contemporary Australia, the organiser of King Vic, Bumpy, has stated that the motivations for setting up this forum came from being exposed to a London drag king performance. This capacity for influence has been, and is, characteristic of Australian culture[9] and, in terms of gender fucking, evidently a useful one. Furthermore, Australia's colonial status may provide a key strength behind the dynamic gender play exhibited at King Vic. As Rachel Cook argues 'pioneering women tended to see femininity as a luxury'[10] and the devalued status of hyperfemininity has potentially trickled down through the generations. While this may not be as definitive as Cook contends, the convict element of colonialism can be irrevocably connected to gender play and lesbian history. Writing in the nineteenth century, Dr W. J. Irvine described the sexual relationships between 'normal' looking convict women and the 'pseudo-male' or 'man-woman' at Tasmania's Ross Female Depot.[11] It is thus the young status of Australia's nationhood, and colonial ties, that has perhaps fostered the richness of Melbourne's drag king community.[12]

The importance of the king community to Melbourne translesbian identification, which will be the focus of the next element of this chapter, bears one more connection to Australia's lesbian history. Through the 1950s Val's Coffee Lounge was a locus of Melbourne camp activity and its contribution to lesbian subjectivity and belonging is forcefully communicated through the words of its patrons. Val, the shop owner, recalls one customer telling her 'you absolutely saved my life… [Val's lounge meant] I would have somewhere that I could go where I felt I was somebody'.[13] How Val's coffee lounge aided the negotiation of personhood and a sense of being is certainly accentuated by Billie who states: 'I didn't know the word "lesbian" until I went to Val's Coffee Lounge. But if anyone asked me from there on if I was a lesbian, I'd say yes'.[14] Billie's self concept as a lesbian is integrally tied to her contact with Val's Coffee Lounge. Val's was evidently a place for identifying with other lesbians, and through this relationship, personal lesbian subjectivity was consolidated.

Dragging Up

These identity-forming processes are paralleled in the contemporary Melbourne drag scene. The following section will consider this scene as vital to the Melbourne translesbian community, and by analysing what we might consider the 'desiring audience', King Vic can be located as forming translesbian subjectivity and challenging hegemonic organisations of space and spectatorship.

King Vic was set up in June of 2000 by Bumpy and Tom Urge. Speaking of the response to their first drag king night Bumpy remarks, 'a lot of butch lesbians or whatever, or boy-identifying in some way lesbians, loved it… they were so hungry for something that… reflected themselves a bit'.[15]

For drag king, Aussie Boy, the King Vic scene is a thriving point of union for the community, for 'underneath the glued on moustaches… there is a sense of togetherness'.[16] Chic Magnet, another performer, confirms the radical impact King Vic made on the lesbian scene when she argues that drag 'has really opened the community'.[17] Indeed, from its beginnings in the new millennium, this kinging has provided, and continues to provide, an antithetical celebration to mainstream lesbian sexualities. Inside King Vic, gender-queer trans and butch-femme sexualities are a pulse to the performances.[18] This type of representation challenges a long history of exclusion by lesbian feminism in Australia – a type of political lesbianism lingering since the sixties and seventies[19] – which championed a singular sexuality separated from any practice imitating, or referencing, heterosexual sexual/social organisation.[20] Lucy, a patron of the king scene, argues that the performance element is important as she sees it as 'a recognition of types of lesbian desire – of butch/femme lesbian desire and butch/butch desire'.[21] King Vic, then, provided an important disjuncture to this trajectory of lesbian identification and still offers a space where trans and butch-femme gender play may find expression in Melbourne.

Performing Identity

Literary critic Debra Moddelmog writes that 'desire… is formed within all sorts of identity structurings'.[22] The reverse can also be true; through desire, subjectivity may take form. This premise can be applied to the drag king himself. Performing king, Justin Sider, discloses that dragging up can 'let out everything that had always remained buried'.[23] By staging masculinity, Sider was able to explore parts of his consciousness that would evolve into his concept of self. Sider's adoption of facial hair and male clothing, the binding down of his breasts and the process of packing are, in the words of Julie Hanson, 'the "signs" engaged with and employed by a body in order to literalise and enact its subjectivity'.[24] Hanson's claim that 'performing becomes synonymous with a certain lived and felt subjectivity and corporeality'[25] can certainly be transcribed on the experience of kinging for Sider, and perhaps other gender queer identifying kings. Through the manipulation of the 'signs' of the body Sider has, according to theorist Emily Apter, 'corpor/realised' his subjectivity.[26]

While excursions into masculinity are championed as a definitive element of king performances, King Vic is also a forum where the femme subject, often dissolved in butch-femme relations, is vocalised. As Sue-

Ellen Case explains 'the butch-femme couple inhabit the subject position together'.[27] According to Judith Halberstam, this coupling can frequently render the femme invisible, her lesbianism 'disidentified', because of the prolific assumptions about lesbian masculinity.[28] Some acts, such as those by Justin Sider, do replicate this type of coupling – in which femme queerness is rendered butch-dependent through the absence of speaking femme subjects in his performances. In a show in August 2007, 'Take a Look at my Girlfriend' (by Gym Class Heroes), Sider performed against the backdrop of three 'girlfriends', who each had a number 1, 2, 3 printed onto their tops. At moments in the performance one of the three 'girlfriends' turned around and Sider sang, to the audience 'take a look at my girlfriend, she's the only one I got, not much of a girlfriend, I never seem to get a lot', and following this, the 'girlfriend' walked off stage, without the opportunity to assume any interactive speaking role. In this organisation of stage and play, it was the queerness of Sider's masculinity which lent sexuality and subjectivity to the 'femme' girlfriends – a precise rendition of Halberstam critique of butch/femme coupling and its unequal deployment of lesbian identification.

The performances of Gwendolyne, however, are quite different. Her shows provide an antithesis to Sider's type of performance and decentralise the masculine-based queerness they propose. In some acts, Gwendolyne (coupled with another drag king), performs such songs as the Black Eyed Peas' 'Pump It', where she dresses in high femme attire (including a wig) and assumes the female singing part. In these roles Gwendolyne does not actualise her lesbian subjectivity through the adoption of masculinity but is one of the most popular 'femmes' to perform at King Vic. In another act, Gwendolyne does a duet with a drag queen, in which both perform to a Britney Spears song and where the femme position is doubly assumed in a femme and queen extravaganza. Gwendolyne also explores her off-stage femme subjectivity on stage when she performs as a king in the outfit 'Dykes to Men'. Not only does Gwendolyne, then, succeed in making space for femme identities on stage she also reveals, and consolidates, a flexibility within her presumed monolithic femininity, a dimensionality that is often not accorded the femme position in lesbian cultures. These King Vic performances acknowledge feminine versions of same-sex desire and decouple Halberstam's femme/butch dyad by exploring independent femme desire. In this way, Gwendolyne's acts help to secure a public position for femme subjectivity in the Australian queerlesbian community.

The Desiring Audience

These self-concept forming processes of the desired drag king/femme performer are extended to the audience who observe such performances. Writing on discourses of desire, Tara Pauliny states that 'the relationship between the king, her act, and the audience mimics that of the writer, text and reader';[29] it is the audience which helps to 'create meaning' in the drag king setting.[30] For those who watch, the drag king becomes a site of desire – they constitute the 'desiring audience'. This desire is multi-faceted and needs careful deconstruction. First, in desiring the body of the king in a sexual sense, the audience member corporeally experiences her lesbian/queer subjectivity. This type of exchange can be no truer than the desire accorded Melbourne heart-throb, Rocco D'Amore, whose sex-imbued performances have transformed him into a icon of the antipodean drag king world. Furthermore, in the drag king scene it is the gender ambiguity of kinging that can be seen as a key factor for the desiring audience. For the audience, the 'double body' of the female king, that is being simultaneously masculine and feminine in exterior and interior, works, in the words of Alexandra Warwick and Deni Cavallaro, at arresting the 'flow of the gaze whilst simultaneously stimulating it, by provoking and increasing the desire for discovery and possession, hence effecting a magnification of the erotic'.[31] Saturated in the visceral experience of lesbian (and/or queer) desire, King Vic works like Val's Coffee Lounge, offering a space where lesbian subjectivity is corporeally sanctified in a way which constructs and sustains the Australian translesbian community.

The second element of the desiring audience considers a subjectivity which transcends, and complicates, the traditional exchange of sexual desire between performer and patron. Recalling her experience as a drag show audience member, Alan Kumbier writes that she simultaneously wanted 'to be them and fuck them'.[32] She goes on to explain that 'female fans are empowered with the knowledge that we, too, can possess that dick, can become the performing subjects of our desire'.[33] This is transference of subjectivity: the audience member inhabits, through consumption of the show, the body of the drag king and sometimes become kings themselves. Jess, also known as Bust Herr, says that, since seeing a drag performance in Sydney many years ago, he 'wanted to be up there, to be that'.[34] It is important to note that this adoption of roles does not often go 'full circle'; for some, such as for audience member Rachel Valentine, the mere fantasy landscape of what Torr and Czyzselska call becoming 'more than [what] a conventional gender role permits',[35] is for her, 'simply enough'.[36] In the words of Judith Butler, by 'taking the body as a point of departure for an articulation that is not always constrained by the body',[37] the audience inhabits the stage, a realm in which, through *disembodiment*, they may embody different gender subjectivities.

Before turning to a consideration of how queer is developed in the drag king scene, one more idea surrounding the relationship between performer and audience begs attention. The King Vic space exists as a potent arena where hegemonic arrangements of gaze and spectatorship are challenged. According to film theorist Laura Mulvey, 'pleasure in looking'[38] is historically constructed along the dualisms of active/male and passive/female. This organisation of 'looking' dispossesses and dislocates; beneath the male gaze 'she', to quote Mary Anne Caws, 'can neither speak nor think... she may be lit or framed, but she is not whole'.[39] Modes of seeing in lesbian/queer communities constitute an opposition to this power divide. The theatre of drag king acts, especially their performance at Opium Den King Vic nights, creates for Australian lesbian communities, in the words of Jan Goulden, a 'public arena where an ideological transaction'[40] between audience and performer might take place. This exchange, especially in how closely it relates to the layered passions already explored, excludes the sexist [male] gaze[41] and authors a subjectivity birthed, from what Jill Dolan describes as, 'a new economy of desire'.[42] By partaking of this economy the audience members of King Vic transcend the traditional subject-object division of spectatorship. In King Vic, Mulvey's analysis of the female spectator as the transvestite viewer is rid of its pejorative connotations; for it is the transvestite, the butch and the femme, the trans, the poofter fags and sissy dykes who constitute a radical spectatorial community.[43]

Theory in the Physical

Following on from considerations of community, audience, desire and spectatorship, King Vic can also be framed as a space where queer is formulated. The politics of queer, especially in its deconstruction of gender, finds a suitable platform at King Vic, because of its centralisation around lesbian and trans experience and its performative 'fucking' with gender on stage. The lesbian subject is in a position, to quote Dolan again, 'to denaturalise dominant codes by signifying an existence that belies the structure of heterosexual culture and its representations'.[44] Lesbian and trans people are what gender theorist Jason Cromwell terms 'fearful Others'[45] as they challenge traditional concepts of fe/maleness. King Vic, then, provides a space for those already on the sexual and gender borderlands to be involved in a performance-based ethic which subverts the social order by presenting people who approximate other genders, but never fully become them. Current King Vic drag king, Koko Ma$$, presents this intermediate place between genders in one performance where she assumes masculine attire and body language for the duration of the song (passing considerably) but concludes her show by undoing her shirt to reveal her bound breasts beneath.

Similar segues into gender ambivalence are perpetuated by the stunning acts of Maniacal Hutchence. In a 2008 performance, Maniacal sang a male cover of 'I am Woman', the deep drawl of the vocals enhanced by his suave swagger and costume. The performance's seemingly analogous arrangement of gender markers was radically undermined by one detail – Maniacal's shirt was unbuttoned to reveal a lacy bra encasing voluptuous fake breasts. Any lateral organisations of sex and gender continued to be unravelled throughout the show. At one point Maniacal pulls from his pants his drag king bulge, a long red balloon, twisting it into a U shape and reuniting it with his crutch – this time as his vulva. The shows' enigmatic gender fucking reached a climax at the song's last line 'I am Woman'. Maniacal throws his fake breasts into the audience, removes his sunglasses to reveal painted eyelids beneath and then proceeds to wipe away the glittering make-up and facial hair. In this act, Maniacal waltzes without any definite gender identity – stepping towards the audience with a female marker, only to immediately withdraw it. As this playful to and fro heightens, its radical possibilities are magnified, until in a final flourish, Maniacal abandons all significations. Phallus is deserted, breasts are discarded, make-up and moustache are removed and Maniacal completes the miming of his lyrics; standing for one brief moment outside of the song, inside a body released from the gender markers which had, three minutes ago, defined it. These non-passing 'dangerous actors' of King Vic present a lived experience of queer, revealing the arbitrary relationship between the signifier and the signified in gendered organisations of dress and demeanor.

In the masquerade of both femininity and masculinity, King Vic engages with the queer agenda. Here, gender is revealed to Judith Butler's words, as a 'persistent impersonation'[46] socially constructed as real. Elviro, a performer at King Vic, can be seen as corporeally investigating theories such as Luce Irigaray's notion of mimesis, where the effects of phallocentric discourse on womanhood are *undone* through their *overdoing*.[47] Elviro frequents the King Vic stage with the markers of femininity pushed to the extreme; adorned in wigs, flamboyant makeup and stilettos. Her femininity, however, is not played out in the same celebratory manner as Gwendolyne's. On the contrary, Elviro often performs to heavy raw songs and presents characters that synchronise with their guttural qualities as she draws both her protagonists, and the attentive audience, through pain, grief, sorrow... even murderous rage. Elviro's hyperfeminine aesthetic, which she sometimes assumes while on stage, aligns her performances with Irigaray's notion of mimicry – that conscious display, the repeated 'doing' of gender.

The emotional potency of Elviro's acts means, however, that her mimicry is not lost to the trappings of gender binaries, with the disturbing atmosphere evoked further rendering her deconstruction efficacious. Masculinity is played out in a similar way during one of Bumpy's early performances at King Vic. A duet between himself and another masculine drag king concluded with Bumpy eating his partner's penis – a vegan sausage. King Vic's 'kinged up' drag acts show that, in the words of Judith Halberstam, 'masculinity does not belong to men'[48] and certainly, in the eating of the penis, Bumpy reduces this ultimate sign of dominant masculinity and power to the consumable – inside the King Vic community the phallus becomes a fallacy.

Finally, King Vic's adaptation of queer provides local Australian access to this intellectualised political framework, and carves a distinct place for translesbian communities in what is a traditionally gay-male dominated definition of 'homosexuality'. According to Tasmin Wilton, 'the contemporary queer/lesbian and gay subcultural infrastructure is dominated by economically privileged gay men',[49] and this is certainly true in an Australian context, where white gay men receive the social benefits not accorded female/trans and/or Indigenous counterparts. The translesbian community is strengthened through the vehicle of queer, and according to audience member Alicia, queer politics are 'sustained within the pulsing environment of drag king performativity'.[50] Drag Kings' subversive dealings with gender testifies that camp and queer narratives are no longer part of a cultural sensibility only available to male homosexuality and, also, that these themes do not only exist within the postmodern framework of Western academia, but as an integral lived experience of Australia's translesbian community.

In Conclusion...

Gender performativity in Australia can be historically documented, extending back to settlement and, as this chapter proposes, related to colonisation and convict histories. In this rich history, female adaptations of gender are, for some, a self-conscious radical play; for others they are an integrated expression of identity. Whatever the motivations, these types of gender excursions provide a historical framework with which to view the contemporary Melbourne drag king scene at King Vic. Drag kinging in Melbourne is an integral component of the sustainability of the local translesbian community. Through performance, it is the performers and the audience, both teetering on the edge of sexual and gender limits, which construct subjectivity, and community, through an exchange of a multifaceted desire. This community is a place where new concepts of spectatorship are negotiated and in which queer becomes a lived experience in Melbourne. King Vic is a site where subjectivity, bodies, space and spectatorship are radically reinscribed: challenges which are integral to the Melbourne translesbian community, and indeed, vital to the diversification of Australian culture.[51]

Endnotes

1   This type of description does not assume the gender or sexual identity of the performers considered in this paper and 'he' will be used as a generic pronoun in order to respect on stage, and off stage, identifications. LaGrace Volcano and Judith Halberstam are considered the pioneers of drag king theory in the international scene producing photographic and literary commentaries on kinging.

2   King Victoria has been the first systematised drag king performance night in Melbourne. Established in 2000, its key organiser is Bumpy and the venue for its duration had been Star, recently re-named the Opium Den.

3   Drag king space is a site in which issues of race are explored, although this chapter is too narrow a forum to investigate these issues. For further discussions, see, Judith Halberstam, 'Mackdaddy, Superfly, Rapper: Gender, Race, and Masculinity in the Drag King Scene', *Social Text*, no. 52/53 (1997), pp. 104–131.

4   The term 'translesbian' was developed by Bumpy to explain the intersections between lesbian and trans communities (namely to female-to-male) and the overlap of identities, genders and sexualities that occur within this diverse community.

5   Frank Van Straten, *Tivoli*, South Melbourne: Lothian, 2003.

6   Chris Beck, 'On the Couch: Interview with Jan Hillier (Gay Entrepreneur)', *Age*, 7 December 1996.

7   Noel Tovey, *Little Black Bastard: A Story of Survival*, Sydney: Hodder, 2004, p. 121.

8   Carroll Smith-Rosenberg, 'Discourses of Sexuality and Subjectivity: The New Woman, 1870–1936', in Martin Duberman et al., eds, *Hidden From History: Reclaiming the Gay and Lesbian Past*, London; Ringwood, Vic.: Penguin, 1991, pp. 264–280.

9   Ian McLean has argued that across history non-Aboriginal Australians have consistently sought to 'negotiate a subjectivity' as a result of the status of Australia as a colonial nation. This is done, he argues, 'by either purloining the identity of their origin, or by seeking a new nativism sprung from a *terra nullius*'. The traditional dependency on England, or new alliances to America, for example, are an expression of this struggle for

identity and a key element of Australia's cultural permeability. Ian McLean, 'Gordon Bennett's Existentialism', in Ian McLean and Gordon Bennett, eds, *The Art of Gordon Bennett*, Roseville East, NSW: Craftsman House, 1996, pp. 65–71.

10 Rachel Cook, 'An Interview with Judith Halberstam', *Slit Magazine*, p. 28.

11 Kay Daniels, *Convict Women*, St Leonards, NSW: Allen and Unwin, 1998, pp. 165–166.

12 This analysis of history can of course be seen as aiding king communities in other parts of Australia, however, as this chapter considers the microcosm of King Vic, Melbourne becomes the point of reference in this discussion.

13 Ruth Ford, 'Val: The Interview', in *The Travelling Mind of Val Eastwood*, Melbourne: Australian Lesbian and Gay Archives (ALGA), 2010.

14 Billie, interview with Lucy Chesser, 31 March 1993, ALGA Collection.

15 Bumpy and Lee Bruce Lee, interview with Daniel Vaughan, 21 September 2001, ALGA collection.

16 Sally, also known as Aussie Boy, interview with Daniel Vaughan, 29 September 2001, ALGA collection.

17 Chic Magnet, interview with Daniel Vaughan, 13 October 2001, ALGA collection.

18 King Lee Bruce Lee states that 'the transgender element is really important as well, King Victoria has always pushed that side of it, to not be afraid'. See, Bumpy and Lee Bruce Lee, interview with Daniel Vaughan, 21 September 2001.

19 While radical feminism has its roots in English and American feminism, Australian radical feminism developed slightly later. The inclusion of radical feminist politics at institutions such as Melbourne University (where Sheila Jeffrey researches and teaches) and the existence of websites such as http://www.the-fury.net/ (a young radical lesbian source) show radical feminism's still-relevant position today.

20 Judith Roof, '1970s Lesbian Feminism Meets 1990s Butch-Femme', in Sally R. Munt and Cherry Smyth, eds, *Butch/Femme: Inside Lesbian Gender*, London: Cassell, 1998, pp. 28–29.

21 Jess also known as Bust Herr and Lucy De Kretser, 15 October 2007.

22 Debra Moddelmog, *Reading Desire: In Pursuit of Ernest Hemingway*, Ithaca: Cornell University Press, 1999, p. 5.

23 Justin Sider, interview with Bree Taber, 23 February 2008.

24 Julie Hanson, 'Drag Kinging: Embodied Acts and Acts of Embodiment', *Body and Society*, vol. 13, no. 1 (2007), p. 74.

25 ibid.

26 Emily Apter, 'Acting Out Orientalism: Sapphic Theatricality in Turn-of-Century Paris', in Elin Diamond, ed., *Performance and Cultural Politics*, London: Routledge, 1996, p. 23.

27 Sue-Ellen Case, *Feminism and Theatre*, USA: Routledge, 1994, p. 34.

28 Judith Halberstam, 'Between Butches', in Munt and Smyth, eds, *Butch/Femme*, pp. 57–58.

29 Tara Pauliny, 'Erotic Arguments and Persuasive Acts: Discourses of Desire and the Rhetoric of Female-to-Male Drag', *Journal of Homosexuality*, vol. 43, no. 3/4 (2002), p. 229.

30 ibid., p. 231.

31 Alexandra Warwick and Dani Cavallaro, *Fashioning the Frame: Boundaries, Dress and the Body*, Oxford; New York: Berg Publishers, 1998, p. xxi.

32 Alana Kumbier, 'One Body, Some Genders: Drag Performances and Technologies', in Donna Troka et al., eds, *The Drag King Anthology*, New York: Harrington Park Press, 2002, pp. 197–198.
33 ibid.
34 Bust Herr and De Kretser, 15 October 2007.
35 Diane Torr and Jane Czyzselska, 'Drag Kings and Subjects', in Nina Rapi and Maya Chowdhry, eds, *Acts of Passion: Sexuality, Gender and Performance*, New York: The Haworth Press, 1998, pp. 237–238.
36 Rachel Valentine, interview with Roberta Foster, 18 August 2007.
37 Judith Butler, *Undoing Gender*, New York: Routledge, 2004, p. 28.
38 Laura Mulvey, 'Visual Pleasure and Narrative Theatre', *Screen*, vol. 16, no. 3 (1975), p. 11.
39 Mary Anne Caws, *The Surrealist Look: An Erotics of Encounter*, Cambridge, MA: The MIT Press, 1997, p. 54.
40 Jan Goulden, 'From Stage to Screen and Back: Tash Fairbanks' *Nocturne* Shedding Some Light on Lesbian Representation, and the Performance of Lesbian Desire', in Rapi and Chowdhry, eds, *Acts of Passion*, pp. 146–147.
41 K. Davy, 'Constructing the Spectator: Reception, Context, and Address in Lesbian Performance', *Performing Arts Journal*, vol. 29 (1986), p. 48.
42 Jill Dolan, 'Desire Cloaked in a Trenchcoat', *The Drama Review*, vol. 33 (1989), p. 64.
43 Laura Mulvey, *The Cinema Book* (Classical Film Narrative), 2nd edn, London: BFI, 1989.
44 Jill Dolan, *The Feminist Spectator as Critic*, Ann Arbor, MI: University of Michigan Press, 1988, p. 116.
45 Jason Cromwell, 'Fearful Others: Medico-Psychological Constructions of Female-Male Trangenderism', in Dallas Denny, ed., *Current Concepts in Transgender Identity*, New York: Garland Publishing, 1998, pp. 120–121.
46 Judith Butler, *Gender Trouble: Feminism and the Subversion of Identity*, New York: Routledge, 1990, p. 30.
47 Tori Moi, *Sexual/Textual Politics: Feminist Literary Theory*, London: Methuen, 1985, p. 140.
48 Judith 'Jack' Halberstam, *Female Masculinity*, Durham: Duke University Press, 1998, p. 139.
49 Tasmin Wilton, *Lesbian Studies: Setting an Agenda*, London: Routledge, 1995, p. 17.
50 Alicia, interview with Roberta Foster, 30 October 2007.
51 The consideration of King Victoria community with the broader Australian cultural setting is one area for potential future research.

Friends and Lovers

Social Networks and Homosexual Life in War-time Queensland, 1938–1948

Yorick Smaal

In early July 1945, Walter,[1] a 40-year-old piano-playing cook of medium build was tried in Brisbane's Supreme Court on one count of sodomy. He was charged with having carnal knowledge against the order of nature with Marvin, a clerk of 13. After four hours of deliberation, the jury was unable to agree on a verdict and the matter was adjourned. Walter was released on bail and required to appear for retrial at the next criminal sittings in August that year. He never showed. A warrant was issued for his arrest, but Walter managed to avoid the authorities, remaining at large for the next three years. His capture in 1948 signalled an end to his run of luck, and when he finally appeared before a second jury, Walter, now 43, was found guilty as charged. In that trial, the Crown Prosecutor alluded to Walter's 'association with criminals and undesirables' including a number of 'convicted sexual perverts'.[2] This claim was refuted by the Defence Counsel. The judge requested further evidence on the matter and the Criminal Investigation Branch hurriedly put together a report on the defendant and his known friends and acquaintances.

The relationship between Walter and Marvin lies at the centre of this particular coterie. The two met at Marvin's place of employment in early 1942 and began a haphazard sexual relationship, consummated on and off at movie theatres and various locations throughout the Central Business District. In mid-1944, the two lost contact for some time before they renewed their acquaintance later that year. Around August or September at his South Brisbane flat, Walter introduced his young friend to another associate, Henry, a 40-something violin-playing piano-tuner who had six convictions between 1941 and 1944 for the sexual assault of pre-pubescent boys. He and Walter had been associates since meeting in Toowoomba on the Darling Downs, many years earlier. The records are unclear on whether Walter and Marvin picked up their sexual relationship immediately where they left off, although we can be sure that on or about the first Tuesday in November 1944, the older man and the youth went for a drink before retiring to Walter's flat in South Brisbane, ostensibly for tea and cards. At about 9 pm that evening, Walter put his arms around Marvin's waist and pulled him onto the bed. He rolled the lad onto his back and switched out the light.

Later that month, Walter and Marvin each found themselves separately involved with another young man, a brown-haired, blue-eyed, 17-year-old named Donald. Walter became sexually involved with Donald after meeting him on Stanley Street, South Brisbane. Marvin and Donald became friends after Marvin (either unintentionally or deliberately – it is unclear whether he had knowledge of Walter and Donald's involvement) introduced himself to Donald at Lennon's Hotel where his new-found companion worked as a drinks' waiter. In his statement to police, made in January 1945, Donald wrote:

> About three months ago I was working as a drink waiter [sic], and I met a boy there named [Marvin], and he used to drink in the lounge at dinner time, and one night he asked me to meet him at the Eternal Flame opposite central station, I went there that night and met [Marvin] who introduced me to a lot of other boys, and I relised [sic] by their talk that they were queens. From that night I started to go to the Flame pretty often and some nights I would go up to Wicam terrace… [sic][3]

The drinks' waiter began soliciting Australian and American soldiers by the Flame before taking the servicemen for a tram-ride to a haunt in the bushes behind the Rainworth tram terminus, where he obligingly performed oral and anal sex.

In December 1944, about one month after they had first met, Marvin and Donald ran into each other on Wickham Terrace (either by chance or assignation), most likely at Wickham Park which was a well-known beat, and the two headed off to the Canberra Hotel on the corner of Ann and Edward streets. Here, Marvin introduced Donald to another friend of his, Joseph, a broadly-built, 49-year-old auditor with a fresh complexion, dark grey hair and blue eyes. That afternoon, the three planned a camping holiday to Palm Beach on the Gold Coast. Away on vacation about one month later, Donald and Joseph took off their shorts one evening and became intimate: Donald fucked Joseph on the top bunk as Marvin listened in, the phrase '[n]aughty, naughty' echoing from the bed below.[4] On returning to Brisbane from their Gold Coast getaway, Joseph secured employment for his younger friend at McWhirter's Department store. He also provided his telephone number and gave Donald a gold cygnet ring.

Joseph also wrote to Donald. This startling piece of evidence, filed among the depositions, and hidden for the last 60 years, gives us a rarely glimpsed insight into the homosexual opportunities available in war-time Brisbane. It reads:

> Things have been happening since I left you at ferry, that young Air Force chap was up at corner of house afterwards, I happened to go out again to the local shop, but did not speak to him. [H]e was all smiles. Next morning got off ferry at town side, I was later than usual, and behold[,] he was standing there on the town side of the ferry: all smiles again[.] I was with some other chaps so never stopped. [H]e sure has been so attentive, and last night I went to town with the intention of going to News Reel, and damn me if he isn't at corner Edward St and Queen St, with 2 other Air Force lads, so more smiles, well can you guess what a botheration I felt[.] [I]t was embarrassing. [H]e is so attentive and my being not interested, as I told you before when I saw him. If only we could all be shuffled up and really sorted out properly, there would be a lot more happier people [sic].
>
> On top of this at lunch yesterday, at my usual café, another Air Force chap came in, really stunning too, sat opposite me and he just wasted no time being really nice, he is just back from completing his course on Canada, he was at Coolangatta on Sunday, but expects to be going down to Sydney, guess I was hard, I didn't raise his hopes, in spite of the hints. Perhaps you really may know how I feel, but it was some day. [W]hether I looked extremely 'it' yesterday I really don't know, but it was certainly an unusual bright day for being in the boom. [W]hat would you do [?] Loyalty to something is much you know [sic].[5]

The letter is undated, unaddressed and unsigned, but the supporting evidence clearly identifies the author and recipient even if it is difficult to know whether Joseph and Donald were friends or lovers at the time it was written. The second last sentence reads like a friend seeking advice rather than a question one lover would ask another, although the last sentence is telling of Joseph's affection and devotion to someone, possibly Donald, especially given the obvious and tantalising availability of other encounters.

There are two final nodes in our network. Both involve Walter, the piano-playing cook. In early February 1945, Walter invited an old associate Ernest along with an Indonesian man, Harold, to share his bed at his South Brisbane flat, presumably for a *ménage à trois*. When they awoke the next morning, Harold discovered that £70 had been stolen from the pocket of the pants he had slung over the back of a chair the evening before. Exactly what happened next is unclear, although we do know that the police later recovered Harold's money from none other than his fellow bed mate, Ernest, a known 'sexual pervert' who apparently produced the tightly-packed notes from his anus after being confronted by the authorities. The final thread in the web involves Walter's attempts to solicit a 13-year-old boy behind a butcher's shop in suburban Brisbane, where he enticed the youth with a 'nude photograph' of Ginger Rogers and Fred Astaire.

This remarkable urban network allows us a window into a broader, multiplex male-centred world; one encompassing adults and adolescents, civilians and servicemen, and Australians and Americans. Taken with other extant evidence – namely, contemporary criminal depositions (both part of, and separate to, the central cohort described here), police and government files, newspaper reports, and a limited number of oral histories – this particular Brisbane case study elucidates some of the processes that informed, enabled and sustained a sense of common identity. This group of friends and lovers met in public bars and on Brisbane streets; they enacted social scripts in public space; used indecent images to solicit others; made mutual friends; went on holidays together; wrote letters, gave gifts and found others employment. And while there are a number of congruent processes at play here, it is those influenced most acutely by home-front realities that reveal the characteristics of Queensland's contemporary subculture. The overwhelming presence of American servicemen (and local military personnel), male uses of public space, the prominence of intergenerational relationships, and, the exchange of visual imagery, came together to produce a sense of self that would continue in the post-war era. Drawing comparisons to other contemporary Australian urban centres, particularly Melbourne, allows us to extrapolate beyond state boundaries, gesturing to wider national patterns.

The following analysis attempts to recover some of the social and cultural processes that helped define male homosexual life in Queensland in the World War II years and beyond. In particular, it focuses on those who understood themselves to be part of an exclusive social world; those camp men who extracted a sense of self from their communion with others of the same sex. In doing so, this chapter argues that the pre-liberation era did not forge a cohort of powerless and miserable actors blighted by inequality; rather, it reveals a group of individuals who developed coping strategies to operate successfully within the confines which cast them as outlaws and deviants.

Australian and American Servicemen

When American servicemen began arriving in Queensland in late 1941, many women, and, for that matter, adolescent girls, found the exotic allure of these well-mannered, smartly-dressed and affluent foreign men in uniform hard to resist. Joseph's letter to Donald provides a fascinating insight into the potential parallels of homosexual encounters. Reliable estimates suggest that somewhere around 2 million American servicemen passed through Queensland between late 1941 and 1945, and it is possible that at least 80,000 and as many as 200,000 American servicemen in Queensland were homosexual, or at least inclined towards male-to-male sex.[6] A small, but persuasive body of work on homosexuality and the Australian armed forces indicates that ostensibly heterosexual service personnel also participated in male-to-male situational sex, alongside those who preferred the exclusive sexual and social company of men. As Garry Wotherspoon explains, 'homosexually-inclined men who wished to fight did in fact get into the forces'.[7] They did so by keeping 'that aspect of their life hidden; in the terminology of the time, they acted "square"'.[8] His observations are supported by Clive Moore, who argues that men from the camp subculture willingly enlisted in the services.[9]

There are 21 incidents from the Queensland court records between 1939 and 1948 involving combinations of civilians, soldiers, sailors and airman. One of the best examples involves Vernon, a 25-year-old Australian soldier, with a medium build, fair complexion, brown hair and grey eyes. He had an affair with Jack, an American soldier whose details remain unknown. In his statement to police, Vernon wrote:

> About the middle of December, 1943, I met an American soldier named [Jack]… in the bar of the Grand Central Hotel, Queen Street, Brisbane.

> We had a few drinks and got into conversation. We had dinner together that night at the Belle Vue Hotel, and we became friends. About a week later I met him again at the Grand Central Hotel. We had some drinks, and had tea at the Marie Theresa Café. We then went down… into a side laneway. I cannot remember just where the laneway was. As we walked along the street we were holding hands, and we both seemed to know what was what. I knew that [Jack] was a queen. After we went into the laneway, we put our arms around each other and hugged each other.[10]

They dated frequently after this, often enjoying drinks together, or taking in a show. Nothing of a sexual nature transpired again until mid-May 1944. By then, young Vernon had left the army and taken residence in Astor Terrace, where the men became intimate once more. Soon after, Vernon moved again, and it was here that Jack came to live with his Australian lover, staying five nights a week for almost two months, before both men were finally arrested by police.

Arguably, the war changed the nature of the Australian camp scene. Interactions between the soldiers who took their pleasures where they could find them, and those men happy to meet their comrades' requirements, must have exposed an uninitiated, although unquantifiable group of men, to new sexual pleasures and cultural experiences. For some, this exposure informed and confirmed their sense of sexual self. And while the war did not impact upon the development of a homosexual subculture in Queensland in the same way it did in major cities in the United States, the arrival of US servicemen edified local experiences.

Moore argues that some of the American troops would have been camp when they arrived in Queensland, and as Wotherspoon explains, these men would have fitted into the subculture here, passing on information about bar life in large American cities such as San Francisco, New York and Chicago.[11] The adoption of an American vernacular by some Queensland men is one clue which suggests that the American influence lingered long after the troops had departed. The term 'fruit', for example, which was part of the terminology circulating in Los Angeles hotels during the late 1930s, was adopted from the 'cultural baggage' imported by US troops.[12] The American phrase 'blow-job' also appears in the records in 1944; picked up by our Australian soldier Vernon:

> we have done 'Blow-jobs' for each other on a fifty-fifty basis. I mean by this that sometimes he sucks me off and sometimes I suck him off.

When he comes in my mouth I spit it out and I have seen him doing the same thing.[13]

'Cock-sucker' also appears to have entered the Australian lexicon during the war, and the words 'fairy' and 'queer', self-imposed labels by American homosexual men, were also used here by visiting servicemen.[14]

Public Space and Camp Infrastructure

It is well recognised that public space has been a defining feature of modern homosexual subcultures.[15] Donald's testimony indicates that the Eternal Flame was important landmark for like-minded men in wartime Brisbane and this is borne out by other court material. The oral evidence of Errol, another contemporary Brisbane teenager, also supports Donald's claims. It was on the steps of the Shrine that Errol first met his friend, 'Diana', and while he was unaware at the time that it was a beat, he remarks with hindsight that it was aptly named 'because it was "like moths gathering around a flame"', a reference to its popularity among homosexual men.[16] It is tantalising to speculate whether Errol might potentially have been part of the network detailed here: was he in fact one of the 'young queens' Marvin introduced in late 1944? We do know that Errol was part of another contemporary (effeminate) network involving men known as 'Gladys', 'Diana' and 'Christine de Winter'. This group shared literature, such Noel Langley's English novel, *There's a Porpoise Close Behind Us*, and participated in more complex rituals on the streets of Brisbane.[17] Errol calls these practices 'carrying on', an attitude that was 'all fluttery, and high pitched and sending up'.[18] He remembers that his friends used to delight in 'send ups', often in front of family and friends. They'd clap their hands and say, 'up you go Mary… up you go Mary, up to the chandelier, dear'.[19]

Other public spaces were also an integral part of male-only networks. Donald's forays to 'Wicam terrace' were most likely to Wickham Park, one of Brisbane's oldest beats. Nearby Albert Park also operated during and beyond the 1940s; the Botanical Gardens next to the Parliament House were a favourite haunt for heterosexual and homosexual liaisons alike, and the North Quay precinct, including the William Street bus-shed and Victoria Bridge, appear repeatedly in the records.[20]

Added to this were a number of commercial venues. Like other establishments in Sydney, Melbourne, and Adelaide, they were not homosexually-exclusive, but nonetheless provided a range of raffish and demi-monde settings for camp men to gather with other unconventional folk; to exchange ideas, to gossip, and to generally find fellowship with other men and women who pursued alternative lifestyles. Moore has detailed a number of Brisbane establishments including the infamous Pink Elephant café along with other less prominent venues such as Littleboys café, the Colony Club, Christies, and Casa Mara.[21] We can add to these the Dingle Dell tearooms, 'situated in the City Buildings, Edward Street', where the proprietor, Paul, took young air-force men for tea,[22] and the Marie Theresa café, where Vernon and his American lover had a romantic outing in late December 1943.

Public bars were also part of camp infrastructure on the home-front, but unlike the gay-specific venues of large American cities during the period, Australian establishments were mixed venues which brought together a patchy, but male-only clientele.[23] Even so, the camp community recognised their utility for social gatherings and sexual pick-ups even if, as one contemporary observed, you had to watch your 'Ps and Qs' around other patrons.[24] There were reputed bars in both Sydney and Melbourne, and a host of establishments in Brisbane, located in and around Queen and George streets. The most popular of these was the Grand Central Hotel, where Vernon and Jack met. Others included Lennon's, where Donald was employed, the Long Bar at the Criterion, the Circular Bar at Her Majesty's, the Grisham, and perhaps the Windsor Hotel.[25]

On entering these bars, a clear division between the crowds was evident to the astute observer. The camp men would meet in one spot and squares would congregate in another. The two spheres remained separate until closing time when, as Errol recalled, you could 'always [find] a bit of trade from the straight section that you could drag up to your net'.[26] Clearly, trade was more likely to sidle up to the camp end of the bar after imbibing their fill of drink, less concerned than they otherwise would have been about the implications. A close reading of the sources discloses that alcohol was a factor in about one-third of the cases examined here. It could be used to mitigate any potential resistance from the object of one's desires, especially where adolescents were concerned, but it also acted as a social lubricant for others, allowing some men to act on feelings they usually kept repressed or hidden. In these circumstances, drinking was used by defendants to excuse, or at least explain, their activities if they were caught. 'I have managed through the use of a bit of will power to control myself', one Brisbane man recorded in a typical statement from 1942, but 'when I have a few drinks that sort of thing always comes over me'.[27]

Intergenerational Relationships

The relationships between Joseph and Donald and Walter and Marvin suggest that meaningful interaction between older and younger men was not uncommon on the Queensland home-front. Detailed analysis of the criminal depositions shows that at least seven youths under the age of 17 were indicted on charges of male-to-male sexual activity. Information from the 'Report of the Commissioner of Police' indicates that in the four years between 1945–1946 and 1948–1949, juveniles under the age of 21 committed around one-fifth of sex offences.[28] And if we examine the age of all complainants (where they exist) for offences of sodomy, attempted sodomy, and gross indecency between 1939 and 1948, we find that more than one quarter were boys aged between 14 and 16, with a further nine young men aged between 17 and 19. These figures exclude the indecent treatment of boys under 14 and as Walter himself noted, age was an important factor in finding an apposite same-sex partner. Before introducing his piano-tuner friend, he told Marvin: 'H[enry] has got himself into trouble. It's his own fault. If he wants to play around with boys who can't blow, he deserves what he got'.[29]

This is not to suggest that boys could who 'blow', to borrow Walter's phraseology, were complicit in homosexual activity, nor to belie the very real trauma suffered by those who experienced sexual violence or predatory advances. But what the numbers do show is that a significant number of adolescents and young men were caught up in homosexual behaviours prosecuted in the courts. And although none of these younger complainants was charged, a critical reading of the evidence suggests that some may not have been the powerless recipients of unwanted advances the authorities often considered them to be.[30] Justice Mansfield, for example, recognised Marvin's complicity in Walter's actions, even though he placed responsibility for the offence with the older man:

> this is a very very [sic] serious offence, the debauching of a boy of 13 [h]owever willing or perverted the boy, himself, may have been, the blame must rest with you because if it were not for people of your description this boy would not have had an opportunity of following his inclination in the way he did.[31]

Commenting on the lax moral standards on the Queensland home-front, one Reverend in 1947 lamented, that 'many [city] children and adolescents' had 'illicit sexual knowledge' during the war;[32] an awareness arguably compounded by shortages of war-time accommodation and the overwhelming influx of Americans. In his assessment of the war, Moore has noted that '[w]illing youths joined the more seasoned camp men in competing with their sisters for American largesse in short and long term sexual relations'.[33] He cites the case of one 14-year-old Townsville youth who performed sexual services for willing American troops while his mother thought he was cycling to the shops on other errands.[34]

Supporting oral testimony from war-time Melbourne bears out this pattern. One man, Philip, thinks that these age-disparate relationships would have been about 'fifty-fifty'.[35] Bob, born in 1918, recalled that that 'in my day we always went with men… at least ten to fifteen years older, twenty years older than ourselves'.[36] One reason he gives for this phenomenon was the economic freedom older men provided during the Depression.[37] For Michael and Reginald, born a decade after Bob, older men represented social freedom. They suggest that for many people still living at home, it was less suspicious to go out at night with someone older. Older men were also more likely to drive a car, which proved another avenue of liberty.[38] Other men note that the presence of a father figure was important, and this may have been accentuated during the forties with many fathers absent serving in the war. It is important to note that these relationships were not financially motivated. As Reginald recalls, 'I think we sought somebody who was experienced in the homosexual world and we felt a little bit more relaxed and comfortable and protected by them'.[39] In his landmark study of New York, George Chauncey also acknowledges the prominence of intergenerational relationships, noting that older men could be mentors, introducing their lovers to the hidden world before them: '[t]hey… taught newcomers slang, folklore and how to survive in a hostile world'.[40] Most importantly, they introduced their young lovers to their circle of friends.[41] Was Walter expanding Marvin's world when he introduced Henry at his South Brisbane flat (although Henry's identity was geared towards pre-pubescent boys rather camp sensibilities, and our young clerk was already very familiar with camp life)? Perhaps Walter was also at Lennon's the night that Marvin and Donald met? The speculative possibilities are enticing.

Indecent Images and Health Magazines

In an era when homosexual pornographic material was difficult to obtain, visual material – ranging from sexually explicit photographs, to bodybuilding pictorials, to innocuous and artistic images of the male nude – was a secret source of erotic contentment for openly camp men and those unwilling or unable to acknowledge their desire for others of the same sex. During the 1930s and 1940s, Queensland police received numerous public complaints about the circulation of indecent material, usually publications such as Sydney-based magazines, *Man* and *Man Junior*, which contained 'numerous photographs and drawings of nude or near-nude females'.[42] Tijuana Bibles, pornographic comic books produced in the United States between the 1920s and the 1960s, were popular with American servicemen visiting here and immoral photographs, it was alleged, were in wide circulation in hotels in Brisbane city and suburbs.[43] There are three cases between 1939 and 1948 where adult men attempted seduce youths using these kinds of images: one example is Walter's use of a 9 inch x 6 inch photograph of nude movie stars.

There is an additional Brisbane case from 1943 which focused on representations of the male form. It involved 33-year-old Watson and three youths who spent an afternoon developing photographs following a nude romp and anal sex. And while there is no reference in the 1943 file as to what these photos actually were, the details from an earlier case in 1938 clearly indicate that Watson had a history of keeping pictorial mementos of sexual exploits and a penchant for collecting other sexual imagery.[44] In that matter, the police discovered a 'very comprehensive photographic record' in Watson's possession: an astonishing 700 images.[45] The collection contained pictures of the complainants and defendant, along with 'indecencies of every description'.[46] So shocking was the material that the judge ordered that all images be 'sealed and lodged in the safe of the Registrar of the Supreme Court, and burnt after the expiration of twenty-one days'.[47] The 1943 evidence suggests that Watson was not deterred by his earlier conviction nor did he seem concerned with the corroborative potential of photographs; indeed, he appears to be repeating older patterns, possibly beginning a new collection of provocative images to replace those destroyed by the authorities five years earlier.

Unlike Watson's pictorial record of offences, bodybuilding images were one source of erotica that were unlikely to arouse the suspicions of the authorities. As Alasdair Foster explains, 'the man's body could be looked at, admired, venerated and even desired, safe in the knowledge that one was only interested in abstracted aesthetics, a concept which was reinforced by the use of "physical culture"'.[48] In short, they were legitimised partial nudity. These images of sculpted and athletic male bodies could be found in the pages of magazines such as *Physical Culture*, a New York publication roughly spanning the first half of the twentieth century. And although these kinds of publications were not designed exclusively for homosexual consumption, a commercialised industry of physique magazines increasingly catered to a camp audience by the end of the 1950s. These later magazines varied in style, ranging from those promoting health and fitness to artistic periodicals and poorly disguised homosexual erotica.[49]

But how widespread was the use of photography and magazines by camp men during the 1940s and did they contribute to the development of identity and subculture? They were certainly recognised as a source of personal satisfaction by the men of the era. One young Melbourne youth, who attended high school in the late 1930s, remembers being aroused by photographs of attractive men and collecting these images.[50] Michael and Reginald remember the 'health and strength' magazines of the late 1940s and early 1950s well: 'in those days you could buy a particular brand of physique pictorial or something – it was Dutch or Danish, and the bodies were clad only in an inked g-string that covered the loins'.[51] They went on to explain that if you were lucky enough to find one of those, you could wet your finger, erase the ink, and 'see cock for the first time'.[52] While Foster acknowledges that these magazines were a 'potent if limited source of sexual fantasy', he argues that they 'kept the individual in isolation' and did little to indicate the existence of a coterie, or promote a sense of community.[53] There is, however, evidence from the 1940s which suggests otherwise.

An article published in the Adelaide *Truth* (also syndicated in Melbourne) illustrates how these magazines operated outside the individual sphere, not only to provide images for private viewing, but also it seems, contact with other like-minded individuals.[54] The story, which ran in 1941, concerned Sydney, a 'star window dresser', who was charged with sending an indecent photograph through the post after he wrongly addressed a letter bound for Melbourne. The correspondence contained three photographs and the proof of a photograph, all of an 'indecent character'. When the police subsequently searched the floor walker's home, they found hundreds of similar images along with notebooks containing the names and addresses of 'scores of men in other states'.

> According to the police investigations [Sydney] was first inspired to this strange choice of 'careers' as one of a number of exchanges for international smut by gazing on pictures in certain magazines that tell how measly weaklings become supermen by submitting to a course of treatment.[55]

It turns out that Sydney had actually collected a global network of pen-friends with whom contact had been initiated through health magazines.

The article also articulated the connections between nudism and perversion, reporting that the purveyor of the images was a confessed nudist.

In Queensland, health magazines were also the medium of choice for one mysterious man named 'Henry', whose request for youths interested in nudist adventures, was detailed in a Brisbane *Truth* exposé in late 1940.[56] For other men, these publications may have also provided clues on how they might present an image of sexual availability to like-minded others as the conversation between one defendant and a police officer reveals:

> I [the police-officer] said... you then caught the bottom portion of your coat with your hands and pulled it open and at the same time pulled your trousers tight and said... 'Look at mine. Isn't it nice [?] Is yours like mine?'...
>
> I [the police-officer] said 'What did you mean when you pulled your coat and trousers tight and passed that remark [?]'
>
> Defdt [sic] said 'There is nothing in that. I dress on the right side and was wondering if he did. A lot of men in France dress like that.'
>
> I said 'How do you know [?]'
>
> Defdt said 'I have read about it in health books.'[57]

Together, these cases suggest that indecent images, photography and physique magazines, not only provided pictures of semi-clad or naked male bodies for individual erotic consumption, but that the collection and exchange of these images fostered a postal network of men interested in the male form, which, depending on the nature of the images, provided a legitimate social avenue for men seeking contact with men.[58]

Friends and Lovers

The negative construction of male homosexuality so prominent in the justice records belies the diverse nature of these relationships and the wide range of feelings and emotions experienced by men who desired the social and sexual company of other men. And while elements of situational circumstance are recognisable in a good portion of the criminal cases, there is deliberate and intentional motivation in others. At least 11 men had a prior history of homosexual offending or were repeatedly charged in the period under review. A further 15 had a suspicious criminal past, and either acknowledged their penchant for other men during police questioning, or were dogged by persistent rumours. When confronted by the police in 1943, one 46-year-old, for example, admitted: 'I have been doing these things since I was a kid and I can't help myself when anyone lets me have them on'.[59] Our central actor, Walter, was confident in his conception of self. For him, the female form held no sexual allure: '[l]ook, if a nude woman stood in front of me I wouldn't get a kick out of it', he said, 'but if I'm out with a boy, or in a room with a lot of boys I just can't hold myself'.[60] Donald's identity also appears self-generated; he bluntly rejected any negative construction of his sexuality when he was questioned by the police:

> I [Detective-Constable] said 'Do you mean you had sexual intercourse with him against the order of nature [?]'
>
> He [Donald] said 'Yes, if that's what *you* call it.' [my emphasis][61]

Wotherspoon has observed that 'many men who had plenty of previous homosexual experience, and thought of themselves as camp, continued to have homoerotic experiences and even love affairs during the war'.[62] Sparing the feelings of his long-term companion, Alfred, Dingle Dell tearoom proprietor, Paul, explained to one Detective-Constable why he had asked an undercover agent (who he had solicited) to lie about how the two of them had met.

> Defdt [sic] said 'I didn't want to hurt Alfred's feelings.'
>
> I said 'How could you hurt Alfred's feelings by introducing him to a friend of yours [?]'
>
> Defdt said 'You don't understand. Alfred and I have been mates for a long while.'[63]

Alfred later clarified that he and Paul had been involved:

> for about the past seven (7) years and [I] have visited his home practically two or three times a month for the Sunday evening meal. On occasions I have stayed at [Paul's] home, and on such occasions I have occupied the same bed as he.[64]

Two other men, Alvin, a 33-year-old nurse, and Howard, a 19-year-old apprentice electrician, also maintained an intimate relationship, residing together for over 12 months in a two bedroom house in Scott Road, Herston, between 1946 and 1947.[65] Sharing the residence with Howard's sister, Betty, the two men slept in a three-quarter bed in the main room. During the first three months of 1947, young Howard was confined to bed with rheumatic fever and during this time he was nursed by Alvin.

While many men got practical and emotional support from other men, Chauncey argues that 'they were also likely to be enmeshed in similar relations of independence with their natal families, work mates and other non-gay associates'.[66] He calls this 'the double-life'. The process of 'coming out' was not the rite of passage which is now synonymous with contemporary gay identity. By keeping a strict division between their private and public life – between their square work world,[67] family life, and their private world – men were afforded some measure of protection in a community generally hostile to love between men.[68] Errol did not reveal his life to anyone outside his camp circle of friends, and certainly not his family. He made excuses to get into city when he needed to, especially on weekends.[69] One Melbourne man who was in his early forties during the war kept his sexuality a secret despite suspecting his mother 'sensed his position'.[70] For many relatives of camp men, the idea that their sons, brothers, or nephews might have been attracted to other men was never countenanced. Despite never finding a girlfriend or wife, Milton another Melbourne man, was simply considered by his kin to be 'a heterosexual man that never married'.[71]

However, with social expectations of marriage and children, many men were pressured to find a companion of the opposite sex and suppressed their desire for other men. The court records show that more than 8% of the defendants charged with homosexual activity were married. Vernon (who maintained a love affair with American soldier Jack) had been living apart from his wife, while another man in this study, Roger (whose story appears below), was certainly leading the 'double-life'. Of course, not all men appeared to keep this side of their lives hidden from their families. Betty, who lived with her brother, Howard, and his partner, Alvin, must have had some suspicions about the nature of their relationship and despite his protestations that any court case would 'kill mother', Paul was quite open about his sexuality in company with his family, much to the shock of the undercover operative lunching with them.[72]

Conclusions

Along with the central network explored here, and the cohort described by young Errol, another police report alludes to one other potential plexus by way of introductory services provided by Andrew, a fifty-something bald shop walker and window dresser at Finney Isles department store.[73] The information on this particular network came about after police were tipped off by a suspicious wife whose mistrust was aroused after her husband, Roger, began arriving home late with no explanation. His acquittal on a charge of gross indecency 18 months earlier would not have eased her fears. During that trial, she had discovered a letter in her husband's pocket which read: '[l]ad, It was nice seeing you on the ---- of December, Hoping to hear from you soon. If you ring B4290, and don't ask for anyone, as I will answer the [t]elephone myself. [Andrew]'[74]

After some amateur sleuthing, Roger's wife traced the phone number listed in the letter to a man (Andrew) whom she believed to be a known 'pansy... the leader of a group of perverts... [who] makes the meeting place of different men'.[75] Suspecting her husband's predilection for other men, and assuming that her husband was again meeting 'men for the purpose of committing [i]ndecent [a]cts', Roger's wife contacted the police in late January 1943 and provided the evidence she had earlier discovered. Four months later, her husband was arrested in company with another soldier on a charge of gross indecency. This time he was convicted. Although other correspondence filed with this case indicates that Andrew was in fact 'a reputed sexual pervert', no information was found linking him to Roger.[76]

That we can find evidence for two or possibly three distinct homosexual networks operating in Brisbane during the 1940s speaks to the relatively complex urban infrastructure of commercial coffee shops, tea houses, bars and hotels, and certain public spaces that enabled communion between camp men. These men aligned themselves with like-minded groups of social misfits in the bohemian world, generated social networks through nudism and physique magazines, and read novels, which ostensibly cast them as deviant, for pleasure. It is difficult to assess accurately the impact of the US servicemen on the Queensland home-front and this is an area which warrants further research in order to tease out fully the interactions between the local subculture and foreign homosexual visitors. But despite the limited information, it is clear that US servicemen passed on ideas about subcultures in large American centres, which may have served as a model for the development of an Australian identity in later decades.

Taking an uncritical reading of the justice records, it would be easy to assess generally these groups as sexually mechanical, devoid of any richer emotional tapestry. And while some relationships were quick and furtive, satisfying little more than a physical need, these must be set among others involving deeper, passionate connections and enduring companionship. The ways these actors met, socialised, leisured, and fucked, brought together different strands of interest, experience, and friendship informing a camp sensibility in war-time Queensland; one which echoed into the decades beyond. Men like Walter, Marvin, Donald and Joseph formed complex webs of emotional support, companionship, and sexual outlet; a world of friends and lovers.

Acknowledgements

I'd like to thank Chris Brickell, Lisa Featherstone, and Graham Willett for comments and criticisms on earlier drafts of this chapter.

Endnotes

1. In accordance with the conditions governing the use of restricted state-held criminal records, the names of defendants and complaints have been changed to protect anonymity. In each case the initial of Christian names is correct although the name itself is altered.
2. Deposition no. 115/48, in Information, Depositions and Associated Papers in Criminal Cases Heard in Sittings in Brisbane, 10 May 1948 – 28 June 1948, Queensland State Archives (QSA), SCT/CC436.
3. Deposition no. 27/45, in Information, Depositions and Associated Papers in Criminal Cases Heard in Sittings in Brisbane, 26 February 1945, QSA, SCT/CC410.
4. ibid.
5. Deposition no. 26/45, 1945, QSA, SCT/CC410.
6. Here, I have used Allan Bérubé's reckoning. Applying Alfred Kinsey's civilian war-time surveys to the military, he calculates that at least 650,000 and as many as 1.6 million American servicemen were homosexual. See, Allan Bérubé, *Coming Out Under Fire: The History of Gay Men and Women in World War Two*, New York: Free Press, 1990, p. 3.
7. Garry Wotherspoon, 'Comrades-in-Arms', in Joy Damousi and Marilyn Lake, eds, *Gender and War: Australians at War in the Twentieth Century*, Melbourne: Cambridge University Press, 1995, p. 212.
8. ibid.
9. Clive Moore, *Sunshine and Rainbows: The Development of Gay and Lesbian Culture in Queensland*, St Lucia, Queensland: University of Queensland Press, 2001, p. 105.
10. Deposition no. 200/44, in Information, Depositions and Associated Criminal Cases Heard in Sittings in Brisbane, 6 November 1944, QSA, SCT/CC408.
11. Moore, *Sunshine and Rainbows*, p. 108; Garry Wotherspoon, *'City of the Plain': History of a Gay Sub-culture*, Sydney: Hale and Iremonger, 1991, p. 96.
12. Walter Stewart Cornyn, 'Hotel Slang', *American Speech*, vol. 14, no. 3 (October 1939), p. 239. Moore records the memories of one effeminate young Australian soldier who was told by an American counterpart: 'My God, you are "fruit"'. See, Moore, *Sunshine and Rainbows*, p. 108.
13. Deposition no. 200/44, 1944, QSA, SCT/CC408.

14 Moore, *Sunshine and Rainbows*, p. 108; Gary Simes, 'The Language of Homosexuality in Australia', in Robert Aldrich and Garry Wotherspoon, eds, *Gay Perspectives: Essays in Australia Gay Culture*, Sydney: Department of Economic History, University of Sydney, 1992, p. 55; Gary Simes, 'History of Naughty Words', *Outrage*, no. 57 (February 1988), p. 20; Wotherspoon, *'City of the Plain'*, p. 97.

15 See, for example, George Chauncey, 'Privacy Could Only be Had in Public', in Joel Saunders, ed., *Stud: Architectures of Masculinity*, New York: Princeton University Press, 1996, pp. 224–266; Matt Houlbrook, *Queer London: Perils and Pleasures in the Sexual Metropolis, 1918–1957*, Chicago: Chicago University Press, 2005, esp. ch. 2, 'Geographies of Public Sex', pp. 43–67.

16 Errol, interview with Barry McKay, 10 November 2000, Australian Lesbian and Gay Archives (ALGA), typescript log, p. 6.

17 Noel Langley, *There's a Porpoise Close Behind Us*, London: Arthur Barker, 1936. Although only one person amongst his group had a copy, 'it was passed on from one to another… and considered *the* thing to read at the time' [original emphasis]. See, Errol, interview with Barry McKay, typescript log, p. 7.

18 Errol, interview with Barry McKay, typescript log, p. 6; see also, Michael and Reginald, interview with Graham Carbery, 9 November 1993, ALGA, transcript, p. 6.

19 Errol, interview with Barry McKay, typescript log, p. 6.

20 See, Yorick Smaal, 'Revisiting Queensland's War-Time Sex Panics: Moral Alarm, Male Homosexuality, and Policing Public Space, 1939–1948', in Robin Archer and Shirleene Robinson, *Crime Over Time: Temporal Perspectives on Crime and Punishment in Australia*, Newcastle Upon Tyne: Cambridge Scholars Press, 2010, pp. 111–141.

21 Moore, *Sunshine and Rainbows*, p. 130.

22 Deposition no. 90/42, in Information, Depositions and Associated Papers in Criminal Cases Heard in Brisbane, 29 June 1942, QSA, SCT/CC396.

23 John D'Emilio explains that exclusive gay bars were discernable in large port cities such as Los Angeles and San Francisco, and also evident in the relatively smaller centres of San Jose, Denver and Kansas City by the end of the 1940s. See, John D'Emilio, *Sexual Politics, Sexual Communities: The Making of a Homosexual Minority in the United States, 1940–1970*, Chicago: University of Chicago Press, 1983, pp. 31–32.

24 Errol, interview with Barry McKay, typescript log, p. 7.

25 ibid.; Moore, *Sunshine and Rainbows*, p. 130. There is also some evidence to suggest that the lavatories at the rear of the Exchange Hotel, on the corner of Edward and Charlotte streets, were being used for sexual purposes. A 41-year-old labourer propositioned a 16-year-old boy at these toilets at lunch-time on a Friday afternoon in late September 1940. The lavatories at the Brisbane Hotel were also used during weekday lunch hours by one defendant who was having sex with a 15-year-old boy. See, Deposition no. 18/42, in Information, Depositions and Associated Papers in Criminal Cases Heard in Sittings in Brisbane, 23 February 1942, QSA, SCT/CC394; Deposition no. 136/40, in Information, Depositions and Associated Papers in Criminal Cases Heard in Sittings in Brisbane, 1 April 1940 – 20 May 1940, QSA, SCT/CC384.

26 Errol, interview with Barry McKay, typescript log, p. 7.

27 Deposition no. 65, 1942, QSA, SCT/CC396.

28 Juvenile offenders accounted for 18.292% of sex crime for 1945–1946; 17.343% for 1946–1947; 15.969% for 1947–1948; and 20.3 percent for 1948–1949. See, 'Report of the Commissioner of Police for the 12 Months Ended 30 June 1947', *Queensland Parliamentary Papers* (*QPP*), vol. 2 (1947), p. 5 [p. 867]; 'Report of the Commissioner of

Police for the 12 Months Ended 30 June 1948', *QPP*, vol. 2 (1948), p. 5 [p. 629]; 'Report of the Commissioner of Police for the 12 Months Ended 30 June 1949', *QPP*, (1949), p. 8 [p. 658].

29 Deposition no. 115/48, 1948, QSA, SCT/CC436.
30 In Queensland, boys were not considered capable of physical penetration if they were under the age of 14 years; see, *R v Moody* (1897) 8 QLJ 102. For further discussion, see, Yorick Smaal, 'More than Mates?: Masculinity, Homosexuality, and the Formation of an Embryonic Subculture in Queensland, 1890–1914', MPhil Thesis, University of Queensland, 2004, pp. 125–126
31 Deposition no. 115/48, 1948, QSA, SCT/CC436.
32 'Lax Parents Blamed for Obscene Scribblings', *Courier-Mail*, 14 March 1947 [cutting], in Advertisements (Indecent) (Also includes items relating to Nudism, Indecent Costumes and Film Censorship), 1 January 1896 – 31 December 1959, QSA, A/44695.
33 Moore, *Sunshine and Rainbows*, p. 108.
34 ibid., p. 109.
35 Philip, interview with Graham Carbery and Mark Riley, 14 July 1990, ALGA, typescript log, p. 12.
36 Bob, interview with Graham Carbery, 19 January 1983, ALGA, typescript log, p. 11.
37 ibid.
38 Michael and Reginald, interview with Graham Carbery, transcript, p. 11. This was particularly important given low car-ownership in Australia in the 1940s. Humphrey McQueen notes that during the 1950s, the ratio of car ownership increased from one vehicle for nine people, to two cars for seven people; Humphrey McQueen, *Social Sketches of Australia, 1888–2001*, St Lucia, Qld: University of Queensland Press, 2004, p. 192.
39 Michael and Reginald, interview with Graham Carbery, transcript, p. 10.
40 George Chauncey, *Gay New York: Gender, Urban Culture, and the Making of the Gay Male World*, New York: Basic Books, 1994, p. 277.
41 ibid., p. 278.
42 G. Smith, State Licencing Inspector, to Commissioner of Police, 30 June 1938, typescript correspondence, in Advertisements (Indecent), 1896–1959, QSA, A/44695.
43 'More Immoral Photos in City', n. d. [cutting], in Advertisements (Indecent), 1896–1959, QSA, A/44695.
44 'Newspaper Employee Sentenced: Seven Years' Imprisonment with Male Persons', *Rockhampton Morning Bulletin*, 16 February 1938 [cutting], in Advertisements (Indecent), 1896–1959, QSA, A/44695.
45 '"Should be with Niggers": Scathing Bench Comment', *Truth* (Brisbane), 20 February 1938, p. 23.
46 'Newspaper Employee Sentenced: Seven Years' Imprisonment with Male Persons'.
47 ibid.; '"Should be with Niggers"'.
48 David Bianco, 'Physique Magazines', available at, http://www.planetout.com/news/history/archive/09271999.html, date accessed 15 October 2007; Alasdair Foster, 'Getting Physical', *Outrage*, no. 65 (October 1988), pp. 15–18.
49 Foster, 'Getting Physical', p. 17.
50 Lionel, interviewed by Geoffrey Stewardson, 9 July 2001, ALGA, typescript log, p. 3.
51 Michael and Reginald, interview with Graham Carbery, transcript, p. 6.
52 ibid.

53 Foster, 'Getting Physical', p. 17.
54 'Australian Vice Ring', *Truth* (Adelaide), 22 June 1941, p. 11; 'Sensational Vice Ring Alleged: Swift Action by Police', *Truth* (Melbourne), 14 June 1941, p. 1. For an alternative analysis of this case, see, Wotherspoon, '*City of the Plain*', p. 85.
55 'Sensational Vice Ring Alleged: Swift Action by Police', p. 1.
56 Moore, *Sunshine and Rainbows*, p. 115.
57 Deposition no. 90/42, 1942, QSA, SCT/CC396.
58 Allison Laurie has argued that these magazines formed part of a vibrant, although hidden community during the period; see, Allison Laurie, 'Pre-1960 Transnational Lesbian and Homosexual Connections – The New Zealand Links', Paper presented at the Australian Homosexual Histories Conference, no. 8, Melbourne University, 12–13 July 2008.
59 Deposition no. 74, in Information, Depositions and Associated Papers in Criminal Cases Heard in Sittings in Brisbane, 5 April 1943 – 9 August 1943, QSA, SCT/CC400.
60 Deposition no. 115/48, 1948, QSA, SCT/CC436.
61 Deposition no. 27/45, 1945, QSA, SCT/CC410.
62 Wotherspoon, '*City of the Plain*', pp. 82, 88.
63 Deposition no. 90/42, 1942, QSA, SCT/CC396.
64 Deposition no. 90/42, QSA, SCT/CC396.
65 Deposition no. 24, in Information, Depositions and Associated Papers in Criminal Cases Heard in Sittings in Brisbane, 16 February 1948, QSA, SCT/CC434; Indictments, in Information, Depositions and Associated Papers in Criminal Cases Heard in Sittings in Brisbane, 16 February 1948 – 20 September 1948, QSA, SCT/CC432.
66 Chauncey, *Gay New York*, p. 274.
67 There is some evidence showing that the workplace could play an active part in some men's homosexual life: floor walking and window dressing, for example, were more conducive to the camp lifestyle than other professions.
68 Chauncey, *Gay New York*, p. 276.
69 Errol, interview with Barry McKay, typescript log, p. 6.
70 Ben, interview with Geoffrey Stewardson, 9 July 2001, ALGA, typescript log, p. 5.
71 Milton, interview with Graham Carbery, 11 March 1983, ALGA, transcript, p. 17.
72 Sergeant Morley Box: 'It was very peculiar to grab my penus [sic] while his [defendant's] mother and sisters were there and while we were having tea. It was almost unbelievable. At the time we were on the settee his own mother, brother-in-law and nephew were in the room. This was the time he grabbed K. by the penus. It is almost unbelievable unless you see it [sic]'. Deposition no. 90/42, 1942, QSA, SCT/CC396.
73 Deposition no. 71, in Information, Depositions and Associated Papers in Criminal Cases Heard in Sittings in Brisbane, 5 April 1943 – 9 August 1943, QSA, SCT/CC400.
74 ibid.
75 ibid.
76 Deposition no. 71, 1943, QSA, SCT/CC400.

The Influence of Ageism on Relations between Old and Young Gay Men

Peter Robinson

For at least the last quarter of a century, the body has been a focus of considerable interest and study in sociology, history, and allied fields. As Deborah Lupton and others have observed, the strong emphasis on youth culture, physical prowess and 'beauty' in contemporary culture has meant that age has become a 'negative cultural value'.[1] Youth is now the most valued stage in the life cycle and, according to Michael Mittenauer, the young have now become society's role models.[2] If this is the case, and there seems little doubt that it is – notwithstanding the fact that the first of the baby-boomer generation are entering retirement – it would help explain why old age is rejected and why, according to Simone de Beauvoir, '[s]ociety looks upon old age as a kind of shameful secret that is unseemly to mention'.[3]

In *The Changing World of Gay Men*, I developed the argument that nowhere in contemporary Western society is this emphasis on youthfulness more pronounced than in the gay world. I examined the gay 'scene' – that site of physical display where young men are valorised for their youth and beauty – and then suggested that one might reasonably assume that old gay men would be rejected in the gay world for what they lacked in youthfulness or beauty. What my Australian interviewees told me was that indeed they felt marginalised in the gay world but that they were sanguine about their outcast status and in some cases pitied the young gay men for their superficial preoccupations.[4]

In *Sex and Sensibility*, Arlene Stein argues that as the lesbians she studied grew into middle age, their attachment to the non-heterosexual subculture changed: 'as certainty about their lesbian identity grew, they... feel "at home" in the community with which they mainly identify, but also in numerous other contexts in which they participate and with which they feel some sense of identification'.[5] Although I did not reach the same conclusion in *The Changing World of Gay Men* about the lives of the men in middle age and old age, I find this persuasive. It helps explain why gay men in their mid-40s and older become less concerned with the values and practices of the gay world and tend to lead what Stein calls more 'decentred' lives.[6]

This chapter considers how gay men aged 40 and over understand the ageism that operates in the gay world. It draws on data collected from interviews with 21 Australian and North American men aged between 40 and 79. The Australian men were recruited from Sydney and Hobart and the North American men from New York and Los Angeles – as part of a larger study on ageing in the gay world.[7]

The two primary narratives the men used were first, that gay men were ageist because the gay world was youth obsessed – a public narrative that is common to both homosexuals and heterosexuals – and second, that the young gay men they personally knew were not ageist and respected them. The four secondary narratives comprise stories about (a) respecting old gay men; (b) hustling as a conduit for beneficial relations between different generations of gay men; (c) teenage gays being oblivious to anyone older than 20; (d) old gay men as predatory or sexually undesirable. Both primary and secondary narratives are revealing for what they suggest about the varying influence that public and private narratives can have on gay men's self identity and how they live their lives.

Method and Sample

My understanding of narrative identity theory follows the work of Alistair Macintyre who, along with scholars such as Edward Bruner, David Carr, and Ken Plummer, argues that personal and public narratives are constitutive, that is, the stories people tell about themselves and their place in the social world makes them who they are.[8] With this in mind, I examined the two primary narratives and four secondary narratives that the interviewees drew on when asked how old gay men were regarded in the gay milieu.

The non-representative sample on which this chapter is based comprises 21 gay men, aged 40 and older, 10 of whom were from Australia and 11 of whom were from the United States. Of these men, two men were in their 70s (one from Hobart and one from New York); three men were in their 60s (two from Hobart, one from New York); 10 men were in their 50s (four from Hobart, three from New York, two from Sydney, one from Los Angeles); six men were in their 40s (four from New York, one from Hobart, one from Los Angeles).

The four cities from which the interviewees were drawn are similar in that they are situated in two western, advanced democracies, both of which were established as colonies of Great Britain and at some point in their history developed as white settler societies. New York and Los Angeles are arguably the two most important cities in the USA from the standpoint of culture, fashion, advertising, and public relations. New York is now the pre-eminent international city and is one of the most important international financial centres. Sydney is an international city and possibly the most well-known, influential Australian city but is dwarfed in size by New York and Los Angeles. Hobart, meanwhile, is the small capital city of a large island state. The four cities comprise therefore one megalopolis (New York), one metropolis (Los Angeles), one very large international city (Sydney) and one relatively small provincial capital city (Hobart).[9] As mentioned, all four cities are situated in English-speaking countries that are affluent, advanced democracies.

New York, Los Angeles, and Sydney share in common well developed gay business and social communities, each with its own local idiosyncrasies.[10] As Dennis Altman argued in 1989, the most resilient response to HIV/AIDS occurred in cities where established gay communities existed, for through these, gay men and their friends were able to organise and work together communally in face of the epidemic.[11] These three cities no longer face the same threat to their existence that HIV/AIDS posed in the 1980s and 1990s but as some scholars have noted, many of the gay communities that responded communally and vigorously to the epidemic emerged stronger and more diverse after the epidemic passed. Hobart, on the other hand, is quite unlike the other three cities. It has only loosely developed gay social networks, which is not surprising given that it is a city of only 200,525 people and therefore the smallest of the four cities from which interviewees were drawn for this study. It also has the least developed gay culture and most gay socialising is done in the home of friends.[12]

The 10 Australian men interviewed for this study were all white and with the exception of two upper-class men (one a descendant of rich pastoralists, the other a retired public service head of department), were mostly upper-middle class or middle class. The Australian interviewees were recruited for this study in 2003, by word of mouth or on the recommendation of friends and colleagues. The 11 interviewees from the United States mostly came from upper-middle class or middle-class backgrounds and included two African-American men, two men who were HIV positive, and two upper-class men, both of whom were professors. The US interviewees were recruited for this study in 2009. The class background of the majority of US interviewees was shaped by the manner of recruiting them, which was via the gay and lesbian alumni network of an east coast university. The social network website Craigslist was my initial means of recruiting interviewees in the USA.

The question that each man answered was 'How does the general community regard old gay men, and how do other gay men see them?' For the purpose of this chapter, I am looking at the men's answer to the second part of the question, that is, what views they believed other gay men to hold of old gay men.

Middle-aged and upper-middle class gay men are strongly represented in this sample and old men are only thinly represented. I am not sure that this is a serious weakness on the grounds that, as Christopher Lasch observed in the 1970s, ageism is most acutely felt in early to late middle age.[13] By the time one has reached old age, other concerns take over, and the views of younger people are of less concern.

Primary Narratives

In answer to the question 'How do other gay men see old gay men?', the men interviewed for this study drew on two primary narratives and four secondary narratives. The two primary narratives the men used were first, that gay men were ageist because the gay world is youth obsessed and second, that the young gay men they personally knew were not ageist and respected them.

Youthful Obsession

Fourteen interviewees (or two thirds of the sample) cited the youth culture that prevails in the gay world as the reason for the ageist attitudes or practices also found there. Eight of these men were from Australia and six from the USA; two were in their 70s; three were in their 60s; six were in their 50s; and three were in their 40s. The narrative stream connecting the stories of the interviewees who told of youthful obsession runs as follows. Parry (aged 63), who is African-American and lives in New York City, said ageism was symptomatic of the values of US society in general. Such a view corresponds to what Michel Foucault said about ageism in the gay world in the 1980s, which is that, '[a]s to the worship of youthful bodies, I'm not convinced that it is peculiar at all to gays or in any way to be regarded as a pathology'.[14]

Unlike other interviewees who raised the matter, Parry was neither dejected nor felt worthless because of ageist practices or beliefs. On the contrary, he said that it was understandable that there were sites on the internet where people under 40 were not welcome but he regarded this as the expression of a 'preference', not evidence of prejudice. Interestingly, Parry understood ageism differently from almost all the other men interviewed for this study, that is, as a preference for men over 40. 'When I was younger', he said, 'I liked older men and the older men now are younger men but they're still the same age, in their 40s and 50s… I've always said I'll always have somebody to have sex with and I carry that in my life now'.

By contrast, and speaking for the majority of interviewees, Noel, a 58-year-old man from Hobart, saw ageism in the gay world as a valorising of the young and beautiful, a consequence of the gay lifestyle. 'The image of being gay', he said, 'was a young man in his late teens or early 20s or an older man being able to look young', which corresponded to what another interviewee, Ross, aged 54, said. Also based in Hobart, Ross explained gay interest in youthfulness as follows:

> There is certainly a culture in the gay community of appreciating beauty and youth and muscular development and athleticism. And because those tend to be more and better developed in young people, the focus is more on beauty of… young people.

Five men from this group spoke of the negative consequences of the youthful obsession in the gay world. First, a group of three men said it meant that old men were seen as 'not sexy', in the words of Leslie, aged 74. Second, two men from the United States, both of whom were in their 40s, described a negative consequence that Australian gay men know as 'mutton dressed as lamb', that is, where middle-aged men try to appear younger than they are.

Positive Personal Relations or Experiences

Seven interviewees or one third of the men interviewed for this study reported positive relations or experiences with gay men who were younger than they. Four of these men were from Australia and three from the USA; one was in his 70s; two were in their 60s; three were in their 50s; and one was in his 40s. Chief among the reasons the men gave for positive relations or experiences with younger gay men were (a) respect for the longevity of their relationships and (b) regard for their lived experience. The views of these men are represented by the accounts of Des, aged 50, who lives in Sydney, Parry, aged 63 who lives in the East Village, Manhattan, and Earl, aged 51, who also lives in Manhattan.

According to Des, who works as a health manager and has been in a relationship with his partner (aged 59) for more than 30 years, the young gay men in his friendship circle admire what he, his partner, and their friends in long-term relationships have achieved:

> They did not know that it was possible. They think that we are lucky to have experienced it and wonder if they will too. They ask what it was that we did to make our lives possible. We find ourselves being lovely mentors to young gay people.

Parry's experience of good relations with young gay men occurred in the setting of his HIV counselling as a volunteer. Young gay men are, he said, 'attracted to my age, my stories about what it was like in the 1960s and 1980s… or the piano bars'. Earl's views on positive relations between old gay men and young men were based on the regard that he as a 51-year-old has for old gay men. Earl's previous partner was an older man who supported him in many ways and from what he observed of his previous partner's friends, life is tough for old, gay men if they are not in his words, 'big men'. It is also possible that his memory of his father, another of his 'big men', coloured his understandings of older gay men. 'There is a mystique', he said, 'if you are a powerful fellow, a successful one. God forbid that you're not powerful because then you are definitely marginalised and you fade in the background'. More discussion of respect for successful men follows in the section on secondary narratives, below.

One thing that struck me about gay life in certain districts of Manhattan was the greater ease with which relations were conducted between old gay men and young gay men. Sometimes money lubricated the social/sexual relations, sometimes not. But quite a sophisticated understanding seemed to exist of the give-and-take between young and old and a great deal less angst was associated with it than exists between gay men in Australia. Attitudes in Los Angeles were more like those in Australia – possibly because the beach culture and the cult of the body beautiful accentuate the divide between young and old.

> In each city we might say there in one body type, the Platonic type for that locality… In L.A. the body is slender, the buttocks pneumatic with youth, the trail of gold dust shading the hollow just above the

coccyx and between the pecs. Something fragile about the clavicle and tender about the nape causes the figure to oscillate between boyhood and maturity. The eyes are blue.[15]

In support of the observations that Edmund White made of Los Angeles in 1980, a 46-year-old man from Los Angeles I interviewed in 2009 said that in West Hollywood, 'there is a strong youth culture that they don't even befriend older people'.[16]

One other possible explanation for the greater acceptance of age difference in Manhattan might be the very high price of real estate and related high cost of rent. For example, one interviewee said the rent for his bed-sitter in Manhattan was approximately $3000 per month, admittedly it was situated around the corner from Fifth Avenue and within five minutes walk of Grand Central railway station. Even so, a number of the men who I interviewed in New York who had secure, middle-class jobs as a social worker or an accountant, could not afford to live in Manhattan and lived instead in one of the neighbouring boroughs such as Brooklyn or Queens.

Secondary Narratives

As mentioned, the four secondary narratives that the men interviewed for this study drew on comprised stories about first, respecting old gay men; second, hustling as a conduit for meaningful relations between different generations of gay men; third, teenage gay men being oblivious to anyone over the age of 20; and fourth, old gay men as predatory or sexually undesirable. The narratives represent only a small number of men interviewed for this study. Two men spoke about 'respect' and another two men spoke about 'predatoriness'; then a different man spoke about each of 'hustling' and 'teenagers' ageism'.[17] The stories are included nonetheless because of what they say about obstacles that can exist to better relations between gay men from different generations and because they have been observed by other scholars.[18]

Respect

Two men spoke of the respect with which they had seen young gay men treat older counterparts. Both men live in New York, are university educated and in their 50s. Hilton is 53 and works as a drug and alcohol counsellor with men who are HIV positive. As one of the HIV-positive men in the sample, his account of the respect with which young gay men regard the survivors of the HIV/AIDS epidemic has an autobiographical reference point:

There's a sense that a lot of them… got through because they were lucky or they were… the most resourceful and adaptable people in general because they had so many challenges and barriers to survive. Gay men can be respected either because they lived through the HIV/AIDS epidemic or only if they have been successful.

Coincidentally, Hilton shares the other interviewee's view that success is the other reason young gay men might respect older gay men. Earl's view of success was made clear in an earlier section on 'positive personal relations or experiences' where he declared that unless an older gay man is powerful, he is 'marginalised and… [fades] in the background'. In Earl's view, the respect an old gay man receives depends on the success he has achieved in his working life, which is a particularly North American view of life course and the world of work. If a person has not been successful, in the eyes of this upper-middle-class man, he can seem comical: 'they're generally… fuzzy wig types and you watch them, especially the older, heavier ones that are like Buddhas, mob kingpins or something'. Successful men, however, can live a blessed life in New York.

> I know an 85-year-old fellow. He's my father's age [and he] served in the War. He's been married, has a great grandchild now… He is now in a second marriage essentially, to a man. He's had… a major career as… a corporate attorney… and he was… way up there… [but] not out until the end of a 30-year marriage. He had sex during the war with a guy. He writes about the whole thing in his book. It is quite a story and I have a great deal of respect for him. He lives with his lover in a penthouse apartment on Christopher Street… beautiful fireplace, massive terrace, gorgeous. He is very comfortably well off, very well regarded. His kids come back for his birthday parties…

From Earl's description, this successful man would seem to have all that anyone could ask for: love, affection, and respect from his children, grandchildren, and male partner. How his ex-wife feels about his success would be for another chapter. The man's life also exemplifies studies of the dual life that many men were forced to lead who were born in the decades between the 1920s and 1940s and even sometimes later depending on their circumstances and birthplace.[19]

Hustling

The idea that young gay men can develop rewarding, affective relationships with older counterparts through the means of prostitution was raised in the account of one man only. Colin is in his early 70s and lives in New York. Still actively involved in the local S&M scene, he is a well respected, upper-class artist who is also a reformed alcoholic. His initial response when asked how he understood young gay men's view of old gay men was to say that they would hold negative views because old gay men are seen as sexually uninteresting or undesirable. He then added that when money changed hands, it was possible for something different to develop.

> If you're a young, beautiful man and an older man pays you, you can like them because the money makes it okay. I have a friend who does a lot of hustlers and has really developed a lot of connections, even relationships, with them which go well beyond the money. But the money makes it possible. They can relax, it takes it out of the bed. I'm only with him for the money but it isn't that at all.

Colin believes that the money that changes hands between a male prostitute or hustler and his client allows for an emotional sleight of hand whereby the young man may allow himself to develop a closer relationship with the older man in a way that would be impossible if they met under any other situation. Similar accounts of such 'situational logic' were more common in published research on pre-liberation homosexual sexual practices.[20] The sleight of hand in Colin's view is that the hustler may justify his emotional closeness simply as a consequence of the money he receives for the sex he has with his client, whereas in Colin's mind it is something other than this, something more resembling a quasi-relationship.

Teenagers' Ageism

This narrative appeared in the account of one man, a secondary school teacher who discovered when on a summer vacation camp that the gay teenagers in his care displayed a startling lack of interest in the past. Timothy who is 46 said that the views that gay men in general held about anyone older than them were 'also very complicated' but that when he worked with young, gay teenagers in an upper-middle-class suburb of New York, he and his fellow volunteer workers were 'a little stunned… that the kids didn't really appreciate how far things had come and how much had been done for them'. Timothy was surprised that the teenagers he met on the camp were unaware of the work previous generations of gay men had done so that they could enjoy their relatively easy lives. In his view, the teenagers were simply mirroring the views of the broader gay community where he sensed that older gay men were seen as 'pioneers in some way, but then there is another sense that people do not want to pay attention to that because it was yesterday' and that young gay men see old gay men as distantly as they would their grandparents but possibly with less affection. Cultural ignorance is not something peculiar to gay teenagers; their unwillingness, however, to engage with or take up the unfinished social agendas of their parents' generation of gay people might be a feature of their identity, as Ritch Savin-Williams explains in the North American context: '[y]oung [gay] people have little interest in subverting American civilisation... Besides... [they] never joined up to be members of a marginalised gay group in the first place'.[21]

Old Gay Men as Predatory or Sexually Undesirable

These two narratives that at first appear mutually exclusive are linked here because of an argument I developed in *The Changing World of Gay Men*, which was that an important reason young men spurned older men was that they resented their presence in social spaces where sexual exchange was available and expected.[22] Depending on their age, a young gay man can regard any approach from someone he regards as 'beyond the pale' as un-cool, insulting, predatory, depending on the age of the man approaching them. One man spoke of old gay men's predatoriness and one spoke of their sexual undesirability. Both topics have been previously explored by other scholars.[23]

Ross is 54 and as mentioned is from Hobart. Like a number of other men interviewed for this study, he admitted that there existed a variety of views toward older gay men. In his eyes they were spurned because of the regard for 'beauty, youth, muscular development, and athleticism' in the gay world. Linked to this in his mind, however, was the suspicion of old men 'hanging around young men and being a nuisance and... unattractive and a threat. And the possibility of their preying on vulnerable, young men'. The last fear he described is of the 'stranger danger' that conservative governments publicised in Australia in the mid- to late 1980s.

Colin, whose views on hustling appeared in the subsection above, lives in New York and is still sexually active and involved in the club scene. As discussed, with the exception of hustling as a conduit for the development of rewarding, affective relations between old and young gay men, Colin suspected that young gay men did not view their older counterparts positively. And that this was so because they were regarded as not sexually desirable, because young men were, in Colin's words, 'not wanting to be sexual with [them]'.

Conclusion

The narrative stream connecting the interviewees' stories linked the following points. First, that mainstream society has a history of ageism, which the gay world simply mirrors; second, that gay identity is associated with youthfulness; third, that consequences for gay men of the ageism that exists in the gay world are (a) old men being regarded as sexless; and (b) middle-aged gay men trying to act as though they are 20; and (c) that the youthful obsession of gay men made growing older harder.

Stories of older gay men's experience of positive personal relations with young gay men point to evidence of their decentred lives, to use Arlene Stein's phrase. That is, their lives are now less focused than they used to be on the social networks and institutions of the gay world and they can call on a wider variety of experiences and relationships to fill out their lives and identities.

The collection of secondary narratives that interviewees drew on strongly suggest the absence of a universalising view of old gay men. As the discussion showed, in the eyes of a subset of the sample of men interviewed for this chapter, old gay men can be seen as respected figures either because they lived through the HIV/AIDS epidemic or only if they have been successful; young gay men can develop affective relationships with them through the means of prostitution while very young gay men can regard them as distantly but with less affection as they would their grandparents.

Finally, despite the different cultural milieux from which the interviewees were drawn, a sense of commonality pervaded the stories they told of how old gay men were regarded and treated in the gay world, that is, by other, younger gay men. One explanation for the common strand running through their stories might be the internationalising effect of gay culture that has come about for a certain class of western gay men with the advent of relatively cheap air travel since the late 1970s and then more significantly, the advent of the internet since 1989.

Endnotes

1. Deborah Lupton, *Medicine as Culture: Illness, Disease and the Body in Western Societies*, 2nd edn, London: Sage, 2003, pp. 41–42.
2. Michael Mitternauer, *A History of Youth*, trans. G. Dunphy, Oxford: Blackwells Publishers, 1992, p. 41.
3. Simone de Beauvoir, *Old Age*, trans. P. O'Brien, Harmondsworth: Penguin Books, 1977, p. 7.
4. Peter Robinson, *The Changing World of Gay Men*, Basingstoke; New York: Palgrave Macmillan, 2008, chs 5 and 9.

5   Arlene Stein, *Sex and Sensibility: Stories of a Lesbian Generation*, Berkeley: University of California Press, 1997, p. 152.
6   ibid., pp. 152–153.
7   The larger research project comprises 60 men recruited for a book I am writing for Palgrave Macmillan, UK. The interviews were collected 2009–2010 from men from Australia, England, Hong Kong, India, New Zealand, and the United States.
8   Alasdair MacIntyre, 'The Virtues, the Unity of a Human Life, and the Concept of a Tradition', in Lewis P. Hinchman and Sandra K. Hinchman, eds, *Memory, Identity, Community: The Idea of Narrative in the Human Sciences*, New York: State University of New York, 2001, pp. 241–263; Edward Bruner, 'Ethnography as Narrative', in Hinchman and Hinchman, eds, *Memory, Identity, Community*, pp. 264–280; David Carr, 'Narrative and the Real World: An Argument for Continuity', in Hinchman and Hinchman, eds, *Memory, Identity, Community*, pp. 7–25; Kenneth Plummer, *Telling Sexual Stories: Power, Change and Social Worlds*, London: Routledge, 1995.
9   Hobart (200,525), Sydney (4,119,190), Australian Bureau Quick Stats, October 2007. Los Angeles (9,862,049 [2008 estimate]), New York (19,280,753 [2005–2007 estimates]), US Census Bureau Quick Facts.
10 For discussion of some of these cities' idiosyncrasies, see, Edmund White, *States of Desire: Travels in Gay America*, London: Pan Books Ltd, 1986; Graham Willett, *Living Out Loud: A History of Gay and Lesbian Activism in Australia*, St Leonards, NSW: Allen and Unwin, 2000; Garry Wotherspoon, *'City of the Plain': History of a Gay Sub-culture*, Sydney: Hale and Iremonger, 1991.
11 Dennis Altman, 'AIDS and the Reconceptualization of Homosexuality', in Dennis Altman et al., *Homosexuality, Which Homosexuality*, London: GMP Publishers, 1989, pp. 35–48.
12 When I visited Hobart in January 2003 to interview men for this study, the city had two gay bars, 'Cruise Bar', which opened every second weekend and 'La-La-Land', which was open every Saturday night but which has since closed.
13 Christopher Lasch, *The Culture of Narcissism: American Life in an Age of Diminishing Expectations*, New York: W. W. Norton and Company, 1991 [1979].
14 Michel Foucault, 'Sexual Choice, Sexual Act', in Paul Rabinow, ed., *Ethics: Essential Works of Foucault 1954–1984*, vol. 1, trans. Robert Hurley et al., Harmondsworth: Penguin Books, 2000, p. 153.
15 White, *States of Desire*, p. 15.
16 Jude, aged 46.
17 All but one came from New York.
18 Among scholars who have raised these matters are the following: Martin P. Bell and Alan P. Weinberg, *Homosexualities: A Study of Diversity among Men and Women*, Melbourne: The Macmillan Company of Australia, 1978; Raymond M. Berger, *Gay and Gray: The Older Homosexual Man*, 2nd edn, Binghamton, New York: The Haworth Press, 1996; Tim Bergling, *Reeling in the Years: Gay Men's Perspectives on Age and Ageism*, Binghamton, New York: The Haworth Press, 2004; Martin S. Weinberg and Colin J. Williams, *Male Homosexuals: Their Problems and Adaptations*, New York: Penguin Books Inc., 1975.
19 For more discussion of the influence of historical context, class, and birthplace on homosexual sexual practices, see, for example, George Chauncey, *Gay New York: Gender, Urban Culture, and the Making of the Gay Male World, 1890–1940*, New York: Basic Books, 1994; Robinson, *Changing World*; Yorick Smaal, 'Queensland's Emerging Homosexual Subculture and Public Space, 1890–1914', in N. Stead and J. Prior, *Queer*

Space: Centres and Peripheries, University of Technology Sydney, 2007, pp. 1–5, available at, http://www.dab.uts.edu.au/conferences/queer_space/proceedings/rural_smaal.pdf, date accessed 8 October 2010; Wotherspoon, '*Cities of the Plain*'.

20 See, for example, Chauncey, *Gay New York*; Clive Moore, *Sunshine and Rainbows: The Development of Gay and Lesbian Culture in Queensland*, St Lucia, Qld: University of Queensland Press, 2001; Robinson, *Changing World*; Smaal, 'Queensland's Emerging Homosexual Subculture and Public Space'; Wotherspoon, '*Cities of the Plain*'.

21 Ritch C. Savin Williams, *The New Gay Teenager*, Cambridge, MA: Harvard University Press, 2005, p. 202.

22 Robinson, *Changing World*, chs 5 and 9.

23 Bell and Weinberg, *Homosexualities*; Berger, *Gay and Gray*; Bergling, *Reeling in the Years*; Weinberg and Williams, *Male Homosexuals*.

'... And the Theatre was Full of Poofs, and I Thought it was Fantastic'

Researching the History of Gay Men and the Movies

Scott McKinnon

The history of gay men and the movies has often been discussed as a matter of representation and in terms of images on screens. Those boys in the band and their eventful party; Al Pacino's nights in the leather bars of New York; a bus called Priscilla; two cowboys in love. Also the focus of inquiry has been the gay men on and behind the camera. Rock Hudson, Rupert Everett, George Cukor, Gus van Sant. More recently, a growing number of researchers have begun to contemplate and investigate the gay men in the cinema audience. This chapter discusses the use of oral history interviews as a methodology for investigating the history of that audience. It is a valuable tool for exploring gay men's use of the movies in the development of personal narratives around gay identity and subjectivity. The memory stories of gay men also reveal the use of cinema as an access point to gay culture and community. Providing a space for the voice of gay men as cinema audiences adds to our understanding of the role of the movies in the history of that culture and that community.

This paper draws on research conducted for a larger project which investigates the history of cinema and cinema-going within the gay male communities of Sydney from 1950 to 2009. That project uses oral history interviews, the close reading of a range of films and the study of inter-textual sources as the three primary ways to explore the place of the movies within the development of gay culture, community and identity in Sydney. To date,

15 interviews with gay men have been conducted to discuss their life stories and their memories of the movies, both gay and otherwise, and it is these interviews that inform the analysis here. Ranging in age from their 80s to their 20s, these men's experiences of sexuality differ greatly according to the changing attitudes of the society around them. Their movie memories reflect both the changes and also the consistencies in gay experience across that time.

These memory stories suggest the value of thinking about the movies as more than a set of images on a screen or as an industry that can also be an art-form. They reveal cinemas as social venues which have provided access to gay community; they reveal the place of the movies in gay men's sense of their own developing sexual identity; and they reveal the diverse and complex relationships gay men have with the way they are represented on screen.

The ways in which gay men and lesbians have been represented has, until relatively recently, been the major preoccupation of gay cinema history. A sign of the growing visibility and political activism of gay communities in the 1970s and 1980s was the development of a critical voice with which to challenge cinematic depictions of homosexual characters. Vito Russo's *The Celluloid Closet* is the best known example of an engagement by openly gay researchers with the formerly closeted screen-homosexual. Overtly political and unashamedly angry, Russo's work finds homophobia in a broad range of Hollywood films. He states:

> As expressed on screen, America was a dream that had no room for the existence of homosexuals. Laws were made against depicting such things onscreen. And when the fact of our existence became unavoidable, we were reflected on screen and off, as dirty secrets.[1]

The question of the representation of gay and lesbian characters on screen continues to be a focus of research, updated and readdressed to take into account changing notions of sexual identity. In recent years, however, there has been a growing level of interest in the gay male cinema audience. Various researchers have used a range of critical perspectives and methodologies in investigating questions of gay male spectatorship and cinematic reception practices.

Brett Farmer's *Spectacular Passions*, for example, takes a psychoanalytical approach in investigating the ways in which gay men have mobilised 'film as a significant site for the investment and production of their own queer desires, fantasies and meanings'.[2] Farmer argues that research which focuses on the homophobic representation of gay men on screen sits in contrast to gay men's enjoyment of the cinema, and that an interest in gay male spectatorships is more inclusive of those for whom cinema is an 'integral, even foundational' part of their lives.[3] Farmer's work sits within the theoretical frameworks of spectatorship and film theory, and is a specific attempt to offer a non-heterosexual perspective within these fields.

The history of cinematic reception within gay culture, addressed less in terms of psychoanalytic theory and more as historically and spatially-constituted practices, has been investigated by a number of researchers, including Richard Dyer and Janet Staiger. Sitting within significant bodies of work investigating film and film audiences, Dyer and Staiger have, for example, each separately explored gay male readings of the films and the star persona of Judy Garland.[4] Such research encourages a contemplation of movies as not only a set of images projected onto screens, but as objects of social and cultural enquiry whose true importance often lies outside the walls of the cinema.

Movies and Memory

While Dyer and Farmer both quote, to varying extents, from letters sent to them by gay men about the movies, frequently missing from contemplations of the gay male audience is a significant place for the voice of that audience. Memory work obtained through oral history interviews is a valuable approach allowing for inclusion of that voice. By exploring the memories of gay male cinema-goers, it is possible to complicate any notion of a homogenous gay male audience; to locate examples of cinema-going events and practices which are unlikely to have left a written record; to develop a sense of the experience of participating in those events; and to explore the place of the movies within the construction of narratives around gay male identity and community.

Important to this is an understanding of the history of the cinema as more than the story of the production of films; or of the purportedly representative characters seen on screens; or of the experiences of a theoretical spectator. It is a history which acknowledges and addresses the place of the movies in everyday life and which examines the event of watching a movie as being one in which 'the audience is paying to be part of a larger social experience consisting substantially of non-filmic elements'.[5] The history of the movies is as much about these non-filmic elements (the cinema buildings, the reviews, the others in the audience, the talk before and after) as it is about the images that were projected on the screen.

While arguing for the value of oral history as a methodology in researching cinema history, I acknowledge that memory is frequently an unreliable source of information about those images. The moment of reception of a film is fleeting and lost to time. The memories recounted to me in interviews are reconstructed and influenced by a range of factors, including the experiences of the interviewee since that time, the process of the interview itself and the media framing of films. These memories are not simply a record of times past. As noted by Nancy Huggett, 'an analysis of the way in which aspects of cinema-going are narrated can shed light on how practices of cinema-going are situated within wider cultural discourse of the past and present'.[6]

A memory of a movie is rarely a discrete recollection of a particular text but is often one element of more detailed narratives. Several interviewees struggled to remember any specific films, recounting instead cinematic venues or other more general experiences of watching films. Bowles and Huggett have described this as 'the modest role allocated to the movies themselves in... narratives of cinema-going'.[7] So while some interviewees did offer insightful interpretations of particular film texts, more often the outcome of these interviews is a broader understanding of the place of the movies in gay community and of the location of the movies in personal narratives.

The use of cinema memories in such narratives has led in some cases to more difficult topics than I first expected to encounter when asking about going to the movies. As noted by Huggett, '[f]inding out about cinema-going over a cup of tea... is more challenging than it may at first appear'.[8] To ask who you went to the movies with as a child is perhaps to ask about a loved relative that has passed on. To ask what your classmates thought of your schoolboy movie interests is perhaps to remind you of schoolyard cruelty. To ask about movies in which a character died of AIDS is to call up memories of lost lovers and friends. Equally, movie memories are often recounted with a great deal of humour, often at the expense of the interviewee's younger self. Childhood naivety is located, for example, in memories of sexuality on screen, a naïveté which has been lost in the development of an adult subjectivity and identity.

In this respect the movies become less a set of texts that are responded to than threads of discourse which are woven into life narratives. Annette Kuhn, who has used oral history research to investigate memories of cinema-going in 1930s Britain, provides a useful framework for such investigations.

She states that the accounts provided in interviews should be 'treated not only as data but also as discourse, as material for interpretation. Concern is as much with *how* people talk about their youthful picture going – with memory discourse – as with *what* they say about it – memory content'.⁹ Thus memories are treated as both data which is analysed for insights into the place of cinema in people's lives and as material which is read discursively for what it tells us of cinema memory.

Kuhn takes a particular interest in her interviewees' memories of childhood cinema-going, and it is the memories of going to the movies in childhood and adolescence recounted in my research to which I will first turn. I am interested in the ways in which an engagement with particular kinds of movies and particular stars is identified by some gay men as an early sign of their developing identity. These memories speak to the interviewees' current understandings of that identity and often take the form of a humorously recounted narrative of childhood difference in which movies play a strong role.

Childhood Movie Memories: In Love with the Movies

For some particularly avid movie-goers, a childhood interest in the movies that went beyond what was considered to be acceptable masculine behaviour was remembered as giving rise to feelings of difference and isolation. For example Kerry, a 57-year-old man who grew up in rural New South Wales, described himself as 'a movie fanatic from a very early age' who was aware that 'the things I was interested in were quite unusual'.¹⁰ When asked how the other people in his life responded to his particularly strong devotion to the movies, Kerry recounted difficulties with several family members, particularly his father and older brother. Kerry remembered that his father 'was bemused, and let's just say he was extremely negative about my interest in films'. Kerry stated that his brother 'would lay shit on the whole movie thing and I'm sure, well I know, because I've spoken to him, we're much closer now, um, he just thought it was a poofter thing to be interested in'.

Kerry was especially fascinated by Hollywood actor Deborah Kerr and he would carefully create a list each year of his top 20 female actors, of which Ms Kerr was always number one. This love of female stars, for their glamour and beauty, is included in the narratives of several interviewees with a sense of fond nostalgia, yet also an acknowledgement that this love led to feelings of difference and isolation. The love of these stars is placed within a narrative of burgeoning gay identity, with this non-sexual interest identified as an early sign of homosexuality.

John B., a 43-year-old man who grew up on Sydney's North Shore, was also a dedicated fan of the movies from a very early age, and clearly elided his current sexual identity with his childhood cinema-going. He remembered:

> Oh, this is bizarre this is, I mean, this is the most bizarre thing for a nine-year-old boy to be doing, but I went to a double bill, a best actress – I mean what a poof – a best actress double bill of Katherine Hepburn and Glenda Jackson. Katherine Hepburn won the Oscar for *The Lion in Winter* and Glenda Jackson won for *A Touch of Class*. And at nine years of age (laughs) I trotted off to see it with a mate of mine.[11]

John identifies this behaviour as unusual for a child and particularly for a male, and sees this as early evidence of his homosexual identity. This was done with humour and affection for his younger self, an affection that carried through into another story in which his childhood cinematic tastes led to rejection and cruelty from his school-mates. John remembered:

> And guys used to laugh about me, the fact that I was so heavily into movies. You know, 1979, at school we had a Master-Mind quiz competition, and everyone was able to choose their topic, and I chose Barbra Streisand. And I got attacked, literally attacked. And I used to say – like, I was incredulous, I was like, 'What's the difference between choosing Barbra Streisand and choosing, you know, Ian Chappell or Dennis Lillee', you know? 'What's the difference between – sorry, I don't understand, why am I being attacked? You've chosen Dennis Lillee, I've chosen Barbra Streisand'. Some of the teachers thought it was hysterical. You know (laughs) in retrospect, I'd be laughing too.

Both particularly avid movie-goers, in their youth and adulthood, Kerry and John look back to their childhood cinema interests as signposts or clues with which to develop a lifelong narrative around their sexuality. This locates film, as opposed to say, sport, as an uncommon interest for Australian boys and sees certain aspects of film, particularly the glamour of certain female Hollywood actors, as an element of gay culture.

These memories suggest the value of the interplay between the past and present as an inherent element in oral history interviews. They do not reveal the *why* of the attraction many gay men feel to certain female stars in a way that is attempted by the psychoanalytical interpretations of spectatorship theory, but instead suggest the location of that attraction as a significant point of both adult gay identification and memories of childhood experience. Childhood questions about feeling different and isolated because of movie fandom are remembered, reconstructed and answered from the point of view of a current model of adult sexual identity.

Feelings of difference are central to these memories. In considering the use of oral history as a methodology for researching histories of homosexuality, Elizabeth Lapovsky Kennedy has noted that, 'Not being born and raised in a public lesbian and gay culture, each gay and lesbian person has to construct his or her own life in oppressive contexts, a process that oral history is uniquely suited to reveal'.[12] The memories of Kerry and John reveal this construction as having begun in childhood and as being revealed in these cases by memories of the movies.

Childhood Movie Memories: Gazing at Men on Screen

Another element of childhood movie memories noted by interviewees in relation to their burgeoning sexuality is the sight of handsome men, in various states of undress, appearing on cinema or television screens. These sightings are often remembered with a mixture of affection and an acknowledgement of the confusion that such sightings could cause.

One such memory was recounted by Daniel, who is 35 years old and grew up on a farm in northern New South Wales. I asked Daniel about memories of Australian films, thinking that this may elicit memories of Australian films containing gay characters. Instead, Daniel's movie memory was tied to his own sexuality, not that of the characters on screen. He answered:

> An Australian war movie, it might've been *The Lighthorsemen* or *Gallipoli* or something like that, but there was a specific scene where the soldiers were, you know, having a nude romp on the beach and ah, that was just the movie of the week on TV, ah, one week, and I remember watching that and, you know, I remember that quite specifically, just for the naked men that were in it.[13]

A little later in the interview, I asked Daniel if he remembered having any sense that his interest in naked male actors on screen was wrong, and he answered:

> I certainly didn't feel that it was wrong. I knew that it was different and I knew that it wasn't something that I could talk about or say, um, although I remember talking about that, ah, sort of group nude scene in the war movie... ah, with one of my male friends at high-

school, and I think I probably spoke about that a little bit too much and the conversation went a little way and I caught myself thinking, 'Oh, I probably shouldn't continue thinking about this'... But, yeah, I didn't feel that it was wrong but I did know that it was, it was unusual and different, and the other boys weren't focusing on that.

That Daniel could not remember exactly which film this scene had appeared in is largely irrelevant. This movie memory tells us much less about a particular movie than it does about the place of movies in the construction of a narrative around a developing sexual identity. Daniel remembers the scene both for a sexual interest in seeing naked men and for his awareness that this interest needed to be kept hidden. The experience becomes associated with an adolescent feeling of difference, and reveals the need for self-regulation experienced by many gay men from an early age. The memory was located as part of a longer narrative about an eventual acceptance of identity and location of community.

Forming Community at the Movies

This location of community is a significant element of many narratives around sexual identity. The use of oral history interviews in investigating the history of gay men and the movies reveals the cinema as a point of access to that world. Several interviewees described experiences, particularly at gay film festivals, of a feeling of solidarity and community gained through watching a film in a theatre full of other gay people. This is at times contrasted with narratives of isolation and loneliness prior to 'coming out' and/or as an alternative means of finding gay community beyond bar and club culture.

Memory stories of encounters with gay community via cinematic space reveal the particular benefit of oral history to such an investigation as they encompass both the empirical and the subjective. As Elizabeth Lapovsky Kennedy has argued, gay and lesbian oral histories operate to their fullest when the empirical and subjective are seen as complementary. By embracing the subjective nature of memory work, oral history's '"empirical" goals are not compromised but expanded'.[14] Memories of access to gay community through the movies reveal both empirical data about the cinematic venues at which such events occurred and more subjective discourses on the emotional aspects of these experiences.

Janet Staiger has described the underground cinema movement of 1960s America as having contributed to a sense of community which would eventually play a role in the gay liberation movement. She argues that underground cinemas provided the 'potential of finding others like oneself not only for identity but for community building' and that, 'the experience of going to the underground cinema contradicted impressions of isolation as it also elevated images of perverts and subjects gone awry'.[15] My interviews with Australian gay men have revealed examples of 1960s and 1970s cinema-going in Australia which used Hollywood films in 'mainstream' cinema settings but which similarly provided access to community.

One such example was provided by David W., who was born in 1935 and who was an active participant in the gay (or, more correctly, camp) social scenes of Sydney and Melbourne in the 1950s and 1960s. Describing the movies during his time in Melbourne, David recounted a memory from the 1950s of film screenings at a Hoyts cinema organised by the gay cinema manager:

> [He] instituted this revolutionary idea of having a special session at 11.30 or something. Absolutely outrageous. 11.30 pm on a Friday night or a Saturday night, I forget which it was, at which he would show, um, a movie. And so that would be a very gay, a very camp audience that would go... and so he would show, sort of, you know, *The Pride and The Passion*, or um, one of those films about Roman life or the early life of Jesus or something, and we'd all sit there giggling and going through it. And so he developed, also, um – there was an Australian actor called Frank Thring from Melbourne, who had appeared in one of those historical dramas as Pontius Pilate or something like that, and so, no matter what film we were watching, at some point, it would be interrupted while this scene with Pontius Pilate condemning Jesus was played (laughs). And so we'd all wait for that. It's a little bit like sort of going to, you know, *Rocky Horror* and singing along. We were all waiting for that bit of Frank Thring to say, 'I condemn you to death', you know, so silly. And so it would be a romantic comedy and suddenly this would come in.[16]

When asked how people were likely to find out about such screenings, David said:

> How did we know? I think it was advertised in the press, but I think it was only outrageous people like us who would actually be going out at 11 o'clock at night. You know, real people were at home in bed, weren't they? You know, looking after their families and their children and all

that sort of thing. It was the sort of loose-moralled ones who were out and about late at night.

David's memory encapsulates many of the issues involved in the use of oral history to investigate the social and cultural history of the cinema. First, he guides us towards the empirical, suggesting the time and place of a particular example of the cinema as social event. However, David's uncertainty about the particular films involved and the exact time of the screening also encourage caution in the use of this evidence. Frank Thring appeared as Pontius Pilate in *Ben Hur* in 1959, suggesting that these screenings may well have occurred in the early 1960s, rather than the 1950s as David remembers. Yet the uncertainties do not discount the place of the story within a narrative of the camp scene of that time, in which David highlighted, with a degree of nostalgic fondness, the existence of a camp community. The story was a specific attempt to disrupt any notions of the pre-gay liberation era as a uniformly dark time of oppression and isolation.

David's memory reveals a great deal about a sense of community developed through a series of regular cinema screenings. It reveals a degree of enjoyment in being 'other', of not being one of the 'real people' but instead of being 'outrageous' and 'loose-moralled'. The time of night, the other members of the audience and the film content fostered in David a sense of himself taking part in a specific, temporary public which was part of a wider community and which felt pleasure, rather than shame, in being different.

The use of mainstream Hollywood films, reimagined by an appearance from gay actor Frank Thring in each of them, also suggests the importance of looking beyond film texts when investigating the history of gay men and the movies. The inherently camp nature of such films was made explicit by the cinema manager and his audience, in a sense inserting a gay element into films which, due to strict censorship, could not be made with any overtly homosexual content. Taken simply as texts, these films would have less to say to us about their initial reception than they do when taken in the context of David's memories of viewing them at a Melbourne cinema.

Another interviewee, Larry, had similar memories of a gay audience gathering to view Hollywood films. Larry was a young man in the early 1970s, newly out of school and working for Greater Union cinemas in Sydney. He remembered Sunday night double bills at the Randwick Ritz cinema, to which he was first taken by an openly gay colleague and which, for him, became a weekly event.

And they would do things like (laughs) *Space Odyssey* and *Ben Hur* (laughs) and my God and we'd do it. You'd get there at 6 [pm] and come out at 2 [am] in the morning and you could do that when you were young. But, um, I had not seen either *Auntie Mame* or *Gypsy*, knew nothing about them, and they were on – it didn't matter what was on, we were gonna go, cause it was sort of – yeah – and a lot of gay people went... and as soon as it sort of started, I don't know which one was on first, but I got it. You know? I got the camp humour and all that sort of thing and I was really rapt that, you know? (laughs) 'Oh! I know, I get it'. I was laughing at the stuff so I thought, 'Oh, how sophisticated is that?' You know?[17]

Again the camp nature of these films is made explicit through the choices of a cinema operator and the actions of a gay audience. The weekly nature of these screenings may have further encouraged a sense of community; of joint participation in the creation of a gay space. Thus the cinema becomes a social space, not merely for the quiet and isolated consumption of moving images, but for a social event which provides access to and encourages participation in a community.

Larry's memory also evokes the emotional experience of participating in this event. He provides us with the empirical data of the time and place of the screenings and some suggestion of what was watched. He also reveals the more subjective nature of the experience itself and what he remembers it meaning to him. The story was told as part of a narrative of what Larry described as an 'escape' from a working-class background in western Sydney into a world in which he felt more at home. It is the story of a naïve young man finding a 'sophisticated' world, told both with pride and a degree of self-deprecation. His recounting of his experiences at the Randwick Ritz expresses a feeling of happiness at having found, in part through the movies, a community of his own.

Narratives of finding community through participation in gay cinema audiences were part of the movie memories of several of the men interviewed for this project. John B., whose school experiences were quoted earlier and who remains an avid moviegoer, narrated his difficult experiences coming to terms with his sexuality through a series of stories about his relationship with a range of films. He remembered a particular cinema-going experience as part of his growing acceptance of a gay identity:

I remember we went to see *Beyond the Valley of the Dolls*, like, another retro movie at the old Mandolin cinema, which is now the Australia

> Hall. And we just sat there and laughed and the theatre was full of poofs and I thought it was fantastic. I couldn't have done that two or three years before that, but I thought at that stage it was fantastic. And it was interesting, I realised at that point, 'oh, I'm becoming part of a subculture'.[18]

John remembers the experience of the film as being improved by the fact that the audience was made up largely of gay men and places the experience as a signpost in his narrative of 'coming out'. Being able to enjoy the film in that setting and feeling comfortable as part of that crowd is directly elided with the location of community and the acceptance of identity.

For some men who were disinclined to venture into the, perhaps, more threatening spaces of gay bars and nightclubs, the cinema has played a particularly important role in providing access to community and the removal of feelings of difference and isolation. One interviewee, John P., was born in the 1920s and spent much of his life hiding his homosexuality for fear of losing his career as an academic and scientist. He was very keen to stress the importance of both cinema and theatre to him as a counterpoint to the isolating world of the closet. He stated:

> And also to be in a gay audience, so, to me going to a gay film or going to a gay film festival, and just being part of an audience which is gay, has a very important psychological boosting effect. Because it gets rid of the idea that you're doing everything in isolation. When you've spent a lifetime trying to conceal your sexuality, it's very liberating to, um, to be somewhere where you don't have to conceal your sexuality.[19]

These movie memories encourage both a contemplation of the audience when researching the history of gay cinema and also a contemplation of the cinema as gay space when researching gay urban histories. Cinemas are rarely considered in histories of gay city life and yet they have played a role in the development of gay culture, community and identity. George Chauncey, describing 1920s New York, has noted that, '[s]ince movie going was a perfectly legitimate way to spend the afternoon, theatres were places where young men could go to search out other gay men and begin to learn about the gay world'[20] and that these visits served both as opportunities for sexual encounters as well as 'valued social (and socialising) functions'.[21] Cinemas can often sit, along with bars, clubs, beats, restaurants and cafés, as important sites for the development of urban gay life.

Unwelcoming or Threatening Cinema Spaces

It is not my intention to romanticise the role of cinema in encouraging community or to suggest a uniform response from gay men to this, or any, aspect of the social history of the cinema. It is important to note that some interviewees recounted memories of the cinema as a threatening space and/or as a space which held different meanings at different times in their lives. Some described the fear of being 'outed' which came with seeing a gay film. Another described the space created by a gay audience as judgemental and threateningly sexualised.

Knowing that John P. had experienced great fear at times that revelations about his sexuality would end his career, I asked if it had been 'a big deal' to go and see a gay movie. He replied:

> J.: Initially, but not later. So, now I wouldn't have any hesitation. But then it was a – it would have been an effort to actually go, and, ah, and see a gay movie, because of all the inhibition I was carrying in my youth.
>
> S.: And if you're concerned that people might see you going to this movie?
>
> J.: That was it exactly, yes. They might see you going in… and so on. Especially when I was still a university lecturer. But you gradually get over that, so of course now it doesn't matter at all. But then it was quite different.[22]

Thus while having eventually found a sense of community and freedom in the experience of seeing a gay film, that experience had been a threatening one at an earlier stage of his life.

John B. recounted a similar memory. The Hollywood film *Making Love* (1981), which told the story of a married man who leaves his wife for a male lover, was in cinemas when John was still in high school and experiencing homophobic cruelty from his classmates. About the film, John stated:

> And I can still remember when the movie *Making Love* came out. That it was on at Pitt Street. I could not bring myself to go and see it. I was terrified, what would I do if someone saw me go and see it? But I was fascinated. I wanted to know about it. And I read everything I could about it.[23]

This memory story acknowledges the potential significance of a film beyond the projected images which comprise it. *Making Love* plays a role in the teenage memories of a man who did not see it until adulthood. For some, the all too rare opportunity of watching a gay character in a movie finding love and happiness may have been a pleasurable and even liberating experience. For one teenager, the very existence of the film was a source of both fascination and confusion. Thus, in considering the impact of the film we must look at it as more than a sum of its parts. A purely textual consideration of this film would exclude the experience of a young man too frightened to approach the cinema doors.

John B.'s memory also expresses the sense of threat that could lie around the cinematic experience, a threat which was again expressed in terms of eventual acceptance of identity and rejection of homophobia. David C., a 25 year old who came out as gay to his parents and classmates at the age of 16, has grown up with homosexuality as a part of public discourse and has never experienced the fear of having his adult sexuality 'discovered'. However, he did describe ambivalent feelings towards watching a film with a gay audience, noting both the positive aspect of 'shared experience' in a screening in which you know 'that everyone around you is relating to this in a similar way, at least, to what you are', but also feelings of intimidation in the 'sexual energy' of the space. Comparing the experience to a well-known gay Sydney nightclub called Arq, he stated:

> It's like, we're going to watch a film, you know? We're not at Arq, like, at all. Like, the opposite of Arq. And yet, the same behaviour… goes on just in like a more… longer haired, blacker-rimmed glasses kind of way… I don't get sexual energy going to Hoyts, you know?… But like, you go to a gay festival and it's just like, fuckin' gay eyes everywhere, you're just like – it's just incredibly intimidating. I just want to go and watch a film yet instead I feel like I'm being cruised. Not me, personally, usually who I'm with (laughs).[24]

This direct correlation of a festival movie with a gay club further suggests the importance of considering cinemas as social spaces within gay culture. David's memory also suggests the ways in which oral history can complicate notions of a homogenous 'gay audience', with his description of intimidation sitting in contrast to the feelings of community and solidarity expressed by other interviewees. David's thoughts on the movies lead to a discussion on the at times threatening, sexualised nature of gay space.

The memories of those I have interviewed are not meant to be read as representative of all gay men. The intention is to complicate, rather than assert, the notion of a homogenous gay male audience. What these memories do speak to are *some* of the ways in which the cinema plays a role in the personal narratives and in the understandings of identity and community of *some* gay men.

Providing a voice for members of the audience enhances our understanding of the cinema as a focus of social and cultural enquiry and, most importantly, encourages us to look beyond the screen when writing the history of gay men and the movies. Movie memories reveal the place of cinema within narratives around the development of gay identity and the location of gay community. They also reveal cinemas as important spaces within gay history. These memories both complicate and illuminate the history of gay men as a movie audience and suggest the significant role of the movies within the history of gay male culture, community and identity.

Endnotes

1. Vito Russo, *The Celluloid Closet: Homosexuality in the Movies*, New York: Harper and Row, 1987, p. xii.
2. Brett Farmer, *Spectacular Passions: Cinema, Fantasy, Gay Male Spectatorships*, Durham; London: Duke University Press, 2000, p. 19.
3. ibid., p. 5.
4. Richard Dyer, 'Judy Garland and Gay Men', in Harry Benshoff and Sean Griffin, eds, *Queer Cinema: The Film Reader*, New York; London: Routledge, 2004, pp. 153–166; Janet Staiger, *Interpreting Films: Studies in the Historical Reception of American Cinema*, Princeton, NJ: Princeton University Press, 1992, pp. 154–177.
5. Kate Bowles, '"Three Miles Of Rough Dirt Road": Towards an Audience-Centred Approach to Cinema Studies in Australia', *Studies in Australasian Cinema*, vol. 1, no. 3 (2007), p. 250.
6. Nancy Huggett, 'Everyone was Watching! Strategies of Self-presentation in Oral Histories of Cinema-Going', *Studies in Australasian Cinema*, vol. 1, no. 3 (2007), p. 273.
7. Kate Bowles and Nancy Huggett, 'Cowboys, Jaffas and Pies: Researching Cinema-going in the Illawarra', in M. Stokes and R. Maltby, eds, *Hollywood Abroad: Audiences and Cultural Relations*, London: British Film Institute, 2004, p. 75.
8. Huggett, 'Everyone was Watching!', p. 261.
9. Annette Kuhn, *An Everyday Magic: Cinema and Cultural Memory*, London: I. B. Taurus, 2002, p. 9.
10. Kerry, interview with Scott McKinnon, 22 July 2009.
11. John B., interview with Scott McKinnon, 26 November 2008.
12. Elizabeth Lapovsky Kennedy, 'Telling Tales: Oral History and the Construction of Pre-Stonewall Lesbian History', in Robert Perks and Alistair Thomson, eds, *The Oral History Reader*, London: Routledge, 1998, p. 345.

13 Daniel, interview with Scott McKinnon, 19 May 2009.
14 Kennedy, 'Telling Tales', p. 354.
15 Janet Staiger, 'Finding Community in the Early 1960s: Underground Cinema and Sexual Politics', in Harry Benshoff and Sean Griffin, eds, *Queer Cinema: The Film Reader*, New York; London: Routledge, 2004, p. 125.
16 David W., interview with Scott McKinnon, 17 September 2008.
17 Larry, interview with Scott McKinnon, 24 June 2009.
18 John B., interview with Scott McKinnon, 26 November 2008.
19 John P., interview with Scott McKinnon, 18 February 2009.
20 George Chauncey, *Gay New York: Gender, Urban Culture, and the Making of the Gay World, 1890–1940*, New York: Basic Books, 1994, p. 194.
21 ibid., p. 195.
22 John P., interview with Scott McKinnon, 18 February 2009.
23 John B., interview with Scott McKinnon, 26 November 2008.
24 David C., interview with Scott McKinnon, 21 October 2009.